THE SURREAL VISIONS OF
JOSEPHINE TOTA

THE SURREAL VISIONS OF JOSEPHINE TOTA

Edited by
Jessica Marten

Essays by
Janet Catherine Berlo
Jessica Marten

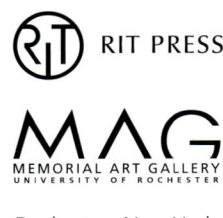

RIT PRESS

MAG
MEMORIAL ART GALLERY
UNIVERSITY OF ROCHESTER

Rochester, New York

This book is published by RIT Press in association with the Memorial Art Gallery of the University of Rochester on the occasion of the exhibition *The Surreal Visions of Josephine Tota*: Memorial Art Gallery, July 14–September 9, 2018. Additional exhibition venues arranged by International Arts & Artists.

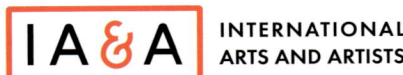 **INTERNATIONAL ARTS AND ARTISTS**

This exhibition and catalog have been made possible by Pamela Miller Ness and Paul Marc Ness, Rosamond Tota, the Gallery Council of the Memorial Art Gallery, and the Robert L. and Mary L. Sproull Fund. Additional support is provided by the James and Jacqueline Adams Fund, the June Alexander Memorial Fund, the Nancy E. Hyman Charitable Fund, and Marguerite and James Quinn, Jane Labrum, Lisa Rosica, and The Century Club of Rochester.

Published and distributed by:
RIT Press
90 Lomb Memorial Drive
Rochester, New York 14623
http://ritpress.rit.edu

Cover image: Josephine Tota, Untitled, completed May 16, 1982. (cat. 30)
All Josephine Tota artwork was photographed by Andy Olenick, Fotowerks, Ltd.

ISBN 978-1-939125-50-7

Library of Congress Cataloging-in-Publication Data

Names: Marten, Jessica, editor. | Binstock, Jonathan P., 1966– writer of foreword. | Berlo, Janet Catherine. Tears of blood. | University of Rochester. Memorial Art Gallery, organizer, host institution.
Title: The surreal visions of Josephine Tota / edited by Jessica Marten ; essays by Janet Catherine Berlo and Jessica Marten.
Description: Rochester, New York : Memorial Art Gallery of the University of Rochester : RIT Press, 2018. | "Published on the occasion of the exhibition The Surreal Visions of Josephine Tota at the Memorial Art Gallery from July 14, 2018 to September 9, 2018." | Includes bibliographical references.
Identifiers: LCCN 2018010334 | ISBN 9781939125507 (softcover : alk. paper)
Subjects: LCSH: Tota, Josephine, 1911–1996–Exhibitions. | Surrealism–United States–Exhibitions.
Classification: LCC ND237.T597 A4 2018 | DDC 759.06/63–dc23
LC record available at https://lccn.loc.gov/2018010334

Design: Marnie Soom
Typefaces: Avenir Next and Poliphilus
Paper: Huron Gloss
Printing and binding: Thomson Shore, Dexter, Michigan

CONTENTS

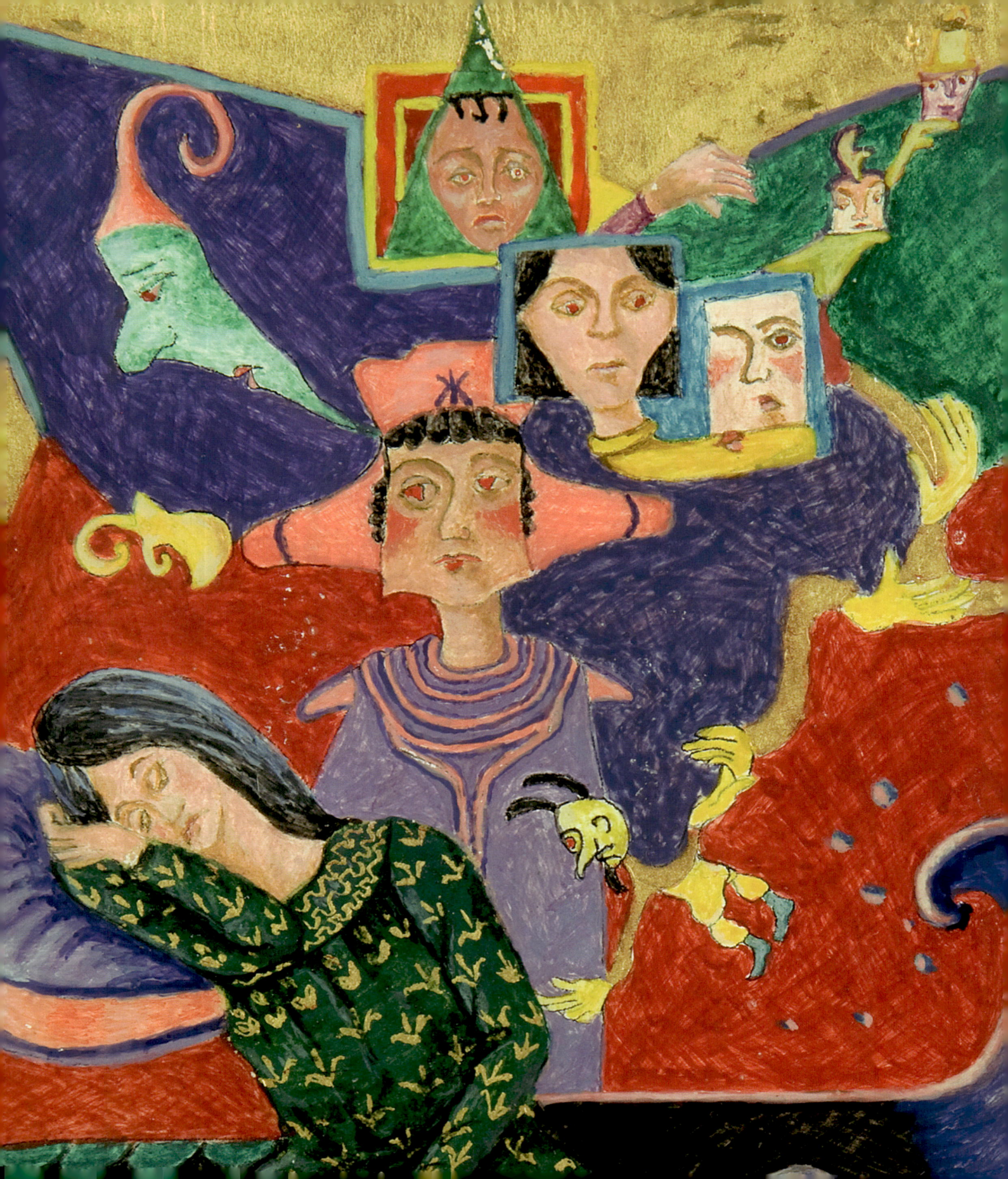

FOREWORD

Jonathan P. Binstock
*Mary W. and Donald R. Clark
Director, Memorial Art Gallery
of the University of Rochester*

The Memorial Art Gallery forges new territory in the introduction and exploration of an unconventional artist with the exhibition and catalog *The Surreal Visions of Josephine Tota*. MAG's effort reflects a growing appreciation among scholars, museums, galleries, and collectors for artists who do not fit neatly into generally received art world categories. We are proud to offer this scholarly examination in recognition of the quality of Tota's work and the importance of her story. Through her single-minded pursuit of her artistic vision, Tota is an example of the power of underappreciated or marginalized figures to disrupt established perceptions of artistic value and enliven conversations and debates about the limits of our art-historical knowledge.

I would like to recognize the efforts of museum staff whose dedication has made this project possible. The talented and intelligent Jessica Marten—MAG's Curator in Charge/Curator of American Art, and the curator of this project—thanks the individuals who have contributed to its success in the acknowledgments of this beautiful volume. Jess has worked for many years to bring Tota's art and a deeply considered assessment of it to the public. I congratulate her for this hard-won and outstanding achievement. I would also like to thank contributing author Janet Catherine Berlo, Professor of Art History/Visual and Cultural Studies at the University of Rochester. Berlo's excellent essay examines Tota alongside her peers within the history of visionary women artists of the twentieth century.

On behalf of MAG's Board of Managers and staff, I express our sincere gratitude to the artist's daughter, Rosamond Tota, and great-niece, Lisa Rosica. Without their support, counsel, and trust, this

Untitled, undated, 1980s (detail of cat. 12)
Egg tempera and gold leaf on panel
6 ⅛ × 6 ⅛ in.
Collection of Rosamond Tota, daughter

exhibition and catalog would not have been possible. We are thankful also to the exhibition's lenders for sharing their personal treasures. Many of them are family and friends of the artist, and deeply passionate about Tota's work and legacy.

The exhibition, catalog, and programming are possible thanks to the generous support of Pamela Miller Ness and Paul Marc Ness, Rosamond Tota, the Gallery Council of the Memorial Art Gallery, and the Robert L. and Mary L. Sproull Fund. Additional support is provided by the James and Jacqueline Adams Fund, the June Alexander Memorial Fund, the Nancy E. Hyman Charitable Fund, and Marguerite and James Quinn, Jane Labrum, Lisa Rosica, and The Century Club of Rochester.

I extend my gratitude to all members of our Board of Managers for their support and confidence. It is because of the active engagement and commitment of our board that MAG is able to realize the important scholarship, exhibitions, and programming demonstrated by *The Surreal Visions of Josephine Tota*.

INTRODUCTION

Jessica Marten
*Curator in Charge/Curator
of American Art,
Memorial Art Gallery of the
University of Rochester*

During a routine inventory of art storage in 2010, I first encountered two Josephine Tota paintings in the permanent collection of the Memorial Art Gallery (MAG). The intense psychic energy in her personal, meticulously rendered images had a powerful effect upon me. I reached out to the keepers of Tota's legacy—her daughter, Rosamond Tota, and great-niece, Lisa Rosica—and over the course of many conversations in person and via email, they provided me with a great deal of insight into the artist.

Tota's story is rich, complex, and all too common: an artist outlier disenfranchised, excluded from and nearly lost to history. Rosamond soon expressed her interest in donating more of her mother's work to the museum. Unusual paintings like these—near death-defying expressions of a little-known artist's interior world, with incisive inquiries into womanhood, age, and power—rarely find their way inside an art museum's walls. Because of Tota's singular and powerful vision, her historic connection to the institution, and her unique perspective on the immigrant experience, twelve paintings were presented and accepted in 2011, for a new total of fourteen in the museum's permanent collection.

The museum's investment in Tota's art has been cited as an example of the way regional museums can make curatorial decisions that act as "an important corrective to exclusionary studies of canonical artists."[1] Scholarship on unconventional artists, bolstered by the advances of the feminist art and art history movements of the 1970s and 1980s, has reached a new pinnacle in the first two decades of the twenty-first century. Major American museums have invested in self-taught art by acquiring collections, exhibiting it alongside mainstream art, organizing exhibitions, and publishing scholarly catalogs.[2] The value of inviting to the conversation artists who willfully pursue their vision outside of traditional parameters is to highlight the unsatisfactory limitations of these categories.

The Memorial Art Gallery's contribution, *The Surreal Visions of Josephine Tota,* introduces and explores this Italian American immigrant's unusual creative life. With the power of her paintings, their rich connection with her personal narrative, and her magical transformation of centuries of art-historical sources into her idiosyncratic style, Tota deserves careful review. In a broader sense, the exhibition and catalog explore currents within the American experience primed for deeper art-historical inquiry, such as the structural failure of the insider/outsider duality, the far-reaching legacy of Surrealism, the marginalization of female visionary artists, and the relationship between age and creative agency.

NOTES

1   Cynthia Fowler, ed. *Locating American Art: Finding Art's Meaning in Museums, Colonial Period to the Present* (Burlington, VT: Ashgate, 2016), 5-6. The first scholarly publication on Tota was my essay in *Locating American Art,* 73–86. The second was a paper presented at the 2016 College Art Association conference and published in *Panorama: Journal of the Association of Historians of American Art 2,* no. 2 (Fall 2016).

2   Pertinent examples include acquisitions and exhibitions by American museums of James Castle, Bill Traylor, Judith Scott, and Ronald Lockett; collections given by Jill and Sheldon Bonovitz to the Philadelphia Museum of Art and the Souls Grown Deep Foundation to the Metropolitan Museum of Art; critical attention for Massimiliano Gioni's *Encyclopedic Palace* at the 2013 Venice Biennale; and the introduction of self-taught artists like that in the *Finding Vivian Maier* documentary (2013) and *The Electric Pencil: Drawings from Inside State Hospital No. 3* (New York: Princeton Architectural Press, 2016). Market forces show a similar focus with Andrew Edlin's 2012 purchase and rejuvenation of the Outsider Art Fair, and the 2016 auction record set for a self-taught artist (William Edmonson).

Untitled, completed May 26, 1983
(detail of cat. 38)
Egg tempera and gold leaf on panel
6 ½ x 6 ^{15}/$_{16}$ in.
Collection of Rosamond Tota, daughter

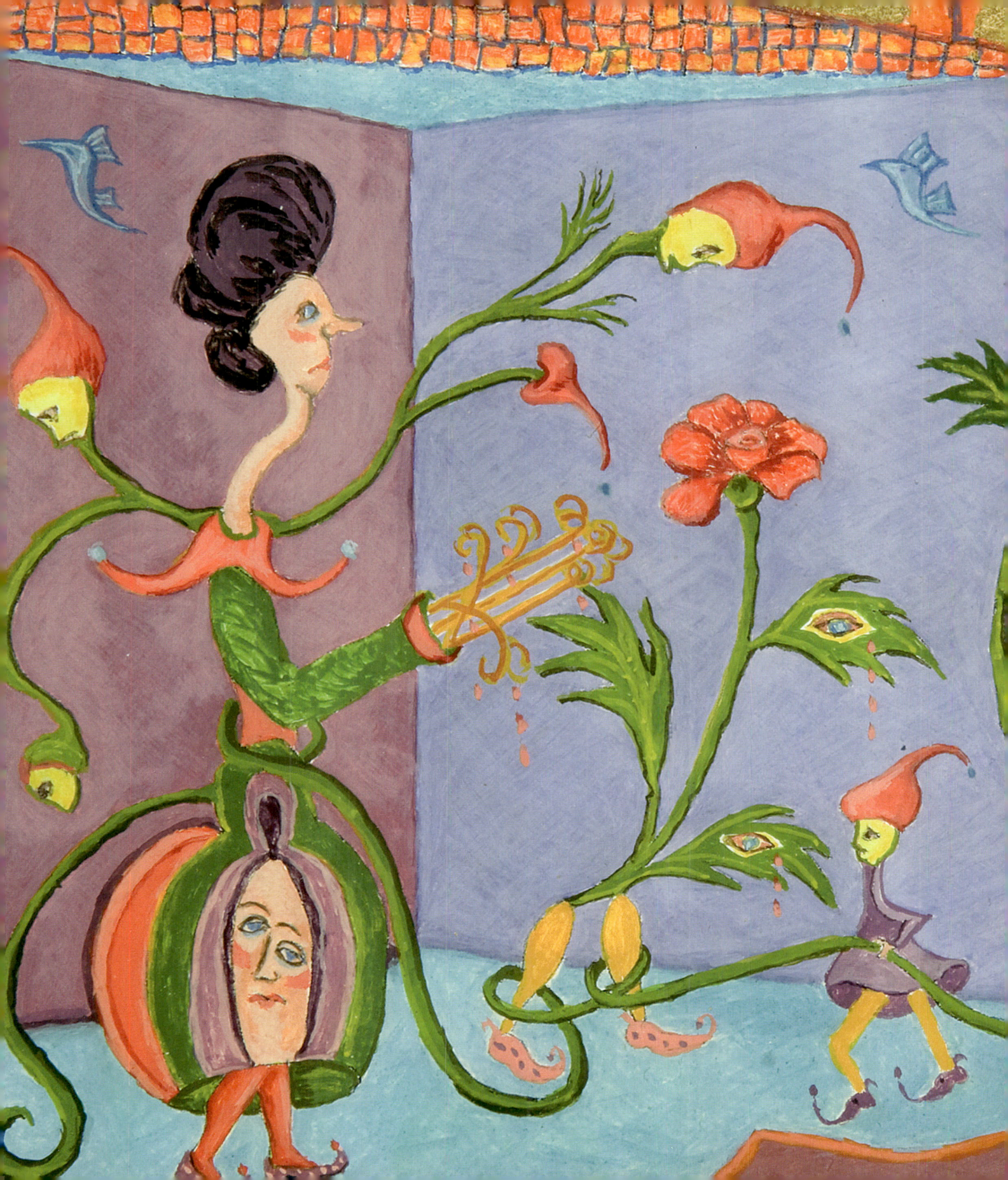

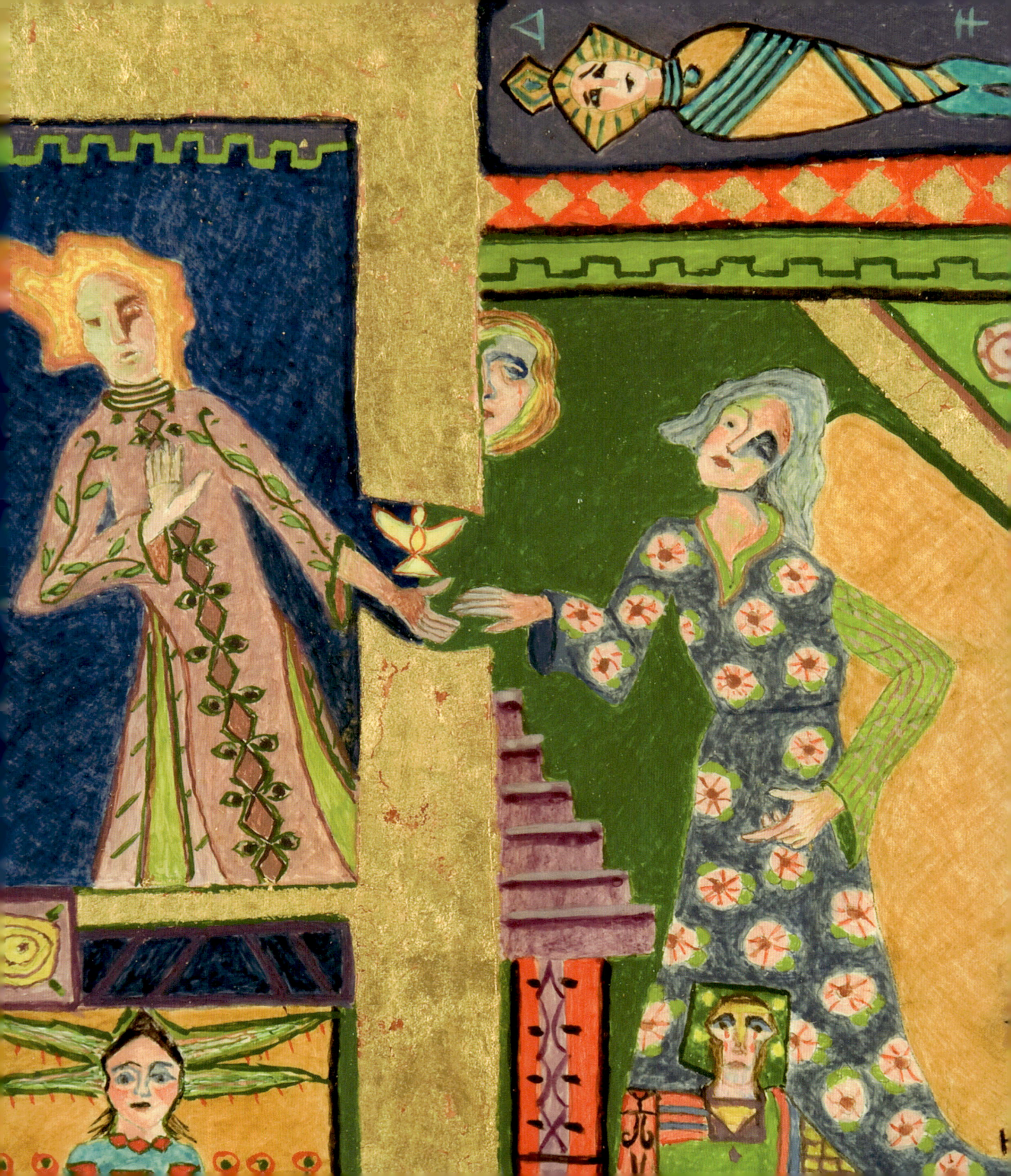

THE SURREAL VISIONS
OF JOSEPHINE TOTA

Jessica Marten
*Curator in Charge/Curator
of American Art,
Memorial Art Gallery of the
University of Rochester*

Josephine Tota (1910–1996) was a seamstress and amateur artist who lived a conventional life among the Italian immigrant community in Rochester, New York. Her awakening to intensely personal subject matter and her discovery of the medium of egg tempera in her early seventies allowed Tota to tap into the stream of her extraordinary creative energy. Her enigmatic paintings show a consistent preference for small-scale, encoded domestic dramas. There are moments of one woman's agony, despair, and quiet alienation, but also of transcendence and hope.

In the 1980s, Tota spent countless hours painting in the privacy of her home, where she imbued over ninety small jewel-like paintings with the richness of her strange imagination.[1] The images sprang from a deep well of memories and dreams, and she reflected upon her life in the only way she could: in paint and pictures. Themes of metamorphosis, family bonds, physical pain, human frailty, the natural world, loss, and tragedy dominate her obsessive and otherworldly depictions. It is this powerful body of work—dozens of untamed paintings in egg tempera and gilding on board, completed at the end of her life—that *The Surreal Visions of Josephine Tota* explores and advocates for inclusion into the canon of self-taught art.

In her small yet formidable paintings, Tota condensed myriad art-historical sources into private images of startling immediacy and timelessness. The formal concerns of her work are unique to her. She was a lively and deliberate colorist, her compositions are dense yet balanced, and her use of line, shape, and narrative serves to attract and repel the viewer. The compact size of her paintings encourages intimate viewing: the smallest painting is about 5 by

Untitled, completed June 1, 1990
(detail of cat. 76)
Egg tempera and gold leaf on panel
8 ¾ x 7 ¾ in.
Collection of Rosamond Tota, daughter

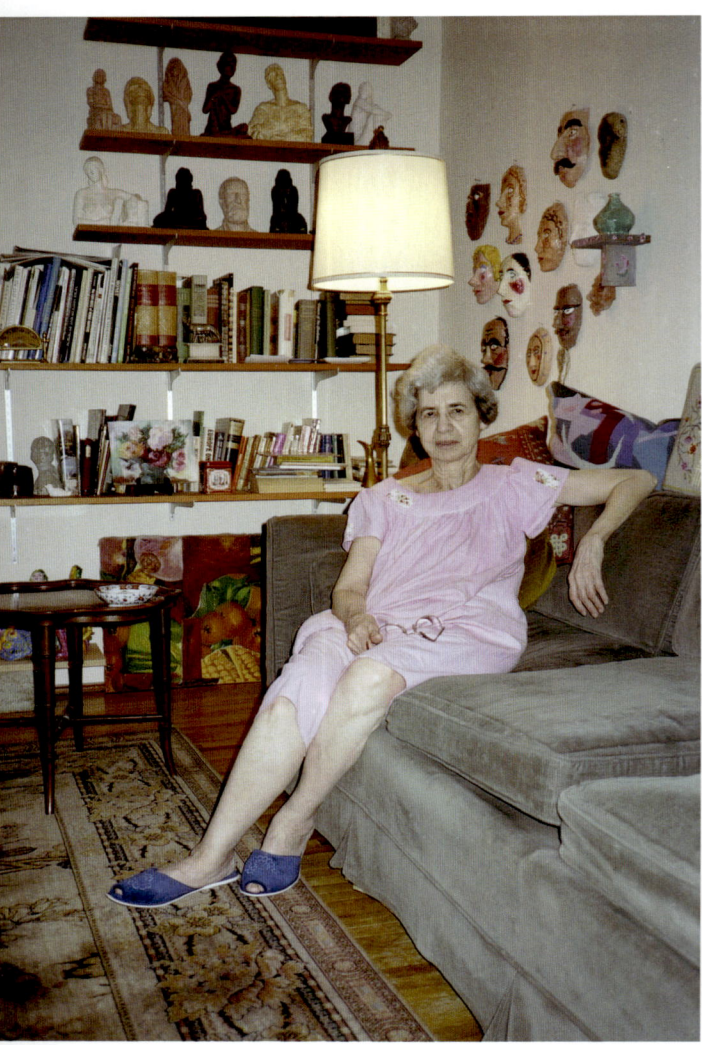

Josephine Tota in her living room,
surrounded by her ceramics, paintings,
and needlepoint, ca. 1980s
Photo courtesy of Lisa Rosica

1½ inches; the largest is 10 by 32 inches.

In a 1982 painting (cat. 30), not much larger than an 8½-by-11-inch piece of paper, figures and organic forms fill the space to overflowing. Trees and vines bracket and infiltrate the scene: the petite tree on the right sprouts an oversized yellow blossom and small breast-like growths on its trunk. Human and plant hybrids take a variety of forms, with everything in a state of germination. A remote and queenly mother figure has bright green leaves growing from the back of her neck. A vine that emerges from the back of her head grows down into the head of the throne-woman upon whom she sits.

This scene takes place in a setting reminiscent of an early Renaissance landscape: lush green grass, small decorative trees, gilded hills, and a night sky the color of the deepest lapis. The stylized depiction of the natural world is pierced on the left by a vertical interior space that has its floor inscribed with the receding lines of one-point perspective. Tota was familiar with the artists who developed these ideas during the late medieval and early Renaissance period, such as Masaccio and Piero della Francesca. Her inclusion of perspective lines—representing a rational articulation of the knowable world—within her surreal, alternate reality illustrates Tota's intrepid and intellectually playful approach to image making.

From this interior space, a woman walks toward the foreground; her body, that of a curvaceous dressmaker's dummy, echoes the hourglass lines of the tall vine to the left. She rests her hand in a comforting gesture upon the young woman who sits in a near-fetal position on the ground. The girl's left hand holds a handkerchief to wipe away her tears of blood; her right hand grasps both the queen/mother's dress and a vine that terminates in a clock on one end and a triangular face on the other. A small, potbellied man enters from the right. His misshapen body is adorned with a black cape. The direction of the path upon which he walks makes clear he will likely walk right past the inscrutable scene. Like us, he is a voyeur or visitor, not an integral player within the central drama.

Viewers of Tota's paintings are strangers within a strange land. We are interlopers upon her most interior explorations, an unexpected audience. Attempts at single-narrative interpretations will be thwarted: in Tota's Wonderland, much like Alice's, nothing is as it seems. Perhaps it would be more accurate to say that everything is also something else, as Tota's visual language is rooted in hybridization, appropriation, and multiplicity. Earlier in the twentieth century, the Surrealists used similar techniques in their exploration of the human psyche and of realms beyond the visible world. Since then, the permissive spirit of the surrealist idiom has proven mutable and well suited to the expressive needs of unconventional, visionary artists within America's vast and diverse population. Both visionary and surrealist impulses are evident in Tota's work.

Her most common motifs include anxious women, human/plant hybrids, the third eye, masks, tears of blood, clothing, and needles and threads. Images like these, not words, were the language in which Josephine Tota communicated. In life, she was a woman of very few words, both spoken and written. No papers or letters exist, and our knowledge of her life comes primarily from the personal accounts of family members.[2] She never wrote an artist's statement, and all that remains of her artistic intentions are these words captured in 1990, "When I am painting, I find peace. . . . My paintings are my inner soul."[3]

By all accounts, when the artist did discuss her work, it was always with a multiplicity of interpretations and associations, sometimes contradictory, within a single image. Her family members have inherited this trait. When asked if a small joyful girl in roller skates was meant to represent her as a child, daughter Rosamond said, "maybe, yes—I did roller skate—but it could also be my mother painting the kind of girl she wished she was."[4]

Our inability to know Tota's interior life or artistic intentions does not diminish our experience of the formal or psychic potency of her work. Time expands and contracts: we see images and symbols of her and her loved ones at different moments throughout their lives. Despite the appeal of her bright, prismatic palette, unsettling narratives hopscotch around shifting spaces. With the power to penetrate time and space, Tota's visions capture and condense anxieties accumulated over a lifetime.

AGE AND NONCONFORMITY

For unconventional artists intent upon pursuing their private visions, marginalization within an art-historical framework is all too common. Early twentieth-century modernist Florine Stettheimer (1871–1944), like Tota, made her best paintings late in life and then almost disappeared from the historical record. Despite notable differences in Stettheimer's and Tota's personal circumstances, both artists' dense

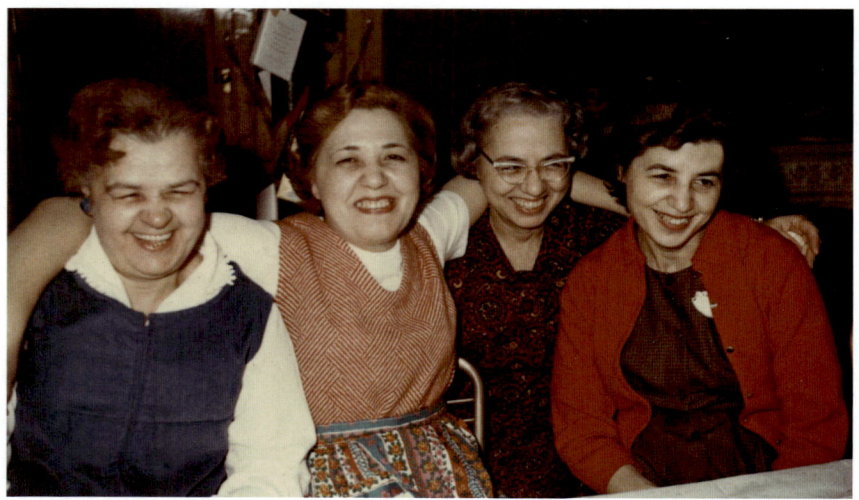

Josephine Tota (*far right*) with sisters
Rose, Nancy, and Louise, ca. 1960s
Photo courtesy of Lisa Rosica

compositions, multiple and female-led narratives, and bright, confectionary colors put them at odds with what has been perceived as the more masculine modernist styles of their times. In the 1990s, art historian Barbara J. Bloemink successfully set out to excavate Stettheimer from the dominant historical record. Like her predecessor, Tota's path to obscurity has been hastened by what Bloemink described as our culture's trouble with "reconciling older women and innovation."[5]

In recent profiles of two canonical male artists of the twentieth century, Chuck Close and Bruce Nauman, the work made in their seventies was described using words like *audacity*, *ferocity*, and *blaring color*.[6] To position an artist in his seventies using this kind of language works against expectations. To do so for a self-taught artist in *her* seventies—to see in her work both innovation and audacity—is a shot across the bow. After a life of impotence within dominant power structures, Josephine Tota did find her audacious and radical voice. In blaring, carefully calibrated tapestries of color, line, and form, Tota painted the wild, fantastical world within her head. There is fear and anxiety in her paintings, but there is also rage and daring.

Tota holds the threat of a subversive female power because her fixed and unabashed self-reflection thwarts the male gaze. Her near complete focus upon what feminist art historian Mary Garrard called "alternative values of female kinship networks" is evident throughout her oeuvre. Tota's relationships with her family, her mother, and in particular her bond with her three sisters, were as complicated as they were formative. In her painted universe, the relationships between women hold the greatest potential for fulfillment and pain; men make only rare appearances in supporting roles.

A horizontal untitled painting from 1983 shows a group of five gray-haired women in long black dresses with small white crosses on their upper sleeves (cat. 39). They exist, forgotten, in a liminal space outside three doors from which brightly dressed women with blond, red, and brown hair peek out. Three phones are mounted to the walls beside each door. Their receivers hang dejectedly; no communication is possible. Tota was a sensitive soul whose creativity gave her great joy, but she often had feelings of depression and social alienation. Cast out and isolated, the artist paints elderly women as modern-day saints, martyrs, mourners, and beggars in a domestic no-man's-land.

Tota's unsettling female-led narratives nearly always take place at the sites of women's bodies: bound, asleep, prostrate, weeping, burned at the stake, and in pain. Her audacious images are rife with women subjugated by the circumstances of life or empowered with mystical and unknowable forces. Her ferocious depictions of danger and disfigurement are what we might expect from medieval martyrdoms or present-day horror films, not an amateur painter in her seventies. As Michel Thévoz observed of so-called outsider artists frequently hitting their stride in retirement age, sometimes "it takes seven decades to turn into an anarchist."[7]

BIOGRAPHY AND INSPIRATION

Josephine Tota's life, dreams, and memories were primary sources for her art. Tota's relationships within her communities—her family, Rochester's Italian American immigrant population, the garment industry, and the mentors and peers from her amateur art classes—are all manifest in her densely imaged, allegorical paintings. The reward for the persistent and curious viewer of Tota's paintings is an engagement with work that unfolds over time in labyrinthian tangles of both art-historical and personal references. Her story is important to us because it was important to her.[8]

Born in Corato, Italy, in 1910, Josephine Tota retained positive memories from her childhood in Italy. She spent long hours absorbed by her imagination in communion with the natural world on her family's farm. As a young girl, she had an active fantasy life in which her imagination was her safe place, and her friends were the fairies who lived under a rock near her family's home. Tota felt a deep and abiding connection with the spirituality and mystery of the natural world. In her seventies, this sensibility found expression in her art, with references to underground realms and human/plant hybrid beings that occupy both the visible realm of the surface and the mysterious world of nature and spirit below. In a 1985 painting (cat. 52), a spindly tree trunk props open a brain-like hill to expose the mouth of a dark cave from which fantastical tadpole-like creatures and sprites emerge. A fairy-tale princess kneels to speak to their Lilliputian leader. In art and in life, Tota followed the essential impulse that drove her: to understand, express, and control the relationship between seen and unseen worlds.[9]

Other early memories included drawing pictures on the slats of wooden crates and lying in the grass to watch the clouds float through the sky. As a deeply sensitive and unusually bright and outspoken child, Tota often felt alienated from her parents and four siblings. These feelings of isolation and marginalization were reinforced by the circumstances of her life, including early experiences of childhood poverty and the trauma of immigrating to the United States.[10]

Tota was ten years old in 1921 when her family emigrated from Italy. The family traveled by boat and entered the United States through Boston. Her mother managed the crossing on her own with Tota and her three sisters and brother in tow. The family then reunited with their patriarch, who had made the trip the previous year.[11] The family's passage to America was like that of so many immigrants who endured inhumane conditions on the boat and upon arrival. As an adult, Tota retained a traumatic memory of being herded through immigration upon arrival at Boston. Due to an illness on board, all the women and girls were disrobed and treated with a fumigant. The artist recalled men looking on as they were sprayed and left to retrieve their shoes and clothing from a vast pile.[12]

Arriving in Rochester in upstate New York, where a relative was working as a tailor, the Tota family struggled with debilitating poverty, a language barrier, and harsh weather unlike the Mediterranean climate of home. In the early 1900s, Rochester had one of the highest percentages of Italian-born populations in the country; these skilled Italian laborers and tailors provided forty percent of the workforce for the city's booming garment industry.[13] The Tota family was subject to the conflicting influences of Rochester's sizable Italian immigrant community and the Americanization encouraged by public schools and settlement houses.[14]

Tota, on the cusp of her own seismic developmental shift of puberty, had to navigate this wholly new cultural environment, one that was constantly shifting as she and her family moved around Rochester repeatedly throughout her young life.[15] The memories of her life in America as a teen were of tension, fear, and emotional isolation.[16] Similar to many immigrant women who have struggled with the

Josephine Tota (*left*) with brother Frank and sister Nancy, ca. 1920s
Photo courtesy of Lisa Rosica

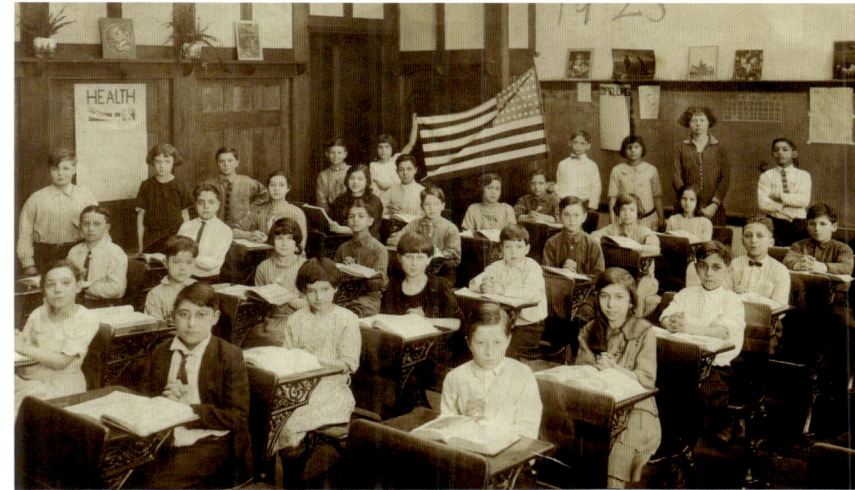

Josephine Tota class photo
(Tota is sitting in the fourth row from the camera, four desks back, wearing a dark shirt and holding a book), Rochester, NY
Pencil notation "1925"
Photo courtesy of Lisa Rosica

displacement and duality of living between their home and adopted cultures, Tota described feeling torn and having a fractured sense of herself throughout her life.[17] This sensation would take visible form, over sixty years later, in her paintings. Like the stories of other self-taught artist-immigrants who have become some of America's most unorthodox and creative citizens—including Martín Ramírez (1895–1963), Simon Rodia (1879–1965), and Morris Hirschfield (1872–1946)—Tota's reinforces a correlation between the immigrant experience, fracturing, and creativity.[18]

Before the age of fifteen, Tota was forced to quit school to contribute to the family's income. She had a sharp mind, and the early termination of her schooling was a loss she keenly felt her entire life. By 1926, the Rochester city directory lists her and her mother Isabella as employees at the tailor shop of the National Clothing Company.[19] Tota worked as a seamstress, a job she would repeatedly turn to throughout her life. Her work put her in the center of Rochester's fashion industry; photos of her as a young woman show her stylishly dressed. Over the course of her working life, the monotonous work of a seamstress would come to frustrate her creative, intuitive personality.

When she turned nineteen in 1930, her family arranged her marriage to a cousin, Frank Tota, who was about twenty years older. They soon moved to the Bronx where Frank lived, and Josephine recalled feeling a great sense of hope and potential at her new life and location. On April 29 of that year, she sent a postcard to her sister Rose with the brief note: "I like N.Y. very much and I hope to see you soon."[20] Josephine and Frank's time in the Bronx coincided with the worst years of the American Depression. Frank felt the pressure

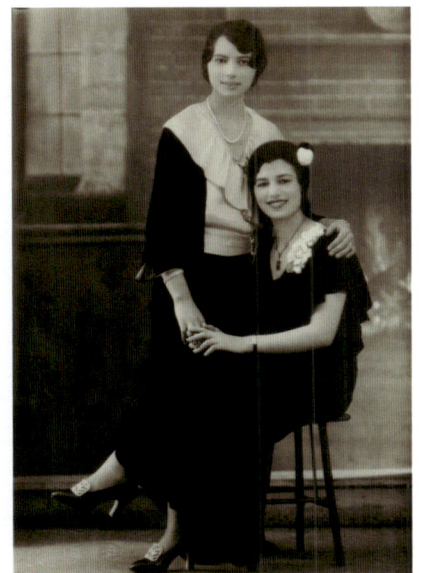

Josephine Tota (*sitting*) with her sister Louise, ca. 1920s or 1930s
Photo courtesy of Lisa Rosica

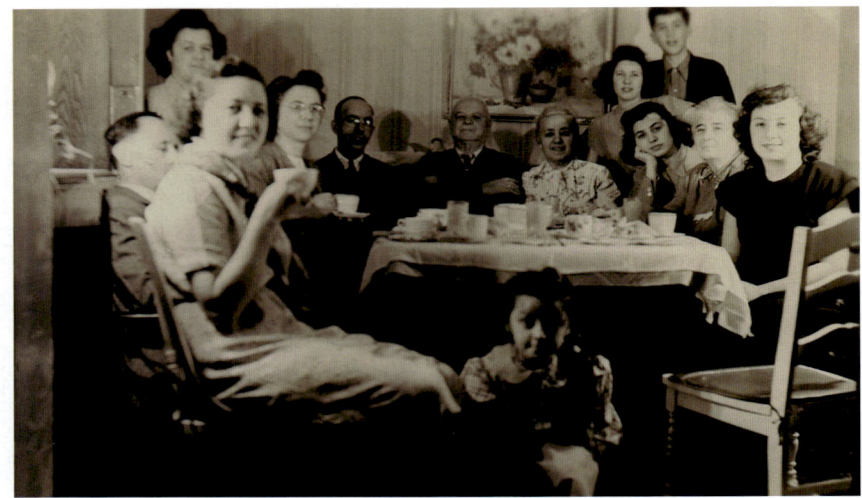

Josephine Tota (*third from right*) at a family gathering with husband Frank (*far left*) and daughter Rosamond (*front*), Rochester, NY, February 21, 1948
Photo courtesy of Rosamond Tota

of providing for his new wife with a struggling bakery business. Josephine did not work outside the home or attend school. Several devastating miscarriages, further exacerbated by her loneliness and lack of creative stimuli, led to a deep depression of her own. By 1937, the shine of city living had worn off. Tota wrote to a cousin in Rochester, "everything is so noisy here."[21]

In a painting completed in the 1980s, Tota depicted her life in the city (cat. 11). The scene is a cacophony of garish colors and angles: a large gold female figure presides over a flat, claustrophobic urban landscape of closed doors, billboards, laundry lines, and fire escapes. The only sign of the natural world in this scene is a single leafless tree. For a woman who yearned for the healing power of the natural world, urban living had become intolerable.

By 1940, the Totas moved back to Rochester, where the artist would give birth to their daughter Rosamond the same year. Josephine eventually went back to work at the National Clothing Company. During this period, she worked in the National's tailor shop with her sisters. After working all day, she would come home to design and make clothing for her family, often sewing late into the night.

Throughout her time at the National, Tota pursued artistic activities to alleviate the drudgery of tailoring clothes. During lunch breaks, she would visit the Rochester Public Library to pore over art books from all periods. By the late 1940s, she was taking weekly art classes open to the public at the Mechanics Institute School of Applied Arts (now Rochester Institute of Technology), and painting became her source of joy and release.

In 1967, Tota's life changed dramatically. The year brought

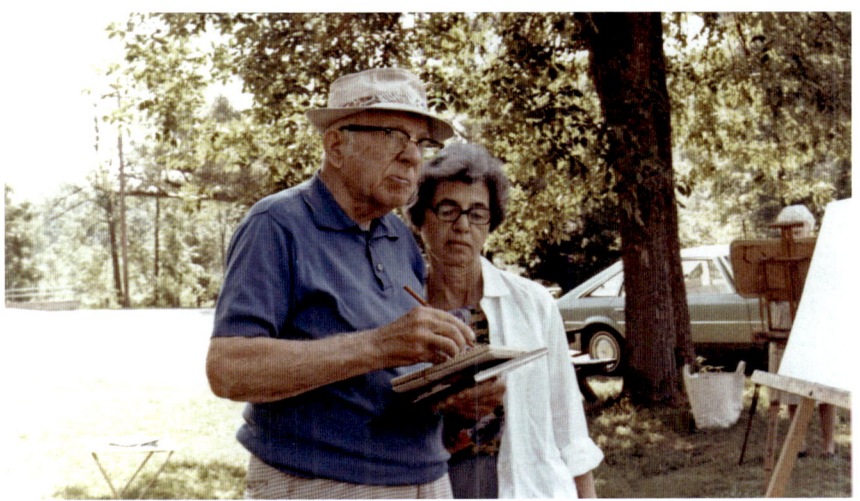

Carl W. Peters and Josephine Tota together at his Creative Workshop painting class, 1979
Photo courtesy of Rosamond Tota

a series of tragedies that included the deaths of her husband in January and her mother in March. Josephine and her sister Louise were both diagnosed with cancer. Tota's was uterine cancer, for which she received radiation treatment that caused chronic neuropathic pain. This she likened to having the lower half of her torso stuck with needles, or set on fire. The storm of personal tragedies led to her retirement and a resulting depression so severe that she was hospitalized and subjected to electroconvulsive treatments.[22]

After her recovery, Tota began to take painting and ceramics classes at the Memorial Art Gallery's community art school, the Creative Workshop. There she developed under the tutelage of Fritz Trautmann (1882–1971), a legendary colorist and instructor. Earlier in the century, Trautmann had joined his close friend the artist/architect Claude Bragdon (1866–1946) in explorations of color, sound, and philosophy. Trautmann's mystical leaning, his emphasis on the power of color, and his desire to bring out each student's "unique and precious individuality" certainly nurtured Tota's path toward her later iconography and style.[23] She credited her time under Trautmann as the period when she truly began to blossom as an artist.[24]

In the 1970s, Tota took extensive plein air classes with regionalist landscape painter, Carl W. Peters (1897–1980), also at the Creative Workshop. Peters, who shared her spiritual connection with the natural world, would take his students around town to paint the rural beauty of Rochester and the surrounding towns. An oil-on-canvas landscape she painted as a student of Peters illustrates her mentor's influence in its loose brush work, natural tones, and lush rural setting (left).

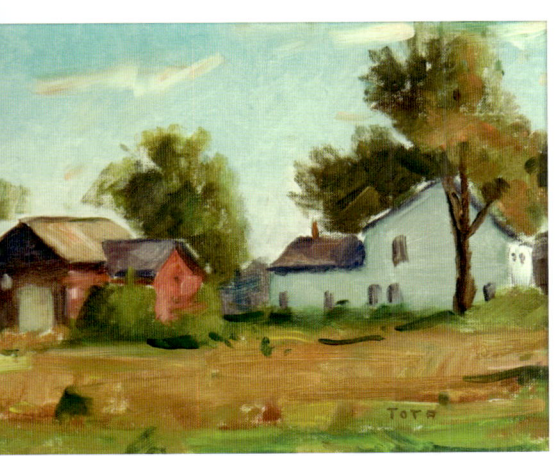

Untitled, undated, 1970s
Oil on canvas panel
11 15/16 x 15 15/16 in.
Private collection

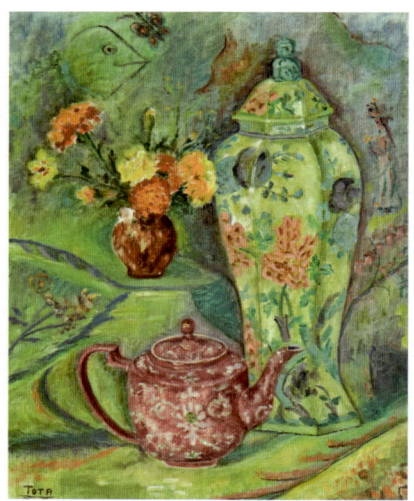

Untitled, undated, 1970s
Oil on canvas panel
19 ¹⁵⁄₁₆ x 15 ⅞ in.
Private collection

After painting in a representational style for many years, Tota experienced her transformative breakthrough in the late 1970s. Losing herself thoroughly to the creative experience while painting a still life, Tota later realized she had painted an abstracted and disembodied bird head in the background of the composition (left). This creative step, one made without conscious choice, was a revelation that led Tota into the depths of her own imagination as a source for imagery and creative inspiration.

During this period, Tota would travel by train a few times a year to visit her adult daughter Rosamond in Manhattan. Their days together were spent absorbing the art on view in the city's many galleries and museums. Tota was as engrossed by the contemporary abstract art in Soho galleries as she was by the medieval and early Renaissance Italian masterpieces at the Metropolitan Museum of Art. Thanks to her natural inclination, further honed by decades of tutelage under excellent teaching artists, and her insatiable visual appetite, Tota developed a sophisticated and independent eye. Now in her seventies, largely freed from the obligations of work, marriage, and motherhood, she would soon find her artistic voice and the "anarchist" within.

LATE PERIOD

The artist described being "hypnotized" by the gilded paintings of the medieval and early Renaissance period at the Metropolitan Museum.[25] It is tempting to imagine Josephine Tota's experience as she stood enraptured by their intimate scale, intense emotions, and bright colors and gilding. Drawing close to each example as she walked through the galleries, Tota absorbed the moments of artistic brilliance embodied by iconic paintings like Giotto di Bondone's *The Adoration of the Magi*. In the late 1970s, the Met reinstalled some of their galleries to highlight recent conservation and new scholarship on its collection of fifteenth-century secular Tuscan paintings.[26] The horizontal cassone paintings and shaped birth trays, like the Master of 1416's *Ameto's Discovery of the Nymphs*, featured humanist and secular subjects and may also have served as models for Tota's late paintings. As an Italian American, the direct and powerful experience of witnessing her rich artistic heritage lit a fire in Tota that would burn bright for the rest of her life.

Driven by her response to these paintings, Tota asked artist and friend Miriam Sellers Lapham to teach her how to work with egg tempera and gilding.[27] The first time she used the new medium, Tota told family members she experienced an overwhelming sensation of

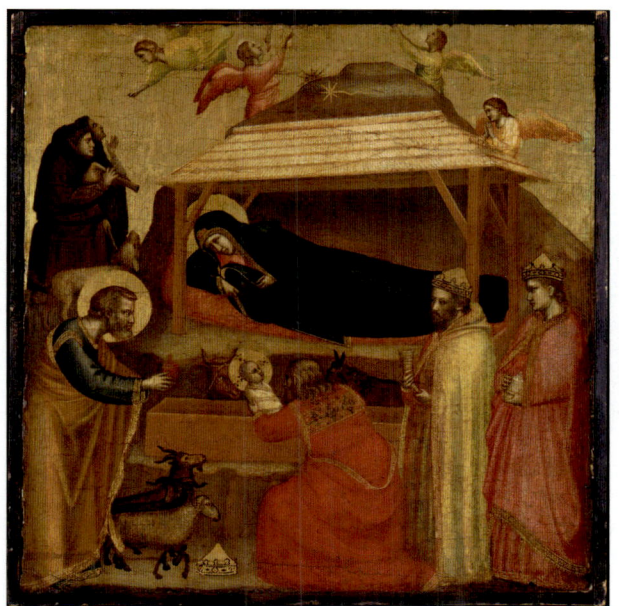

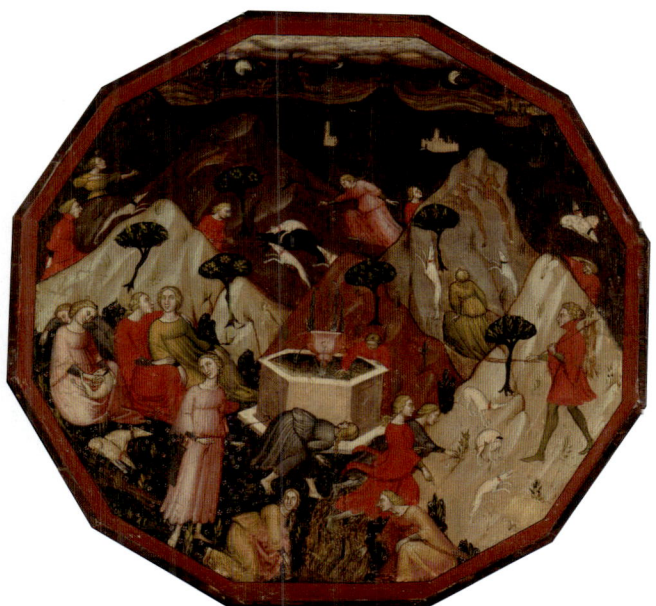

Left: Giotto di Bondone (Italian, Florentine, 1266/76-1337)
The Adoration of the Magi, possibly ca. 1320
Tempera on wood, gold ground
17 ¾ x 17 ¼ in.
Metropolitan Museum of Art, John Stewart Kennedy Fund, 11.126.1
Image source: Art Resource, NY

Right: Master of 1416 (Italian, Florentine, early 15th century)
Ameto's Discovery of the Nymphs, ca. 1410
Tempera on wood, twelve-sided
21 ⅛ x 22 ⅛ in.
Metropolitan Museum of Art, Rogers Fund, 26.287.2
Image source: Art Resource, NY

having done it before. The obsessive, meticulous technique—grinding the pigments, mixing the paints, and building up the image with multiple, small brushstrokes—complemented her creative temperament and provided a controlled process through which she could exorcise the chaotic fears and traumatic events of her life.[28]

The flattened and stylized images typical of egg tempera suited Tota's artistic sensibilities. The small painting *Homage to Miriam,* with its bright, candy colors and patterned surface, is an early example of Tota's exploratory work in this new medium (cat. 1). Tota soon revisited one of her earlier oil landscapes in egg tempera and gilding. Like medieval alchemy, her use of the centuries-old technique transformed a prosaic landscape into an otherworldly scene of bright colors, stylized flowers and trees, and a fantastical golden sky (page 9 and cat. 10).

With this shift to egg tempera, Tota soon turned from traditional landscapes and still lifes to intensely insular images teeming with figures, plants, enigmatic action, and ambiguous settings. In both subject and style, these paintings had no precedent in her previous work. In her late paintings, she depicted the landscapes of her dreams and her interior world, in which women and the natural world exist within a fluid and interconnected physical plane. Descendants of the ancient story of Apollo and Daphne, Tota's women undergo metamorphosis at the will of a cosmic force: they germinate seedling offspring and sprout flowers and leaves from their bodies (cat. 47).

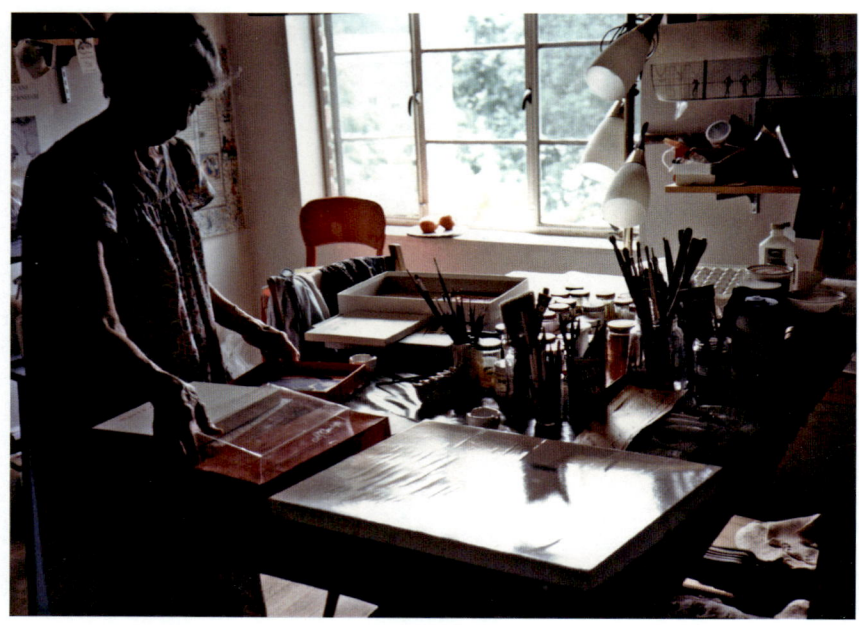

Josephine Tota in her painting studio,
Rochester, NY, ca. 1986
Photo courtesy of Lisa Rosica

The decades-old wounds inflicted by multiple miscarriages and reproductive traumas shaped Tota's interior landscape and took vivid form in her late paintings.

Given the intensely personal nature of the imagery, it is not surprising that Tota soon ended her enrollment in painting classes at the Creative Workshop. With her late style, Tota overturned her earlier amateur training to develop her own idiom, one based on interiority. The second bedroom of her apartment was converted into her studio. From the stylish woman of her youth with dreams of a large family of her own, Josephine Tota in her seventies became a diligent, autonomous artist who went to work each day in her studio, painting for hours in her housecoat. According to family members, she was interested in the act of art making and very little else.

Her paintings were not made in a swirl of visionary trances but rather were the result of slow and meticulous artistic focus and planning. A photo of Tota's studio space shows a tidy collection of repurposed jelly jars full of dried pigment, a variety of brushes, and small vessels for mixing colors. She first outlined the composition on a sheet of tracing paper as it existed in her mind's eye. After coating her board with gesso, she would transfer the image from the paper to the gessoed surface. She did not make other preparatory studies or drawings for her late paintings, and she would discard her tracing papers after they had fulfilled their function.

Egg tempera is a demanding and precise medium. The speed

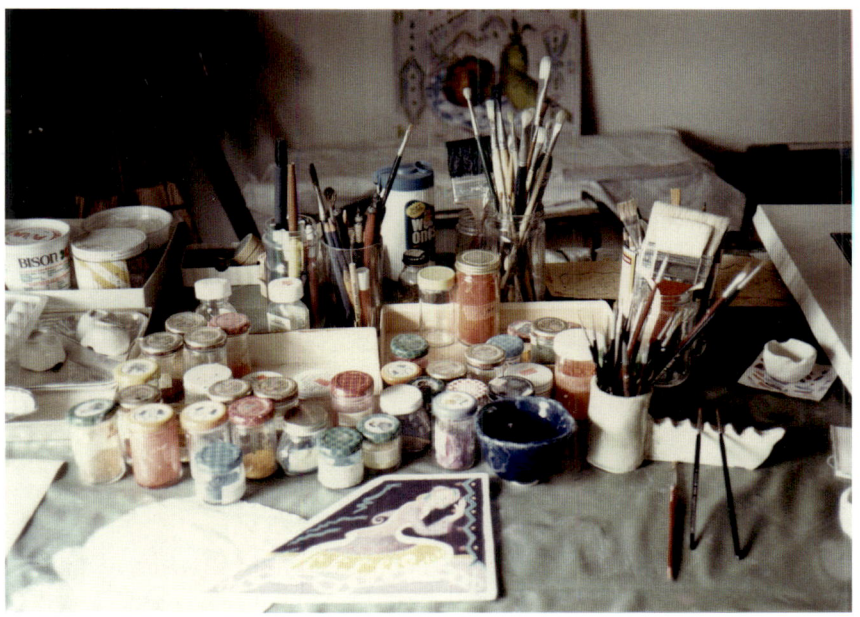

Josephine Tota's workspace and painting materials, 1986
Photo courtesy of Rosamond Tota

with which it dries requires colors and shading to be built up with countless cross-hatched brushstrokes. Tota's predominantly linear, flat, and decorative style grew out of the qualities in her chosen medium, the influence of medieval illuminations and panel paintings, and the artist's aesthetic choices. Modeling to mimic form and mass, something Tota endeavored to do when she sculpted clay figures from live models, was not a priority in her paintings.

Over the course of the twelve years of her late period, only minor changes in skill and style are evident in her work. A precise record of stylistic change or development is difficult to track because so many of the paintings are undated and because her control and quality seem to have fluctuated. Paintings with shaky brushstrokes and chaotic compositions sometimes precede, by only a few months, paintings that mark her most masterful control of paint, color, and pattern. At times, her varnish was unevenly applied or not applied at all. Examples at the end of her life show an application so thick that it is likely her varnish supply had aged, evaporated, and thickened beyond what most artists would considerable viable. These inconsistencies point to the limitations of her informal training, certainly. But perhaps more tellingly, they emphasize how her expressive objectives were inward facing and existed outside the expectation of an external audience.

Tota placed her creative activity in time by marking the day, month, and year of completion on many of her late paintings, in paint on the front or in pencil on the back. The earliest dated egg tempera,

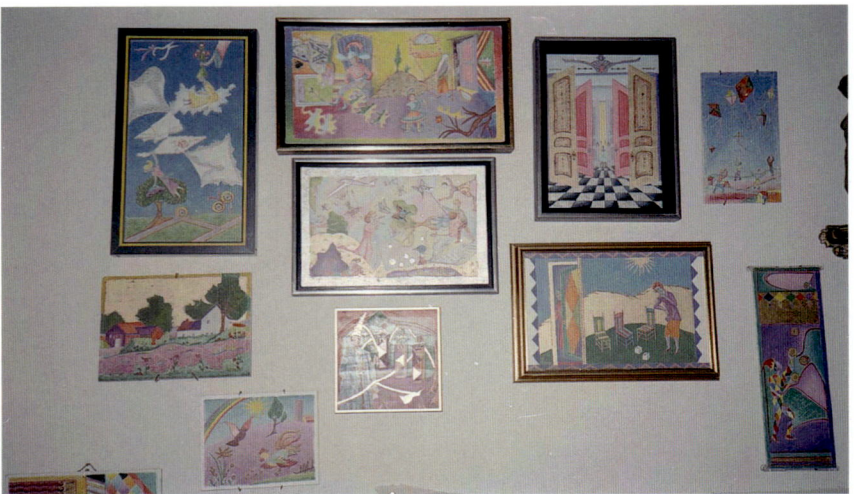

Josephine Tota paintings displayed in
her apartment, ca. 1980s
Photo courtesy of Lisa Rosica

painted when she was seventy years old, is inscribed May 19, 1981.
Inspired by the shaped canvases she admired by Frank Stella, and
possibly the birth trays of fifteenth-century Tuscany, in 1983 Tota
began to paint on shaped boards she had custom-cut at the lum-
beryard. The latest dated egg tempera is inscribed March 1, 1993,
painted three years before her death at the age of eighty-five.

In the small studio where she spent hours every day quietly
and methodically painting her dreams and memories, Tota's small,
subversive paintings were not complete until she inscribed her name:
TOTA©. Her signature in blunt and blocky capital letters thwarts
potential erasure, a fate all too common for women artists through
time. As Anna Chave has observed, "In ways both social and legal, to
inscribe one's name is to lay claim to one's identity, to be counted.
Making a deliberate, contrived showpiece out of this banal and basic
act holds extra resonance for a female artist, however, given that
female artists' identities were historically widely subject to erasure."[29]

Her addition of the copyright symbol began after her transition
to egg tempera, an indication of her awareness of the originality
of her new style. In the true spirit of Tota's appreciation for contra-
diction, these bold declarations of artistic ownership conflict with
her reluctance to show her paintings outside of her home and her
frequent practice of boxing and storing the paintings upon their
completion. Only a small selection of her late egg temperas—primarily earlier and more joyful examples—found a place on the walls of
her apartment (above).

While her daily pursuit of her muse was primarily a solitary
endeavor, Tota was not a stereotypical solitary or isolated outsider.

She called upon family members to help grind her pigments and prepare her paints. With friendships that grew from her art classes, the artist would entertain in her apartment, organize visits to local art exhibits, and visit and make art in her friends' homes. Finding her muse at this late stage of her life was not without its challenges. During her most productive period, as she was newly developing her late style, Tota began to suffer from cataracts. A difficult surgery in the mid-1980s almost led to the loss of her vision. The terror she experienced from the ordeal would affect her for the rest of her life.

To help her cope with her trauma, Tota's psychiatrist invited her to his family farm outside of Rochester for therapeutic visits during long walks. One of the most unadulterated visions of solace and natural splendor is the artist's painting of her doctor and his farm (cat. 65). The long-necked geese that honked alerts with the arrival of new visitors maintain an assertive presence in the foreground, not far from a tree-root fairy who playfully tweaks the horn of a small purple goat. In the background, we see Tota from behind as she peers into a mystical portal, her arms crossed and held close to her body. She leans forward, as though considering whether to proceed. Beyond the patterned barn, rows of cabbages, and leaf-eared pigs, a winged agricultural fairy with a farmer's fork for a head careens through the sky. The figure of her doctor is one of her best-developed representations of a male figure. With his third eye tucked discreetly within his light brown hair and his white coat, he presides over the idyllic scene.

During the most prolific period of her late paintings, Tota continued to take ceramics classes at the Creative Workshop, where she focused her attention on figural sculptures and small wall-hung masks (left). Friends and acquaintances remember her as a sweet, dedicated artist with a quiet sadness who always made a point of bringing in homemade pizzelles at the start of each session. After friends visited her apartment, news of her visionary paintings made it back to the classroom. This is how Alec Hazlett, her ceramics instructor, and Larry Merrill, former director of the Creative Workshop, learned of her late paintings. Merrill recognized their importance and began to appeal to the artist to exhibit her paintings in the school's faculty and student exhibit space. It took Merrill years to earn Tota's trust before she agreed to show her paintings.[30] Like many artists' narratives framed by a "discovery" story in which a figure in the mainstream art world brings them into the fold, Josephine Tota's story will feel familiar. Without Merrill's persistence, Tota's paintings might never have been seen by the public.

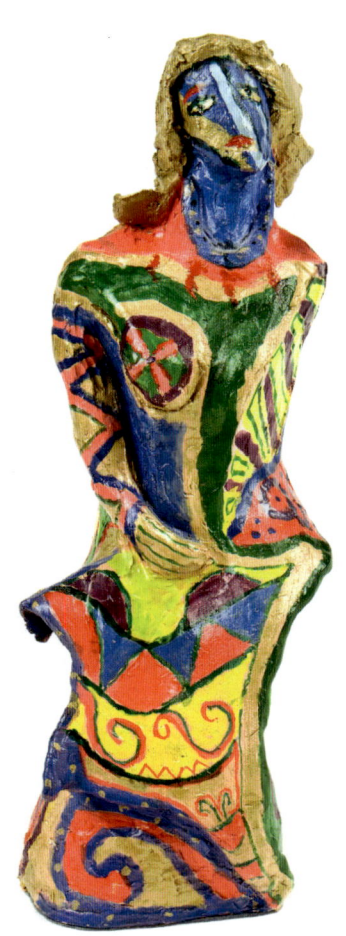

Untitled, 1988
Glazed and painted ceramic
13 ¼ x 4 ⅝ x 3 ⅜ in.
Private collection

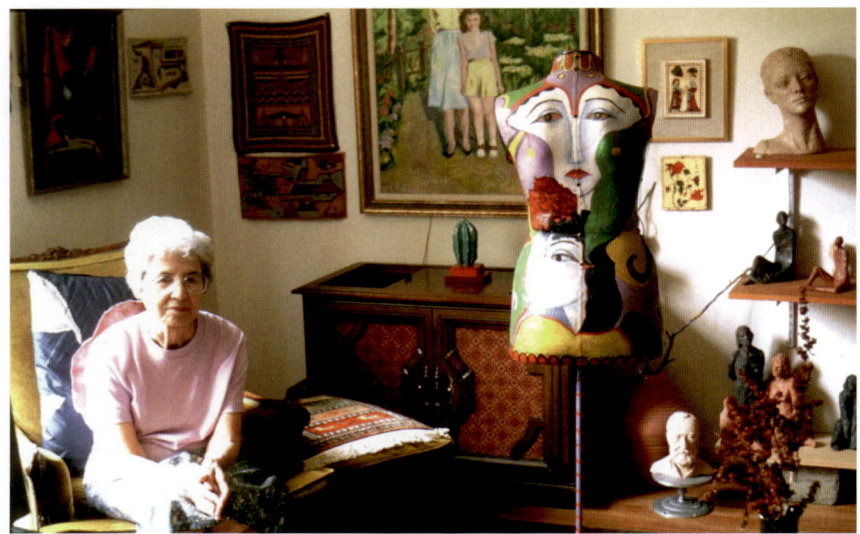

Josephine Tota at home, surrounded by her paintings, dressmaker's mannequin, and ceramics, ca. 1990
Photo by Larry Merrill

On the occasion of her exhibition, Merrill, a photographer by training, convinced Tota to sit for her portrait. He captured her in her apartment surrounded by the paintings and other artistic creations in clay and needlework. The egg tempera paintings became her primary focus in her later years, but her creative impulse found multiple outlets. The results proliferated to such an extent that they eventually filled her apartment and those of family members. Tota's apartment embodied the commingling of her domestic life and her art making and, as both studio and exhibition space, served her primary intended audience: the artist herself.

With no apparent pride or excitement in this moment of recognition, Tota sits slightly hunched with her hands folded on her lap, as though trying to take up as little space as possible. In this photo, as in her paintings, multiple incarnations of the artist are present. In addition to Tota's quiet presence, her surrogates are visible in the large painting of her and young Rosamond standing together in an abundant garden (based on two separate photos of the artist and her daughter in front of a Coca-Cola truck) and in the dressmaker's dummy cast from the artist's own body and painted in her wild, late style.[31]

Merrill organized a two-artist exhibition in the gallery of the Creative Workshop featuring Tota and another more established Rochester artist, Julianna Furlong Williams. When the exhibition opened in January of 1990, Tota was seventy-nine years old. The show was accompanied by a gallery brochure in which Merrill wrote how Tota's "frightening images of women gripped by doubt, fear and pain paradoxically calm her but spook the viewer . . ."[32]

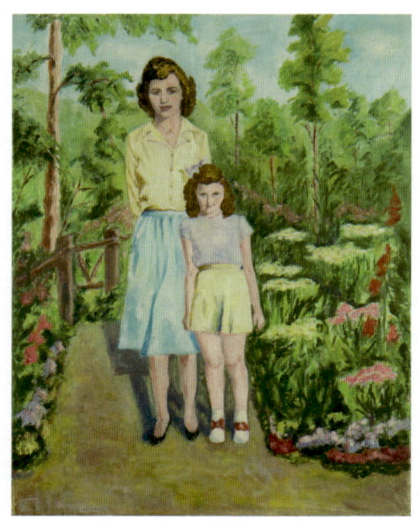

Untitled, undated, 1970s
Oil on panel, 36 x 28 1/16 x 3/16 in.
Private collection

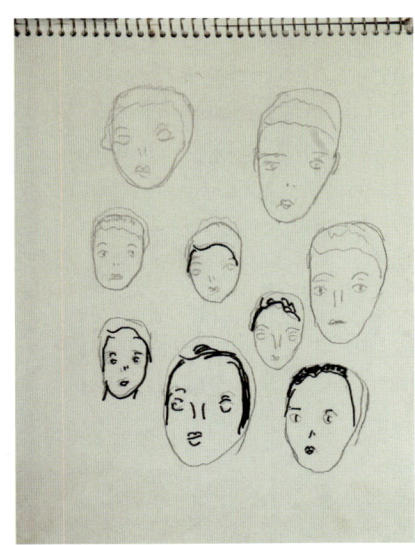

In the Rochester *Democrat and Chronicle*, critic Ron Netsky described her "mysterious allegorical narratives" and their "expressive, 'primitive' quality despite years of training."[33] For an introverted woman who had felt ostracized all her life, the anxiety of exposing herself through her art must have been intense. Yet from all accounts, the positive response to her paintings provided Tota with a welcome affirmation of her talent.

The small but well-received exhibition, which included over twenty of her late paintings and a small group of ceramic figures and masks, was the only time Tota's late paintings were exhibited during her lifetime.[34] Given her insular tendencies, it is not surprising that the public's experience of Tota's work ended here. The paintings were not available for sale; almost everything remained in the artist's possession until her death. The possibility of growth and exposure beyond this exhibition was further thwarted by Tota's diagnosis of progressive dementia in the early 1990s.

The powerful creative impulse that had exerted itself before dementia continued to assert itself in her illness, as evidenced by a sketchbook of drawings made in the last year of her life (left). Like a visual document of an artist all too aware of her decline, Tota's sketchbook revisited potent images and symbols: trees, gazing faces, and her signature, "Tota," written again and again. Josephine Tota died on December 29th, 1996, from complications of vascular dementia. Soon after, the Memorial Art Gallery acquired two paintings from her daughter Rosamond (cats. 24 and 67).

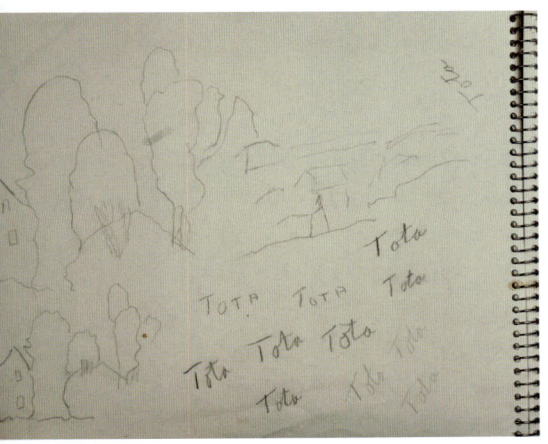

Sketchbook drawings, 1990s
Graphite and ink on paper,
12 ¹³/₁₆ x 9 ⅛ in.
Private collection

TOTA ON THE OUTSIDE

Tota is one of countless individuals who have followed their muse outside of art world conventions. While the work from her late period shows surrealist tendencies in her depiction of dreamscapes, multiple narratives, fairy tales, and destabilized identities, her irrepressible impulse and obsessive imagery links her with artists in the contested and marginalized category of so-called outsider or self-taught art. In 1972, Roger Cardinal first used the term *outsider* to describe artists who fell within Jean Dubuffet's concept of the French *art brut*, or the art of the mentally ill. Over time, outsider art has come to encompass a greater range of creators and artistic practices than Dubuffet's original definition. In recent years, the term itself has become the subject of debate as one built upon implicit social, economic, cultural, and racial biases. The use of *outsider* can stigmatize and further marginalize minority, economically disadvantaged, immigrant, or female artists already excluded from conventional social and artistic systems.[35]

Recent scholarship has favored the term *self-taught*, due to its emphasis upon training. Yet Tota's personal iconography and style grew out of decades of consuming and creating art within the art world infrastructure, however peripheral she may have been. Tota's inspired, vivid depictions of her interior life were made possible because of her artistic training and awareness of art-historical precedents, not in spite of them.

Given the role of dream imagery and her depictions of her interior worlds, she may qualify for a label of visionary as described by the curator Maurice Tuchman:

> A distinct compulsiveness, a visionary tone, a fusion of edgy uncertainty and anxiety with a firm certitude, a sense of exorcism, and the need and intent to get it out and place it down and to grasp and anchor the ephemeral. Such expressiveness verges on the hallucinogenic; it grapples with the unknowable . . .[36]

There is no end in sight for this ongoing debate in which scholars seek neutral terminology to try to encapsulate an expansive, diverse group of creators lacking a shared set of experiences. Despite the absence of a clear path forward in nomenclature, the debate has been successful in bringing to light the powerful and damaging assumptions behind the existing terminology.

These difficult-to-name artists—outsider, self-taught, visionary, marginal, unconventional, nonacademic—do share certain characteristics that are visible in Tota's story. These include an internal drive or compulsion to make art, a life story that often includes trauma of some form, and their rejection of the goals, motivations, or sites of training and production occupied by mainstream artists. Other unifying impulses include an uninhibited expression of self-made worlds, the obsessive focus upon process and the act of art making, and a fluid, almost casual relationship with supernatural realms and forces.

In two paintings, Tota depicts a visit to a fortune-teller and the vision of a past life recounted on that visit. In the painting of the visit (cat. 43), she sits with her hands clasped; a powerful woman stands before her. Both women lack facial features. The fortune-teller is identified by glasses containing her eyes pushed to the top of her head, a necklace with a question mark, and swirling hair. This meeting takes place simultaneously inside and outside: a flowing blue curtain on the left references a stage or interior setting. The walls and floors dissolve into a brightly colored landscape edged by red tatting, a familiar motif for a seamstress. During this visit with the fortune-teller, Tota was told the story of an experience she had during a previous life in which she unsuccessfully attempted to scale a wall in Spain. In the painting of the vision (cat. 63), Tota depicts a woman attempting escape over a spiked stone wall. As a black mass surrounds her, women pull her down from below. Lightning shoots out from brain-like shapes that hover menacingly in the night sky. In the upper left corner, a version of a chaos wheel, representing infinite possibility, hints at the whims of multiplicity and chance in the construction of our personal histories. In both paintings, Josephine Tota peers in from another time and place.

The artist was always watching the world, trying to absorb and understand it. Eyes figure prominently in her paintings. Figures are depicted with eyes that are sometimes whited out, painted black, or distorted in shape and scale. Vast volumes of wordless communication are transmitted through her use of the gaze. The third eye, traditionally associated with psychic abilities, clairvoyance, or access to realms beyond the physical, also appears in Tota's work. Eyes, a powerful source of Tota's magic, were a source of profound anxiety for her as well. Due to her visual nature and the threat she experienced to her sight during her cataract scare, her omnipresent eyes—glaring, seeking, weeping blood—are laden with psychological weight. The blood tears reference her physical ailment, the traumatic surgery, and they serve as a metaphor for her suffering.

Josephine Tota's creative impulses and obsessive imagery reflect many of the characteristics of self-taught or visionary artists for whom the focus is upon the creative process of art making, rather than the reception. When she was deeply engaged with consuming or producing art, Tota described falling into transcendent states in which her physical and emotional pain and losses lifted.[37] During even the longest painting sessions when she stood at her easel, her lifelong foot pain due to fallen arches was alleviated. When the art-making process was completed, she seems to have had little interest in assigning descriptive titles or discussing the work in depth.

Tota's obsessive patterning and *horror vacui* imposed order and control over her difficult memories. By revisiting and reframing them within her decorative, painted borders, she wielded a power and agency not afforded her in life. Similar qualities are evident in female artists who have entered the self-taught canon, like the British visionary artist Madge Gill (1882–1961). Gill, like Tota, suffered from a traumatic childhood and a lifetime of physiological conditions and

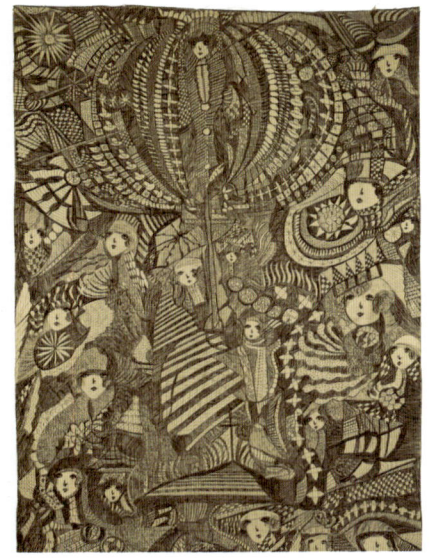

Madge Gill (English, 1882–1961)
Untitled, undated
Chinese ink on calico
83 ⅞ x 34 in.
Collection de l'Art Brut, Lausanne

illnesses. Both proudly self-identified as artists with focused and sustained artistic ambitions. Both artists lost children during pregnancy and childbirth, and experienced threats to their eyesight as adults. Gill had to have one of her eyes removed, a trauma that preceded the initial otherworldly vision that drove her creative activity.[38] While Gill's creative impulse contained a more mediumistic impulse than Tota's, both artists created imagery featuring peering faces with textile-like picture planes replete with decorative patterning.

Due to Tota's disinterest in discussing her work, what little we know about the inspiration for her paintings comes from the memories of family members. In a painting from the 1980s (cat. 24), an interior scene is dominated by a large standing figure in a black dress, likely Tota's younger self with her characteristic downturned eyes. She gazes out at the viewer with a mournful look as she pulls a wedding dress out of a box from which a bouquet has tumbled. Higher on the wall, another bouquet hovers, this one with withered flowers and a blackened ribbon. Oversized threaded needles surround her on the walls, as if contained within the fabric of the house. These ominous presences point at the young Tota's head and torso, their coiling threads like serpents about to strike. All of the tools and accoutrements of a seamstress—needle, thread, fabric, cloth—oppress or threaten to injure the occupants of this domestic scene. On the same plane as the needles are the head and arms of a distraught woman with grey hair, again likely Tota. She holds a handkerchief to her open mouth as though swallowing it against her will. Almost twenty years after having retired from her working life, Tota is made to consume her trade or it may consume her.

The center of the painting is a tumultuous, tilting zone where the private meets the public sphere. Below two trees that grow tortured faces, a table is set for a Mad Hatter's tea party and a metaphysical family reunion. The three chairs at the table—pink, yellow, and blue—likely represent mother, wife, and artist Josephine, daughter Rosamond, and husband Frank, respectively. The trio at the center of the artist's life. The curved line that divides the green and blue tablecloth continues in the line where the floor meets the grass. Divided precisely by gender roles, Tota's pink chair sits in the private sphere of the home, while Frank's blue chair is planted firmly in the public outdoor sphere. Made up of equal parts mother and father, Rosamond's yellow chair straddles the two spheres.

If our bodies are vessels, teacups are an appropriately delicate surrogate. Rosamond's teacup sits directly in front of her well-placed

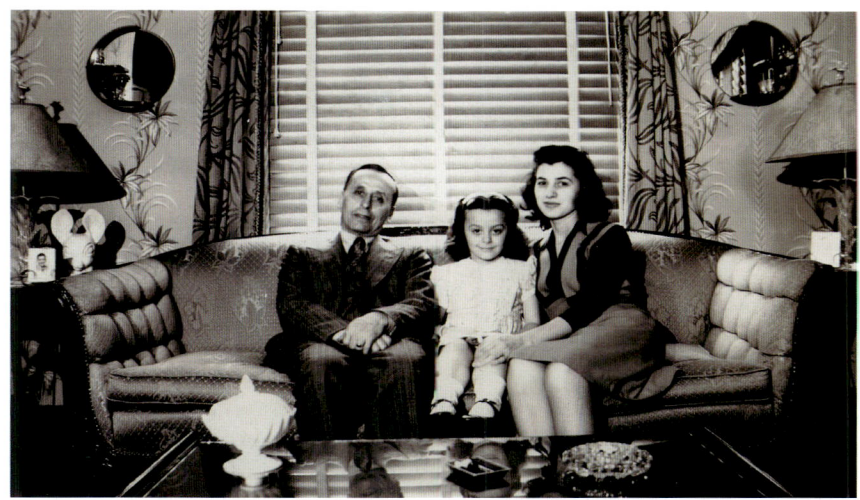

yellow chair: upright, viable, and open to life's experiences. In contrast, Tota's pink chair sits awkwardly at the corner of the table and her cup is pushed to the other end of the green tablecloth, out of reach and noticeably inverted in its saucer. This vessel is no longer performing its intended function. Frank's cup and saucer have fallen to the floor, where they remain shattered—a tragic symbol of her husband's death.

The dichotomous mother/daughter relationship figures prominently in this painting. Indeed, the image is dominated by dualities: female/male, absence/presence, old/young, black/white, mother/daughter, wild/domesticated, interior/exterior, day/night, past/present. Along a path that cuts diagonally across the lower right corner, a woman and a young girl gather nuts into a yellow bag. In the grass nearby, four large dandelions with aggressively reaching leaves crane up and out of the ground. A comical pink squirrel observes the scene. Rosamond Tota recalls collecting horse chestnuts with her mother from a neighborhood tree as a child. The ritual involved bringing the nuts back to their house to be placed in the front yard for the squirrels to eat. Only as an adult did Rosamond discover that the nuts disappeared because her father retrieved them during the night in order to maintain his daughter's illusion.[39] This little vignette offers a poetic memory of that parental impulse to weave magic and fantasy into children's lives. Both mother and daughter have their eyes closed; behind them, two heads that correspond with the figures below sprout from the top of the house and watch with brows furrowed.

The night sky is dotted with bubbles containing totemic eyes that weep blood. The faces that occupy the trees in the center of the composition look out at the viewer, at the mourning figure in black, and off into the distance. They, too, cry blood, grasp their heads in alarm or horror, and furrow their brows in dismay. The agonized figure at the top of the tree who clutches her head and opens her mouth in a primal scream may be the source of the plea written across the sky, "why?" Are these family trees broadcasting ancestral warnings? Are they spirit guides with revelations from another dimension? Viewers of Tota's paintings are voyeurs of the private communications between the artist and herself; no answers are forthcoming.

MANY SOURCES

The tortured artist creating work wrought from psychic pain has become a part of the mythology around both modern and self-taught art. Throughout her life, Tota was plagued by isolation, loss, physical illnesses, and depression, yet we must not assume that all of her imagery is born of personal and psychological turmoil. Like all artists, Tota was influenced by her family, friends, community, and socioeconomic culture. Perhaps more than many self-taught artists, she was particularly attentive to the art of the past and of her own time. Her artistic output was not hermetically isolated, nor entirely insular, but rather a reflection of her unique world view developed over a lifetime. As it is any artist's right to do, Tota absorbed, projected, and remade the world around her.

Tota's most productive period took place during the 1980s, a decade marked by shifting paradigms in the country's studios, museums, classrooms, and galleries under the influence of postmodernism and feminism. By questioning the dominant model of the single "great" (often male) artist and drawing attention to art made by groups presumed to be cultural outsiders, both postmodernism and feminism subverted the existing standards and power structures of the art world. While 1980s postmodern appropriation artists like Cindy Sherman and Sherrie Levine were questioning the very premise of originality, Josephine Tota was inventing her own iconography drawn from popular culture, art history, and the art of her time. Her eclectic tastes encompassed a love for the work of Wassily Kandinsky, Georgia O'Keeffe, the Surrealists Frida Kahlo and Salvador Dalí, and Frank Stella, to name a few.[40]

Ten years prior to Tota's artistic breakthrough, Linda Nochlin's revolutionary 1971 essay "Why Have There Been No Great Women Artists?" inspired feminist art historians to begin excavating exemplary women artists long written out of historical records.[41] One such artist was Kahlo, the subject of a popular biography and a major touring exhibition during Tota's late period. We know Tota admired Kahlo's work, and it is easy to imagine how its psychological intensity might have given her permission to embark upon her own inner journey. As biographer Hayden Herrera described the "strange magnetism" of Kahlo's small paintings, the same words could be used for Tota's: "Taken from separate, poignant moments in her life, each was like a smothered cry, a nugget of emotion so dense that one felt it might explode."[42] As discussed in Janet Catherine Berlo's essay in this volume, both Kahlo and Tota used their art to process lives marred by physical and emotional pain. Both found their unique voices by looking to artistic forms and traditions rooted in their ethnic heritage.

Tota's ability to incorporate a variety of art-historical sources into a singular, personal style accounts for the timeless appeal of her work. In an undated painting (cat. 13), Tota uses the structural form of a Buddhist mandala—one that facilitates healing and meditation—to frame her vision or memory of a young woman contemplating the ghostly apparition of a man in a 1940s fedora. A grand staircase leads toward a gilded sky heavy with incised stars like the vaulted interior of a medieval chapel.

Throughout the modern era, artists have looked to medieval art as a purer or more primitive form of expression. Tota's reliance upon decorative borders, bright colors and gilding, intense emotions, and a magical, lawless approach to depicting space reflects the most important influences upon her late style: medieval and early Renaissance panel paintings and illuminated manuscripts. Her first egg tempera was a direct copy from a fourteenth-century German manuscript that was published in a full facsimile in 1978, the *Codex Manesse* (cat. 2).[43] After that first foray, the artist did not copy as much as absorb. Her 1987 self-portrait (cat. 67) may have been drawn from multiple medieval sources, like this illumination reproduced in black and white in the 1979 book *The Illuminated Manuscript* in the Memorial Art Gallery library.[44] Tota's tightly cropped, boxed-in figure evokes her suffocating isolation; the starlight pattern echoes the effect cataracts had upon her vision. The decorative border that enshrines the medieval martyr imprisons the artist.

The role of the church in the Italian immigrant enclave of Rochester would have been especially important in fostering a sense of community, but the artist's personal inclination tended toward a more mystical, nature-centric belief system. Both in medium and imagery, Tota clearly drew upon the power of Christian models, but unlike the original didactic function of the medieval prototypes Tota

Siegburg Lectionary, German
Martyr Holding a Palm, f. 66v, second
quarter of the 12th century
Color and gold on parchment
10 ⅝ x 6 ½ in.
British Library / GRANGER

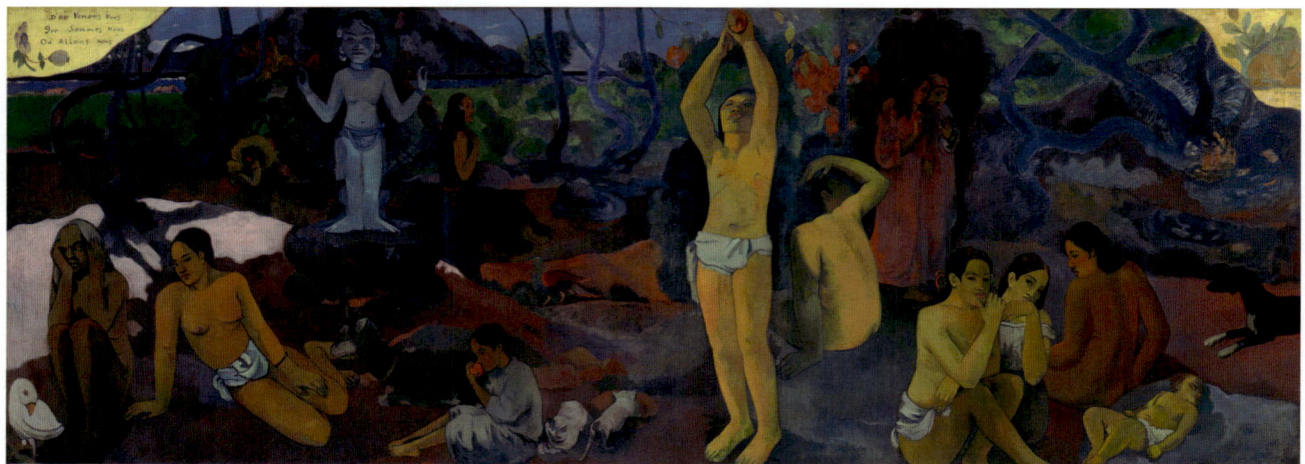

Paul Gauguin (French, 1848–1903)
*Where Do We Come From? What Are
We? Where Are We Going?*, 1897-98
Oil on canvas
54 ¾ x 147 ½ in.
Museum of Fine Arts, Boston, Tompkins
Collection–Arthur Gordon Tompkins
Fund, 36.270

so admired, her chosen imagery was developed toward maximum personal impact.

Her appropriation of traditional Christian imagery is at times overtly iconoclastic, in one instance hitting both the church and the medical profession in equal measure (cat. 66). In this 1987 painting, Tota's subject is the modern "religion" of medicine. An imperious man offers his blessing; above his arm is the caduceus, the symbol popularly associated with the medical field in the United States. The recipients of this benediction are three nearly identical male figures adorned with ivy vines, glowing halos, and stethoscopes that hang from their ears. On each, the bell or diaphragm used to listen to a patient's heart dangles uselessly on his chest. They do not see or hear the tiny figure of Tota who, like the patrons in medieval altarpieces, kneels in fervent prayer. Her tenuous physical health takes visible form in needlelike appendages that point at her body, starbursts that cover her eyes and float in front of her face, and her hip, rear, and feet painted flame red. Her secular saints are imbued with the same remote and mysterious power of their medieval forebears, but their chess-piece bodies reveal another truth: Tota's prayers will not be heard or answered by these Ivy League pawns.

In 1985, Josephine Tota was seventy-four years old and recently recovered from cataract surgery when she painted one of her largest and most significant late paintings. The artist's existential questions took shape in an intense, carefully composed image (cat. 57). Three figures anchor the horizontal composition evoking Paul Gauguin's 1897 to 1898 masterpiece, *Where Do We Come From? What Are We? Where Are We Going?*. The inscribed upper corners, painted orange in Gauguin's painting, become curtains in Tota's work, turning her scene into a staged performance of physical and psychological pain and endurance.

Like Gauguin, Tota divides her image into three sections. Her sophisticated questions about the internal and external forces that shaped her life play out across the painting in which all three figures represent the artist. In the figures' laps, Tota has painted, from left to right, a handkerchief of bleeding eyes, a flower in the form of a bleeding eye, and a swirling black vortex in the place of her uterus. The void in the figure on the right may reference the artist's obstetric troubles. The handkerchief held in the lap of the left figure is so filled with tears and pain accumulated over a lifetime that its saturated fabric has begun to drip onto the floor. Tacks stab exposed feet and torturous blindfolds obscure vision. The central figure, with Medusa-like hair and the all-white eyes of a person in the midst of a vision, is the artist in her most potent state.

SURREALIST SENSIBILITY

Throughout the twentieth century, the average American experienced Surrealism, quite apart from the French movement's rigid philosophy, as a set of visual strategies based in the unconscious, dreams, and imagination of the artist. In her assessment of the qualities and influence of the movement in the United States, scholar Sandra Zalman describes the "elastic contemporaneity" of Surrealism and its relationship with popular culture and mass media throughout the twentieth century.[45] Like many Americans, Tota was aware of the icons of Surrealism in the United States, Frida Kahlo and Salvador Dalí, both of whom she revered. A year before leaving the Bronx, Tota and her husband attended the 1939 World's Fair in Queens, the year Dalí's Surrealist funhouse pavilion was the talk of the fair. Fifty-four years later, Tota fulfilled a lifelong dream when she visited the Dalí Museum in St. Petersburg, Florida, with her niece in 1993.[46]

Beyond Dalí, Surrealism offered women artists—including Kahlo, Dorothea Tanning, Remedios Varo, and Leonora Carrington—a new language with which to explore, in personal and often transgressive images, the fraught relationship between female identity, public and private spaces, and a woman's body. As outlined by Whitney Chadwick:

> In general, the works of women associated with the Surrealists display an affinity for the structures of fabulist narrative rather than shocking rupture, a self-consciousness about social

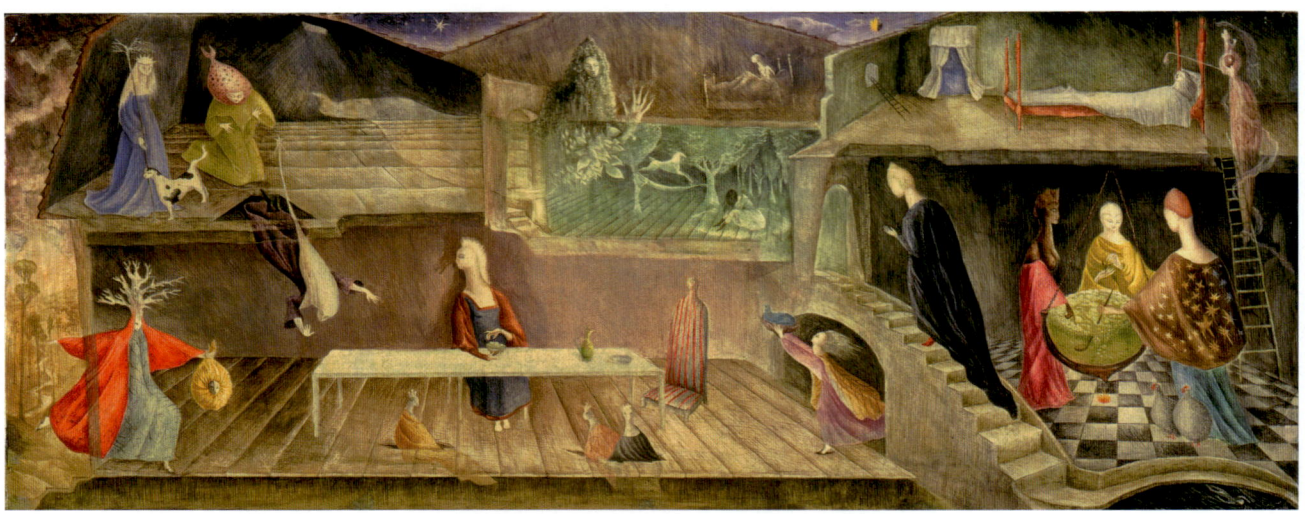

Leonora Carrington
(Mexican, born England, 1917-2011)
The House Opposite, 1945
Tempera on panel
13 x 32 ¼ in.
West Dean College,
the Edward James Foundation
© 2018 Estate of Leonora Carrington /
Artists Rights Society (ARS), NY

constructions of femininity as surface and image, a tendency toward the phantasmic and oneiric, a preoccupation with psychic powers assigned to the feminine, and an embrace of doubling, masking, and/or masquerade as defenses against fears of non-identity.[47]

In their paintings, as in Tota's, women are active agents. They play aggressor and victim, subject and object. Men and boys make only occasional appearances. The potent symbolic association between the female identity, the female body, and the home—a relationship capable of both comfort and oppression—was a frequent subject of the female Surrealists. Their paintings feature inscrutable scenes played out by hybrid creatures in which domestic spaces, normally the domain of female power, are threatened or disrupted.

Delight, despair, and wonder are visible in equal measure in Leonora Carrington's *The House Opposite* (1945) and an untitled painting by Tota from 1982 (cat. 29). Both artists present domestic worlds in which the tangible and intangible commingle. Familiar spaces are transformed into uncanny, potentially magical realms. Carrington's figures cast spells, sprout branches, and dive through floors. Tota's painting includes three playing cards that reference the address of the home in which her family lived the longest, 128 Fairgate Street in Rochester. Two toylike figures dance on the grass below laundry lines. The lines hang upon a rod that sprouts a female head and bleeds from both ends. A faceless guardian holding the ace of spades watches from the edge of the painted frame; a single leaf grows where she grasps an otherwise bare tree. Tota, like the female

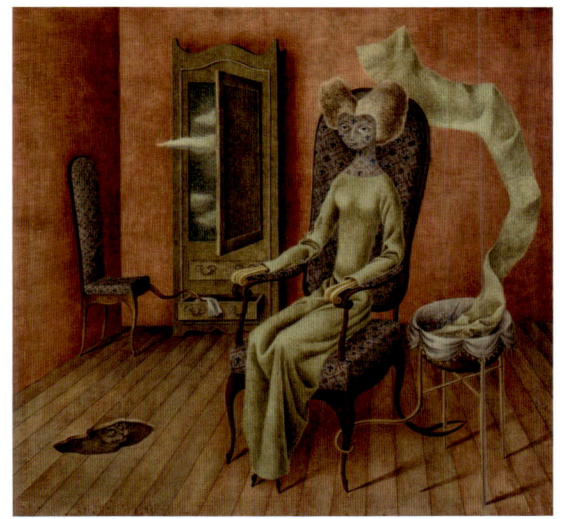

Remedios Varo (Spanish, 1908–1963)
Mimesis (Mimetismo), 1960
Oil on Masonite
18 ⅞ x 19 ⅝ in.
Museo de Arte Moderno, Mexico City,
Collection Isabel Gruen Varsoviano,
in memoriam, Gift of Walter and
Anna Gruen

Surrealists before her, created worlds in which multiple planes inter-
connect in mysterious ways, and where women, children, and hybrid
beings coexist.

The Surrealists and Josephine Tota counted Lewis Carroll as an
influence.[48] Tota's painted world, like that of Alice's Wonderland, is
sometimes delightful dreamland but more often a menacing realm
of teacups, playing cards, and dizzying shifts in scale and vantage
point. Just as Alice had to renegotiate space as she grew and shrank,
Tota and the Surrealists were constantly renegotiating their shifting
identities as artists, women, wives, and mothers. A tendency toward
a fractured sense of self has been observed in the work of female
Surrealists and is sometimes associated with the challenge inherent in
balancing a creative drive alongside marriage or motherhood.[49] Tota
often described feeling "torn" or fractured; her destabilized, unravel-
ing identities take the shape of women with multiple heads that grow
from a single body.

In the 1940s, Carrington and Varo both adopted the medium
of egg tempera used by medieval artists before them. Beyond the
desirability of the medium for its luminous, high-key tonalities, they
appreciated the symbolic value of the egg and its potent associations
with mysticism, reproduction, and domesticity.[50] Remedios Varo, like
Tota, was deeply attuned to nature and found her connection with
another plane of existence in the natural world and in her own kind
of mystical faith. She, too, was a skilled seamstress and had her most
productive artistic period in the last years of her life. Varo's interest in
creating clothing and costumes was so great that the curators of her
1983 retrospective included her sewing machine in the exhibition.[51] In

Mimesis from 1960, the artist sits on a chair in a window- and doorless room. Her body is as stiff as a piece of furniture; her skin and limbs have become one with the chair. While she sits in impotent paralysis, the other pieces of furniture bend, stretch, and gesture improbably around her. A piece of fabric hovers behind her head like a cobra, a cat peers at her through a hole in the floor, and clouds lazily drift into the room through an open door in an armoire.

Carrington's and Varo's images, like Tota's paintings, are typical of the way the Surrealists turned the home and its familiar features—like rooms, doors, furniture, and staircases—into metaphors for relationships or symbols of inner exploration. Over fifty years after the golden age of the Surrealist movement, Tota began her fertile yet solitary artistic journey. Multiplicity, metamorphosis, reproduction, and the domestic and natural environments represent Tota's unique personality and life experiences, what art historian Whitney Chadwick describes as the iconographies of the Surrealist women artists' "feminine unconscious." [52] Tota played her own muse, confronting her demons through her secret mythology. Her paintings illustrate how the language of personal exploration and liberation established by Surrealism has continued to inform the work of women artists beyond the historic moment.

CONCLUSION

The increasing call in the early years of the twenty-first century for the dissolution of the insider/outsider duality has broadened the canon to reflect ongoing battles waged for racial, gender, and social equality. As the term *outsider* has begun to break apart under the weight of its own limitations and biases, conversations about the ability of marginalized individuals like Tota to move the needle of mainstream culture have taken root in the broader culture as well. [53]

Josephine Tota's disruptive visions—not wholly insider, outsider, visionary, or surreal—present a point of view so fierce and uncompromising as to prove nearly unassimilable. Her insistent liminality, exacerbated by our culture's failure to perceive innovation in the artistic contributions of older women, has contributed to her slipping through the cracks of art world classifications.

By championing artists like Josephine Tota, MAG intends to complicate and expand the discourse around noncanonical artists and the history of modern and contemporary art. One steadfast advocate of the integration of so-called outsider art, *New York Times* critic Roberta Smith, wrote in 2015, "Outsider art is gradually being integrated into the widening gyre of 20th-century modernism."[54] Here we can begin to understand Josephine Tota's marginality as an asset, as her agency within these charged spaces on the periphery can wield a remarkable kind of power the artist never had in her life, to transgress categories, level hierarchies, and change the very landscape of the center.

NOTES

1   Most of these paintings remained with family members and friends until recently. Thanks to their care for her legacy and to a 2011 gift from Rosamond Tota, fourteen paintings are now integrated into the collection of the Memorial Art Gallery.

2   I wish to thank the artist's daughter, Rosamond Tota, and great-niece, Lisa Rosica, who have generously shared their rich understanding of Josephine Tota's life and art with me in many conversations and emails over the last eight years. Because Tota did not write letters or keep a journal, their memories are a primary source on the artist's life experiences: conversations between Rosica and the author, September 24, 2010, October 4, 2012, and October 5, 2013; emails from Rosica to the author, September 25, 2010, and July 22, 23, and 28, 2014; emails from R. Tota to the author, November 21, 2010, July 27, 2014, October 8, 2015, July 11, 2016, December 3, 2016; and conversation with Rosica and R. Tota and the author, October 5, 2013; conversation with R. Tota and author, March 23, 2016 and January 19, 2017.

3   "Inside Out: Works by Josephine Tota and Julianna Furlong Williams," *Gallery Notes*, 1990, Memorial Art Gallery Archives.

4   R. Tota conversation, March 23, 2016, paraphrased with permission from R. Tota.

5   Barbara J. Bloemink, "Florine Stettheimer: Becoming Herself," in *Singular Women: Writing the Artist*, eds. Kristen Frederickson and Sarah E. Webb (Berkeley: University of California Press, 2003), 124.

6   Randy Kennedy, "Bruce Nauman, Art Provocateur, Returns. Are You Ready?," *New York Times*, September 8, 2016; and Wil S. Hylton, "The Mysterious Metamorphosis of Chuck Close," *New York Times*, July 13, 2016.

7   Michel Thévoz, "An Anti-Museum: The Collection de l'Art Brut in Lausanne," in *The Artist Outsider: Creativity and the Boundaries of Culture*, eds. Michael D. Hall and Eugene W. Metcalf, Jr., with Roger Cardinal (Washington: Smithsonian Institution Press, 1994), 62–75.

8   When applying a biographical mode of inquiry to unconventional or self-taught artists, one must avoid romanticizing stereotypical qualities like isolation and dysfunction. A meaningful assessment will frame the artist's life within broad and specific cultural influences, including geographic location, ethnicity, race, gender, socioeconomic status, religious affiliations, occupation, and exposure to vernacular art forms and popular culture. For an assessment of the complexities of biographical modes of inquiry and the rich understanding this can provide, see Lynne Cooke, "Orthodoxies Undermined," in *"Great and Mighty Things": Outsider Art from the Jill and Sheldon Bonovitz Collection*, ed. Ann Percy with Cara Zimmerman, exh. cat., Philadelphia Museum of Art (New Haven: Yale University Press, 2013), 204–14; and Catherine Morris, "Judith Scott and the Politics of Biography," in *Judith Scott: Bound & Unbound*, eds. Catherine Morris and Matthew Higgs, exh. cat., Brooklyn Museum (New York: Prestel, 2014), 8–17; Daniel Wojcik, *Outsider Art: Visionary Worlds and Trauma* (Jackson: University Press of Mississippi, 2016).

9   R. Tota and Rosica conversation, October 5, 2013.

10   Rosica email, September 25, 2010.

11   Father, Vincent ("Vincenzo") Tota, arrived in New York, bound for Rochester, in December 1920. Mother, Isabella Tota, and her children—Louisa, Rosa, Josephine (listed as "Maria"),

Nancy ("Nunzia") and Frank ("Francesco")—arrived in Boston, MA, in May 1921. "New York, Passenger Lists, 1820–1957," digital images, Ancestry.com, citing microfilm publication T715, roll 2884. 27, 183; The National Archives at Washington, DC, "Passenger Lists of Vessels Arriving at Boston, Massachusetts, 1891–1943," 4319742; Records of the Immigration and Naturalization Service, 1787–2004, 85, T843, 267.

12   R. Tota conversation, January 19, 2017.

13   Frank A. Salamone, *Italians in Rochester, New York, 1900–1940* (Lewiston, NY: The Edwin Mellen Press, 2000), 19.

14   Salamone, *Italians in Rochester*, 59.

15   The first formal documentation of the Tota family in Rochester took place five years into their life in Rochester, with the 1925 New York State Census. From 1925 to 1930, the family is documented in the census and Rochester city directories as having lived in at least three different locations in the city.

16   R. Tota email, December 3, 2016.

17   Rosica conversation, October 4, 2012. For more on the duality experienced by immigrant women see, Roni Berger, *Immigrant Women Tell Their Stories* (New York: Routledge, 2011).

18   To learn more about these artists, see Brook Davis Anderson, ed., *Martín Ramírez*, exh. cat., American Folk Art Museum (Seattle: Marquand Books, 2007); Luisa Del Giudice, *Sabato Rodia's Towers in Watts: Art, Migrations, Development* (New York: Fordham University Press, 2014); and "Morris Hirshfield," in Charles Russell, *Groundwaters: A Century of Art by Self-Taught and Outsider Artists* (New York: Prestel, 2011), 41–54.

19   Rochester, NY, city directory, 1926. The National Clothing Company, known as the National, was a department store and one of Rochester's largest employers in the industry.

20   Postcard dated April 29, 1930. All that remains of Tota's writing are five postcards she sent to family members in Rochester while she lived in the Bronx. Collection of Lisa Rosica.

21   Postcard dated August 8, 1937, Collection of Lisa Rosica.

22   Rosica and R. Tota conversation, October 4, 2013.

23   Fritz Trautmann letter to Marlene Phillips, August 1961, Memorial Art Gallery (MAG) Archives.

24   "Gallery Exhibit Showcases Works by Tota, Williams," *Brighton-Pittsford Post*, February 1990.

25   *Brighton-Pittsford Post*.

26   John Pope-Hennessy and Keith Christiansen, "Secular Painting in 15th-Century Tuscany," *Metropolitan Museum of Art Bulletin* 38, no. 1 (Summer 1980): 2–64.

27   Miriam Sellers Lapham wrote *Encaustic Painting Revealed* (Rochester, NY: RIT, 1980).

28   Larry Merrill's notes, November 28, 1989, exhibition file for *Inside Out*, MAG Archives.

29   Anna C. Chave, "Feminism, Identity, and Self-Representation: Self-Portraiture Reimagined," in *The Female Gaze: Women Artists Making Their World*, ed. Robert Cozzolino, exh. cat. (Philadelphia: Pennsylvania Academy of the Fine Arts, 2012), 77–83.

30   Merrill email to author, June 19, 2014, and Merrill conversation with author, May 6, 2016. Thanks to Larry Merrill, Josephine Tota's legacy exists at the Memorial Art Gallery.

31   Tota's painted dummy echoes the body cast famously worn and painted by Frida Kahlo.

32   Exhibition pamphlet, *Inside Out,* January 26–March 3, 1990, Lucy Burne Gallery of the Creative Workshop, MAG Archives.

33   Ron Netsky, "Two Artists: Naïve by Design," *Democrat and Chronicle* (Rochester, NY), Arts section, 3D, February 11, 1990. Another notice of the exhibition, more descriptive than analytical: "Gallery Exhibit Showcases Works by Tota, Williams," *Brighton-Pittsford Post*, February 1990.

34   No checklist for this exhibition exists. The approximate number of paintings included was gleaned from physical evidence that remains on the verso of the paintings due to the later removal of exhibition mounts.

35   For some background on the history and changing use of the outsider and self-taught

designations, see Roger Cardinal, *Outsider Art* (New York: Praeger Publishers, 1972); Vera L. Zolberg and Joni Maya Cherbo, eds., *Outsider Art: Contesting Boundaries in Contemporary Culture* (Cambridge: Cambridge University Press, 1997); Valerie Rousseau, "The Oblique Angle: When the Self-Taught Artist Shapes the World," in *Self-Taught Genius: Treasures from the American Folk Art Museum*, eds. Stacy C. Hollander and Rousseau, exh. cat. (New York: American Folk Art Museum, 2014), 43-65.

36   Maurice Tuchman and Carol S. Eliel, *Parallel Visions: Modern Artists and Outsider Art*, exh. cat. (Los Angeles: Los Angeles County Museum of Art, 1992), 10.

37   Wojcik, *Outsider Art*, 216. The author outlines how "creative activities often help construct order out of chaos" and the experience of "flow" as an intense psychological engagement with its own beneficial rewards.

38   Sara Ayad, "Mine Worker's Hands: The Arts and Crafting of Madge Gill (1882-1961)," *Raw Vision*, no. 87 (2015): 26-33.

39   R. Tota and Rosica conversation, October 5, 2013.

40   Rosica email, July 23, 2014; Tota email, July 27, 2014.

41   Linda Nochlin, "Why Have There Been No Great Woman Artists?," *ARTNews*, January 1971.

42   Hayden Herrera, *Frida: A Biography of Frida Kahlo* (New York: Harper & Row, 1983), xi.

43   *Codex Manesse: die grosse Heidelberger Liederhandschrift: Interimstexte zum Vollfaksimile* (Insel, 1978).

44   Janet Backhouse, *The Illuminated Manuscript* (Oxford: Phaidon, 1979), 26.

45   Sandra Zalman, *Consuming Surrealism in American Culture* (Burlington, VT: Ashgate, 2015), 4.

46   Rosica email, July 22, 2014. Tota consumed a great deal of art and culture through books. The diversity of her interests is reflected in the titles barely visible on the shelves of her apartment (page 2) such as: *Drawing on the Right Side of the Brain, Chinese Rugs Designed for Needlepoint, The Cut-Outs of Henri Matisse, Golden Screen Paintings of Japan, Life in the Renaissance, Master Paintings from the Hermitage and the State Russian Museum, Mexican Art, More Needlepoint by Design, Rome and the Barbarians, Treasures of Tutankhamen, World Art,* and books on the artists Pierre Bonnard, Bronzino, Paul Cézanne, Paul Gauguin, Claude Monet, and Robert Vickrey.

47   Whitney Chadwick, "An Infinite Play of Empty Mirrors," in *Mirror Images: Women, Surrealism, and Self-Representation* (Cambridge, MIT Press, 1998), 6.

48   Rosica email, July 23, 2014. The surrealist qualities of Lewis Carroll's story of Alice's adventures and its influence on female Surrealists and subsequent generations of artists was the subject of this exhibition and catalog: Ilene Susan Fort, Tere Arcq, and Terri Geis, eds., *In Wonderland: The Surrealist Adventures of Women Artists in Mexico and the United States*, exh. cat. (Los Angeles: Los Angeles County Museum of Art, 2012).

49   Salomon Grimberg, "Frida Kahlo: The Self as an End," *Mirror Images*, 83-104.

50   "The Alchemical Kitchen: Domestic Space as Sacred Space," in Susan L. Aberth, *Leonora Carrington: Surrealism, Alchemy and Art* (London: Lund Humphries, 2004), 57-96.

51   Janet A. Kaplan, *Unexpected Journeys: The Art and Life of Remedios Varo* (New York: Abbeville Press, 1988).

52   Whitney Chadwick, prologue to *In Wonderland*, 16.

53   Alissa Quart, *Republic of Outsiders: The Power of Amateurs, Dreamers, and Rebels* (New York: New Press, 2013).

54   Roberta Smith, "'Art Brut in America' Highlights Outsider Artists, No Longer Looking In," *New York Times*, October 22, 2015. Smith and her husband, *New York* critic Jerry Saltz, are two influential voices who have long advocated for the integration of unconventional artists.

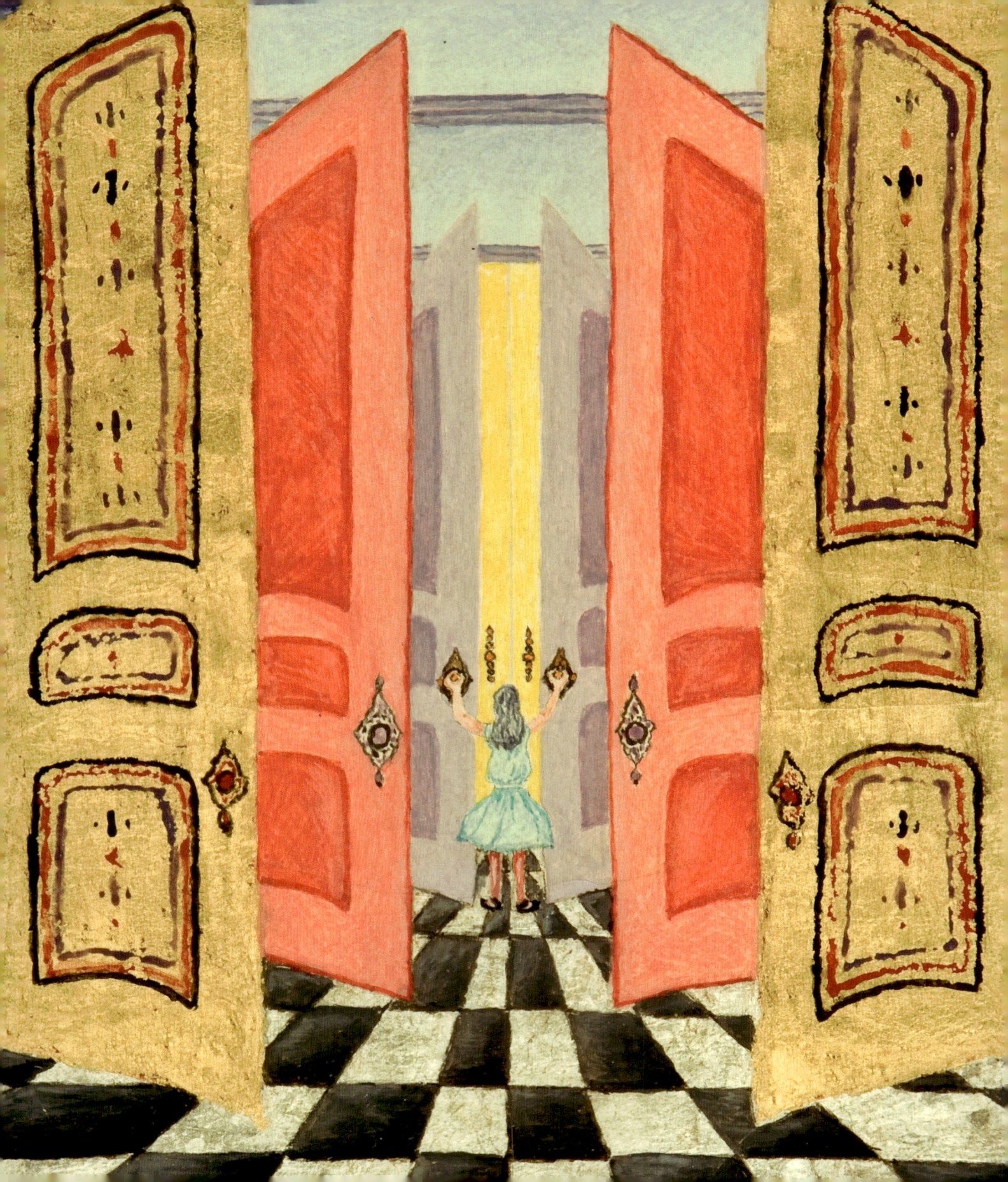

TEARS OF BLOOD
VISIONARY WOMEN AT THE MARGINS OF TWENTIETH-CENTURY ART

Janet Catherine Berlo
Professor of Art History and Visual and Cultural Studies, University of Rochester

In Josephine Tota's enigmatic paintings, women weep tears of blood. They are flattened behind locked doors or boxed in by claustrophobic spaces. They peer through partly opened doors as if afraid of what awaits on the other side. They are tortured by flames, beset by needles and tacks, or hobbled by chains. Threaded needles encircle Tota's women or float menacingly in the background. Rarely does Tota paint a scene that connotes unalloyed pleasure; trouble always besets her female protagonists. Does the woman eyeing two ladders overhead plot her escape, or do the eyes in the sky crying bloody tears signal a warning? Is the girl-child opening successive doors on her way to freedom, or will unknown menaces beset her? Does the woman in the feathered hat find joy in the fabric she cuts into paper dolls, or do the vexing circumstances in her surroundings militate against this? In rare acts of grace, an angel bestows flowery visions upon a sleeping woman, and embroidered hankies lift a woman into the sky.

Josephine Tota's artistic vision is a singular one, but she is part of an artistic sorority that transgresses categories of age, class, race, nationality, education, and intention. Her work resists being pinned down by customary art-historical classifications. Neither outsider artist nor academic painter, she falls between the categories established by the traditional art history canon. As Jessica Marten has observed,

While her singular style and personal iconography developed mainly in the quiet isolation of her home, it grew out of decades of consuming and creating art within an art world infrastructure, however peripheral she may have been. These inspired, vivid depictions of her interior life were made possible because of

Untitled, undated, 1980s (detail of cat. 16)
Egg tempera and silver leaf on panel
10 9/16 x 7 9/16 in.
Private collection

her artistic training and awareness of art historical precedents, not in spite of them.[1]

In this essay, I seek to illuminate Tota's work by comparing both her art and her life with that of other singular women of the twentieth century who participated in the art world to a greater or lesser extent. Some were afforded a measure of success or limited recognition during their lifetimes, while others labored unknown. The Mexican painter Frida Kahlo is the best known, not only to us today but also in Tota's lifetime. Her personal iconography of pain influenced Tota's work, as Jessica Marten points out in her essay. In two southern visionary painters, Minnie Evans and Theora Hamblett (one African American and one white), deep Christian faith is combined with intensely personal revelations set down in paint; it is unlikely that Tota would have come across their work. The German artist Charlotte Salomon, working in the early 1940s, was only slightly known before the 1990s, but her hundreds of intensely personal and autobiographical paintings now stand as a rich revelation of the inner life of a young woman artist under conditions of great social and personal upheaval. I will discuss the correspondences among these images, as well as the varying reception of each artist's work.

As Marten notes, male artists in their seventies are often described using terms that stress their undiminished potency and the boldness of their vision. With few exceptions, the art world is seldom as kind to the older female artist.[2] If she is self-taught or works in the hinterlands, the twentieth-century press routinely feel the need to bring up America's most famous "old-lady painter," Grandma Moses. Anna Mary Robertson Moses (1860–1961) was arguably both the most reproduced and best-known artist of the twentieth century. She achieved fame only in the last two decades of her life.[3] With her folksy Grandma Moses moniker (almost invariably used instead of her given name), her nostalgic primitivist imagery, and her homespun pronouncements about art and life, Moses became an easy stereotype.

But paternalistic and reductive rhetoric about a woman making art in her old age affords little insight into the singular lives and works of some of the artists under discussion here. As I shall discuss, Tota, Hamblett, and Evans all offer powerful examples of artists achieving a complex style and personal iconography later in life. Each deserves to be assessed on her own terms. Because all of the women I discuss were outside the mainstream in diverse ways, and each had an artistic practice that rendered her unusual in her time and place, I suggest a metaphorical affinity with the great medieval artist and intellectual of the Roman Catholic church, Hildegard of Bingen, whose art making was born out of physical pain and celestial visions.

Tota's influences were numerous. She studied art books her entire life and spent lunch breaks from her job in the art section of the Rochester Public Library. As Marten's essay chronicles, after her retirement Tota haunted museums and galleries in New York City when visiting her adult daughter. In her work, one finds echoes of Hieronymus Bosch's *Garden of Earthly Delights* and Joan Miró's early Surrealist abstractions, but it was medieval manuscript painting that fascinated and inspired her to learn to paint in egg tempera, and to use gold pigment and bright lapidary colors. We have no way to determine how much she may have known about Hildegard of Bingen, but I open this essay with some thoughts about this medieval nun as the "patron saint" of the visionary woman artist.

PROLOGUE: HILDEGARD OF BINGEN (GERMAN, 1098–1179)

But when I had passed my first youth and attained the age of perfect strength, I heard a voice from heaven saying "write what you see and hear."[4]

The twelfth-century nun, mystic, painter, and scholar Hildegard of Bingen was unparalleled in the reach of her accomplishments. She began experiencing visions as a small child and was sent by her parents to a convent at the age of eight. Thirty years later she was the Abbess of that Benedictine convent, and in subsequent decades became renowned throughout Christian Europe for her mystical revelations, preaching, healing, and writings on theology and natural science. It was a spectacular vision at age forty-two, accompanied by the celestial prescription to set down on paper what she had seen, that brought her such fame.

All of these unusual aspects of Hildegard's life cause me to imagine her as the artistic forebear of the artists I consider here. As biographer Sabina Flanagan has observed, Hildegard's visions afforded her a way around the patriarchal constrictions of her era. Although literate in Latin, she had not had the thorough grounding in sacred theology that the learned monks of her time would have been given. Hildegard's "divine gifts" were widely accepted as such by church officials; having been ordered by God to set down her visions, her mandate for theological and medical writing, art making, musical

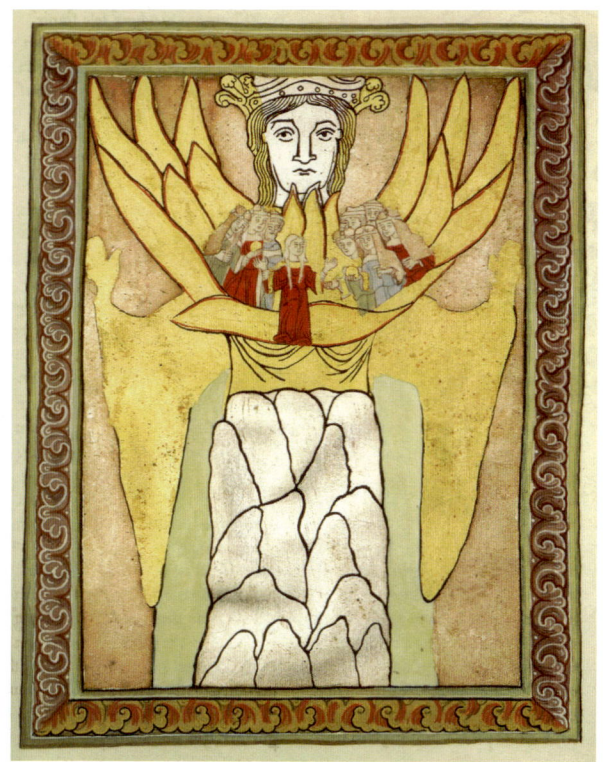

Hildegard of Bingen
(German, ca. 1098–1179)
The Mystical Body from the
Rupertsberger Scivias-Codex,
hand copy on parchment, 1927–1933,
from an original ca. 1175 (destroyed in
1945), plate 14, folio 066
Abbey of St. Hildegard,
Rüdesheim / Eibingen

composition, preaching, and healing was unchallenged.[5]

The six-hundred-page manuscript with thirty-five illuminations that came forth from her pen after the visions Hildegard experienced in middle age is titled *Scivias*. This is a shorthand way of saying "Know the Ways of God." One image depicts Ecclesia (above), a huge, mountain-like personification of the church painted in silver and gold to convey the blinding light that Hildegard experienced in this and other visions.[6] Ecclesia holds within her bosom some nuns from Hildegard's convent, all of whom admire the light-haired virgin dressed in red who stands before them as the essence of purity. Of these figures Hildegard wrote, "These are the daughters of Zion . . . and the voice of all gladness, and the joy of joys."[7] Hildegard conceived *Scivias* as a multimedia work: it encompasses text, imagery, music, and even a play. In the pages that follow, we will see that some of the artists discussed here went beyond the confines of painting, too, in their self-expression.

Today a wealth of pictorial material is available on Hildegard, much of it published around the nine hundredth anniversary of her birth (1998). In Tota's time, less was available, but Hildegard's work appeared in some books on the Middle Ages, and she was featured in the popular feminist installation *The Dinner Party*, which toured the United States from 1979 to 1983 with two accompanying books.[8] When holding Tota's small, jewellike paintings in one's hands, the link with medieval manuscript painting is unmistakable. Each has a private devotional quality. The use of gold pigment and other rich colors and the depiction of scenes ranging from tribulations to visions all recall the devotional paintings made in medieval Europe, as does Tota's use of detailed geometric patterning to embellish empty spaces and borders. A few of Tota's works even conform loosely to medieval stylistic and iconographic patterns. In two arresting scenes, the artist presents herself as akin to the crucified Christ (cats. 74, 73). (See Marten's essay for further discussion of parallels with medieval style, medium, and iconography.)

Illustrations of manuscript illuminations had long been available in scholarly publications, but by the time Tota was making art and scrutinizing art books, beautiful editions had been published for the general public; many were available in both the Memorial Art Gallery library and the Rochester Public Library.[9] I imagine her examining these carefully, or perhaps looking at originals on view in the Morgan Library or the Metropolitan Museum in New York, and then coming home and framing her own experiences in terms of medieval depictions of the trials and scourges of the martyrs. She portrays the burns of medical radiation and her resulting neuropathy with terrifying directness (cats. 70, 86). In this depiction of her physical traumas, she follows the example set by Frida Kahlo.

FRIDA KAHLO (MEXICAN, 1907–1954)

They thought I was a Surrealist, but I wasn't. I never painted dreams. I painted my own reality.[10]

Before Frida Kahlo became an iconic figure in the 1980s, other exceptional women artists such as Louise Nevelson and Georgia O'Keeffe had captured the attention of the art world. But in the 1980s, when Tota was painting, Kahlo's work was ubiquitous.[11] Her subject matter was almost always herself. Many of her paintings were small and were deliberately modeled after Mexican *retablos* and *ex-votos*, small folk paintings on tin made in religious tribute for a prayer offered or answered.

For Tota, Kahlo offered a model not only of a woman artist but one whose life was shaped by physical and emotional trauma and lifelong pain, as Marten discusses. Kahlo's eclectic style was shaped by her knowledge of folk art, of Mexico's indigenous heritage and its

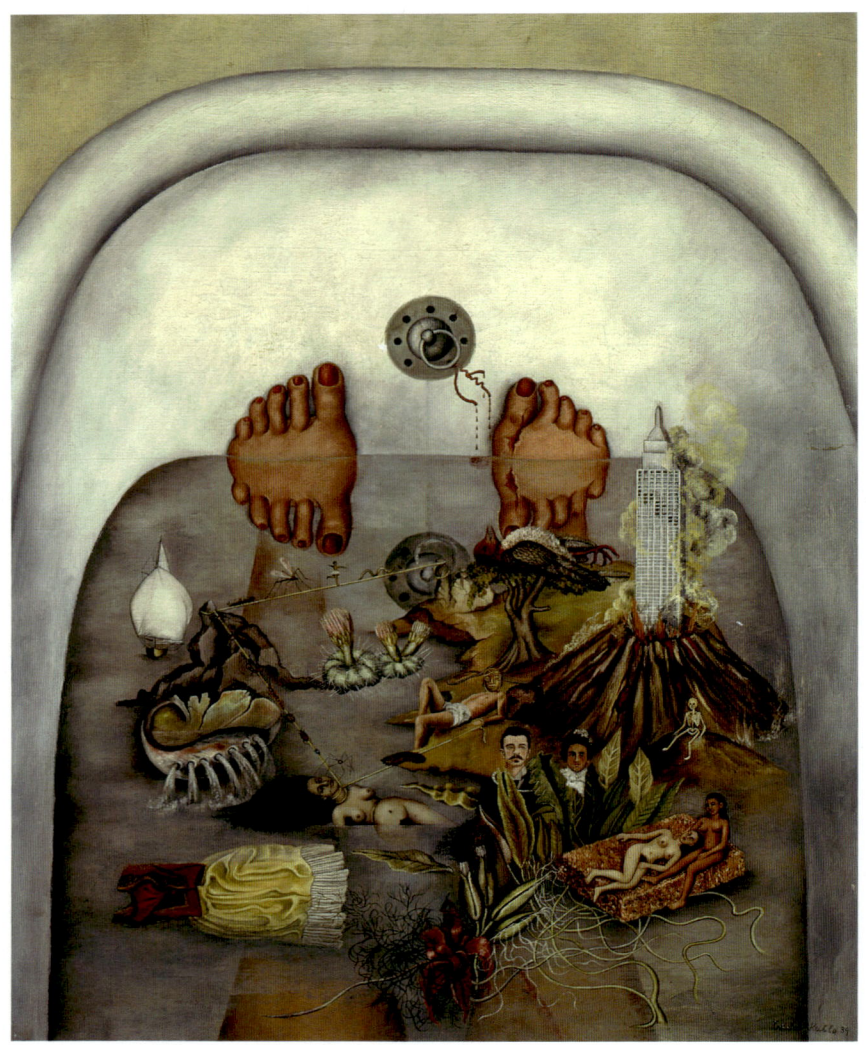

Frida Kahlo (Mexican, 1907–1954)
What the Water Gave Me, 1938
Oil on canvas
34 ⅝ x 27 ⅛ in.
Private collection
© 2017 Banco de México Diego Rivera
Frida Kahlo Museums Trust, Mexico, D.F.
/ Artists Rights Society (ARS), NY
Photo: Schalkwijk / Art Resource, NY

popular art traditions, as well as European painting from Hieronymous Bosch to Henri Rousseau.[12] André Breton, upon meeting Kahlo in Mexico in the spring of 1938, famously proclaimed her a Surrealist; in his essay for her first solo show, held at the Julien Levy Gallery in New York City in November of that year, he described her work as "a ribbon wrapped around a bomb," a phrase much quoted ever since.[13]

What the Water Gave Me, perhaps Kahlo's most unusual self-portrait, was featured in that 1938 New York exhibit as well as in *Mexican Art Today* at the Philadelphia Museum of Art in 1943.[14] In the bathwater extending from her knees to her feet, the artist has painted a collection of images and vignettes that combine autobiography and dreamlike fantasy. In the upper center of the canvas, where the eyes would be in a conventional self-portrait, the artist's feet, with their blood-red toenails, are reflected in the water. The right foot, misshapen both from polio and multiple surgeries, has a slash-like scar across the big toe. Below, on the right, a phallic skyscraper emerges from an erupting volcano. On the land beneath the volcano, a skeleton, a recumbent seminude male with a pre-Columbian mask for a face, and a tree carrying a huge dead bird are arrayed. At lower right, portraits of her parents peer out from behind lush foliage, while in front of them two female nudes recline on a mattress. In the center of the composition is the reclining male previously mentioned. To his left wrist is tied a taut rope that extends out over the water to strangle a floating female nude. On other parts of this rope, a series of tiny insects, a ballerina, and a snake are balanced. The nude, with its long dark hair and prominent eyebrows, is surely the artist herself. As if to corroborate this, the skirt and blouse floating nearby are the distinctive Tehuana-style outfit of indigenous women of Oaxaca that Kahlo often wore, both in life and in her self-portraits.[15] At the bottom of the canvas, between the legs, dark fronds of seaweed recall pubic hair, while the wilted red flower petals and cleft seec pods seem to stand in for female genitalia.

Kahlo's physical and psychic pain provided the subject matter for much of her art. But her inimitable style, like Tota's, drew from a variety of sources. Foremost was the complex cultural heritage that was modern Mexico: the pre-Hispanic substratum onto which Hispanic traditions were placed. These merged with indigenous expressive culture to make a hybrid culture of retablo paintings, mestizo clothing, and other sources, all of which Kahlo drew upon.

A number of Tota's more complex canvasses might be compared to What the Water Gave Me. A work dated "5-13-91" depicts fourteen full or partial figures (cat. 88). The four most prominent females are defined by complex patterned garments, as is the male at upper left. Many of the women weep, and two are confined by chains around their necks. Six other chains fill various parts of the background. The weeping figure at lower left appears to sit in a burning bush. Surely some autobiographical narrative is at play here, though the different hairstyles, hair colors, and facial shapes, ranging from realistic to stringently geometric, allow for the possibility of multiple protagonists. While Kahlo "never painted dreams," instead meticulously chronicling her reality, Tota seems to have done both. In this she bears comparison with Theora Hamblett, a southern folk artist.

THEORA HAMBLETT (AMERICAN, 1895–1977)

What bubbles up in me just has to come out.[16]

On a September Sunday in 1950, an art student at the University of Mississippi in Oxford brought some visitors to the home of a local painter, Theora Hamblett, a fifty-five-year-old woman who had painted some unusual works on panel and had attended some night-school art classes.[17] This Sunday encounter remained vivid in Hamblett's mind, for she had been in a wheelchair, convalescing from an operation for a broken hip. She had just finished a large ambitious work and, as she described it years later,

> I put my name on the painting on Saturday night, and on Sunday some people who were staying with friends in Oxford came by and wanted to see my work. One of them was a New York art dealer, but I thought she was just some lady from Arkansas. She bought the vision painting for $50 and the next thing I knew it had been sold to the Museum of Modern Art.[18]

Betty Parsons, the woman who bought the painting, would be her dealer for the rest of her life, marketing Hamblett's art far beyond the American South.[19]

The Golden Gate or *The Vision* is a self-portrait as well as a vision, for the artist takes an omniscient view, portraying herself in four sequential scenes standing near a small frame house. We see only a corner of her rural childhood home, with a window and doorway illuminated from within. Her back is to the viewer, with her right hand raised, shielding her eyes. She is clad in an orange shirt and pants as she witnesses a vision develop within a white cloud in the night sky. A simple pasture gate—though it is resplendent in gold, rather than ordinary paint, making it a heavenly gate—takes shape. The vision, dazzling enough that it casts a shadow behind the human figure, illuminates the branches of the trees at left, with the branches growing ever brighter as the time sequence moves from left to right. In her artistic autobiography, Hamblett writes,

> I was not a painter when I had that dream. Nearly thirty years later, when telling the dream to a friend, I was told to paint it. My friend and I were dabbling with mixing colors at the time. I did start it, but before I finished it, I broke my hip. When I was on the operating table, I had a strange and compelling

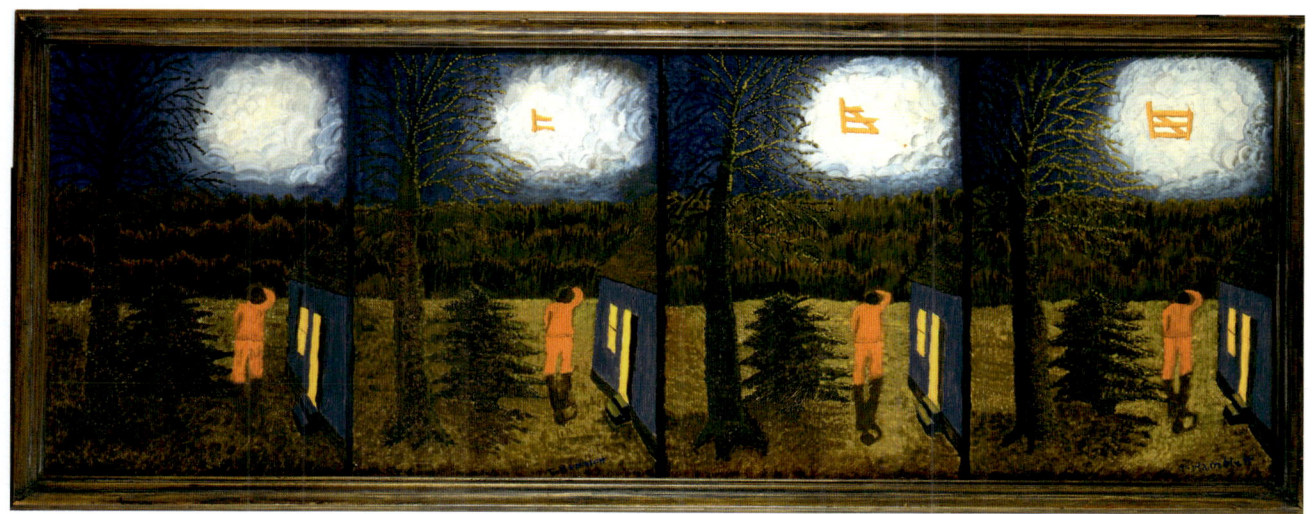

Theora Hamblett (American, 1895-1977)
The Golden Gate or *The Vision*, 1954
Oil on composition board
17 ⅞ x 48 in.
Museum of Modern Art, NY, Gift of
Albert Dorne, 10.1955a-b
Photo: SCALA / Art Resource, NY

experience that made me realize that I must finish painting that Golden Gate. I even prayed and promised my Lord that I would finish the painting if He would help me get well.[20]

While Hamblett painted many visions, this was one of the most significant to her.[21] Like many southern folk artists, she was deeply spiritual, with an abiding personal connection to Biblical scripture and to her Christian God, whom she generally called her "Maker."[22]

It is easy to see what captivated Parsons in *The Golden Gate* or *The Vision*: its restricted color palette, its pointillist style, and its surrealist sense of the four-part progression of an eerie event witnessed by a lone mysterious figure all work together to produce a scene of uncanny beauty and mystery. But why would Parsons, a prominent player in New York's avant-garde art scene, choose to represent the work of a southern visionary painter?[23] When Parsons opened her own gallery in 1946, attracting important contemporary abstract artists such as Ad Reinhardt, Barnett Newman, and Mark Rothko, she was undoubtedly familiar with paintings by the so-called modern primitives celebrated in New York exhibits. MoMA's 1938 exhibit *Masters of Popular Painting* introduced such artists to the public, and over the next decade other exhibitions and books followed.[24] The MoMA catalog advocated that such self-taught artists have "an honorable place in the history of American painting."[25] And Parsons clearly agreed.

In addition to visionary paintings, Hamblett produced many genre scenes: workers picking cotton, quilts hanging on a fence to air, and children playing games.[26] For this reason, reviewers of her exhibits repeatedly called Hamblett "the Grandma Moses of Mississippi,"[27] though this provided little insight into her work or her intentions. At eighteen, Hamblett had sought to attend college to study art—a remarkable aspiration for a poor young rural southern woman in 1913; she spent some years teaching in a series of one-room schools instead. She sporadically took summer art courses and in middle age took a correspondence course with the newly founded Famous Artists School.[28] All her adult life Hamblett had wanted to paint, principally because since adolescence she had had what she called "visions." She interpreted these as messages from God and saw it as her duty to record them visually. Yet, in a scenario that recalls Hildegard of Bingen, she did not begin to do so until she was middle-aged. The painting that Betty Parsons bought was only the second of these vision paintings, and it was remarkable that Hamblett sold it to a stranger, given her deep misgivings about selling any of her visionary work.[29] Yet the artist believed that God had sent Parsons to buy it.[30]

Soon thereafter, Parsons became not only her dealer but her sounding board and mentor. Their correspondence reveals Hamblett to be an ambitious and canny woman—not at all the stereotype of the southern folk artist untouched by the commercial world of art making. She queried Parsons about pricing the work, about what shows she should enter, and whether she should pay good money to have her name listed in various Who's Who volumes.[31] She fretted about having used cerulean blue for the sky in a copy she made of *The Golden Gate* or *The Vision* when cobalt blue would have been a better choice.[32]

Unfortunately, we have no equivalent documents from Tota with which to reveal the complexity of her thoughts, her visions, her ambition, or her life. Both women were semireclusive. But unlike Hamblett, who never ventured to visit her New York City dealer (even when Parsons devoted a gallery show to her in 1958), Tota eagerly visited New York City on several occasions, spending all her time at galleries and museums. As Marten notes, Tota had mentors at the Creative Workshop at the Memorial Art Gallery; but surely she never engaged with any art world figure in the way that Hamblett engaged with Parsons.

MINNIE JONES EVANS (AMERICAN, 1892–1987)

Something told me to draw or die.[33]

While scholars and curators often use the word *self-taught* as a label for those who make art outside the mainstream, Minnie Evans asserted that she was not self-taught:

God has sent me teachers: the angel that stands by me, stands by me and directs me what to do. Time for me to paint a picture and I be tired I say I'm going to rest up for a couple of days. He won't let me. Come down grab my feet and shake me. Beat me. Scared me so bad one night I jumped off the bed and looked. Got up there, I thought some of the children had come in. Nobody in the room. No one.[34]

Minnie Jones was born in rural North Carolina but soon thereafter was taken to Wilmington, North Carolina, where she was raised by her mother, grandmother, and great-grandmother, who all lived together. At age thirteen, Jones started having remarkable dreams, but her grandmother assured her that they were visions, and they continued for the rest of her life. As they had for Theora Hamblett, the visions engendered the work. One in particular seemed to lay out her life's work:

The whole entire horizon all the way across the whole earth was put together like this with pictures. All over my yard, up the sides of trees, and everywhere were pictures.[35]

Having attended school only through sixth grade, Minnie Jones married Julius Evans at sixteen. She was a devout Christian, attending both African Methodist Episcopal and Southern Baptist churches, sometimes even preaching to the congregations.[36] Evans made her first visionary drawing on Good Friday of 1935 but commenced art making as a serious endeavor five years later at age forty-eight, using crayons, pencil, and ink. Her family remembers that often she labored over her art all day.[37] Starting in 1947, Evans sold tickets at the gatehouse to Airlie Gardens, a private home and extraordinary garden that had recently opened to the public. She worked there until her retirement in 1974, often hanging her drawings in the gatehouse and selling them to visitors for fifty cents or a dollar.

While angels may have taught her to paint, Airlie Gardens, renowned for its lush vegetation and spectacular azalea displays, provided Evans with a color palette and floral imagery. In many of her paintings, human faces look out from within botanical and geometric designs. Additional eyes often stare at the viewer, but they are an integral part of the design field, unlike Tota's many works where disembodied eyes appear alone.[38] One work by Evans in the Weatherspoon Museum is characteristic of the way she customarily

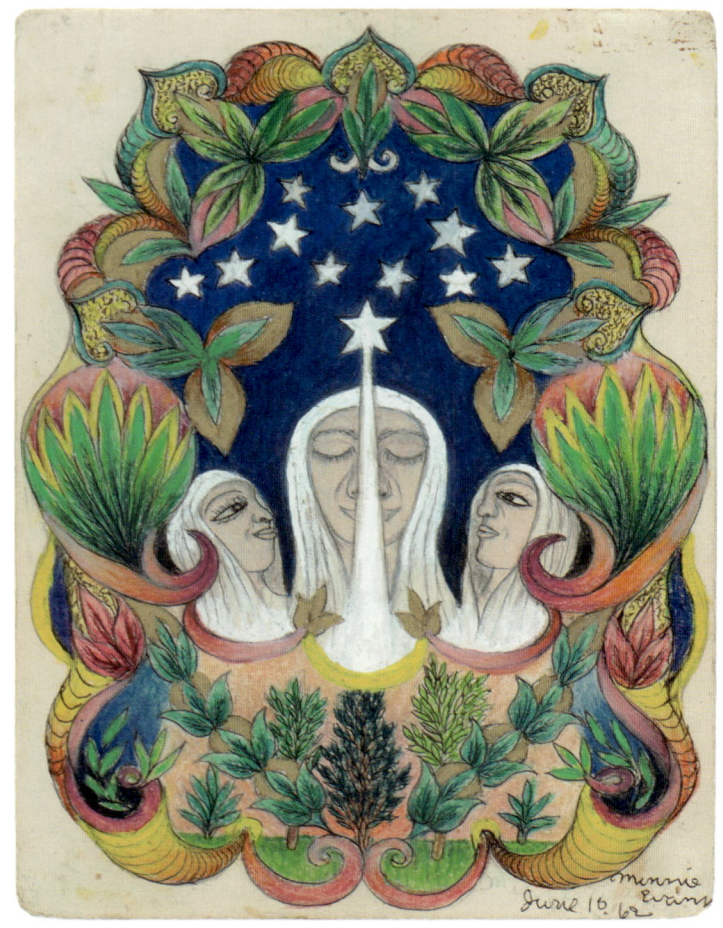

Minnie Evans (American, 1892–1987)
Untitled, 1962
Graphite, ink, and wax crayon on paper
11 ¾ x 8 ⅞ in.
Weatherspoon Art Museum, University
of North Carolina at Greensboro,
museum purchase with funds from the
Dillard Paper Company for the Dillard
Collection, 1981.2878
Artwork © estate of Minnie Jones Evans

fills most of the page or canvas with pattern and color. A swirling image contains, at the bottom, a green ground line with trees and plants growing out of it. Above, three human faces against a blue sky filled with stars are contained within arabesques, curlicues, leaves, and flowers. Using crayons, Evans has portrayed a scene in which the reds, yellows, and greens enframe the star-filled vision in blue and white. As is her custom, the artist favors numerous shades and tints of green, from chartreuse to seaweed to forest green. This recalls one of her most quoted observations: "Green is God's theme color. He paints everything green. Six hundred and some shades of green."[39]

Evans's first exhibition was in a local gallery in Wilmington in 1961. The following year she met a woman who would change her life. For, like Theora Hamblett, African American artist Minnie Evans had a female champion, who saw to it that the last twenty-five years of Evans's life included exhibitions at university museums, commercial galleries, and even the prestigious Whitney Museum in New York City.

Nina Howell Starr had been working on her MFA in photography at the University of Florida when another student showed her some crayon drawings by Evans. Starr photographed them, both in black and white and in color, later realizing that in studying the black and white prints she was "surprised and awed by the graphic power of these images."[40] A few months later, Starr drove from Gainesville, Florida, to Wilmington, North Carolina, to meet the artist. Evans was already sixty-nine, and Starr only a decade younger.[41] A friendship was forged, and Starr became her unpaid agent, dealer, curator, and mentor.

In 1966, Starr organized *The Lost World of Minnie Evans*, an exhibit held at two Episcopalian churches in New York City. Evans traveled north for the openings, visiting the Metropolitan Museum during her stay. Seeing the art of the world upon its walls, she decided to make some of her works larger than the 7-by-9-inch or 9-by-12-inch paper that she had customarily used.[42] Other exhibitions followed, both solo and group shows, and in the summer of 1975, Starr curated an exhibit of Evans's paintings at the Whitney Museum. Her work has been included in numerous exhibits of southern folk art, both in the United States and abroad.

Starr called Minnie Evans an "innocent Surrealist."[43] Bona fide Surrealists such as Max Ernst and Leonora Carrington sought through dreams, visions, and automatic writing an unfettered access to the unconscious (page 26). They hoped this would liberate them from the burdens of being overly intellectual and academically trained. Neither Tota nor Evans carried such burdens. Evans was, however, compelled to "draw or die"; the outpouring of Tota's work (some eight dozen paintings completed over little more than one decade) suggests a similar compulsion. For Tota, art forged a path through solitude, physical and emotional pain, and the thoughts and images that clamored in her brain, waiting to be released through her brush.

Tota's depictions—whether they were visions, dreams, or simply the products of a vivid imagination—share neither the joyous botanical exuberance of Evans's work nor their grounding in religious faith. By all accounts, Tota, though raised in the Roman Catholic Church, was not a devout woman. When she paints trees, fraught and disturbing faces sometimes lurk in their foliage (cats. 24, 34). Tota's visions are most often nightmares rather than divine revelations. In one, a long-haired woman attempts to escape over a tall stone wall but is stymied by the spikes atop the wall as well as the five women who claw at her dark skirt (cat. 63). In one softer vision, two women are taken aloft via floating lace-edged hankies (cat. 18).

CHARLOTTE SALOMON
(GERMAN, 1917—1943)

Foam, dreams—my dreams on a blue surface. What makes you shape and reshape yourselves so brightly from so much pain and suffering?[44]

From the summer of 1941 to the summer of 1942, a twenty-four-year-old German Jewish woman named Charlotte Salomon created a mixed-media work of art about her life and that of her family. With the interrogatory title *Life? or Theatre?,* it combined imagery, texts, snatches of music, and stage directions. Its maker called it a *Singespiel*—a songplay—or sometimes a *Dreifarben Singespiel*—a three-color opera.[45] Salomon had been exiled to Nice, France, in 1939 for her own protection. Those who saw her in Nice, obsessively bent over her solitary task, recalled that she was "always painting, always humming."[46] By October of 1943 Salomon was dead—incinerated in the ovens of Auschwitz. Before her arrest in Villefranche, on the outskirts of Nice, in September of 1943, she entrusted a wrapped parcel containing her work to an older friend, saying "Keep this safe. It is my whole life."[47]

After the war, when her father and stepmother (who had survived in Amsterdam) traveled to Nice in search of information about their daughter, they were given this parcel. It contained a magnum opus of 769 small numbered gouache paintings, plus hundreds of tracing-paper overlays with explanatory texts and dialogue, as well as several hundred other drawings that the artist had excised from the final version of the songplay.

Space is too limited here to outline fully the complicated and tortured family history of this young artist, many of whose relatives had committed suicide over three generations. Charlotte Salomon, known as Lotte, was born to a prosperous professional family in Berlin. She was described as a solitary and nondescript child, yet she must have been prodigiously talented, for she was admitted to the Berlin Art Academy in 1936, at a time when it observed a strict quota of 1.5 percent for Jewish students. In the summer of 1938, all such students were expelled. Just a few months later, in January 1939, Salomon (along with some seventy-eight thousand other Jews) fled Germany.

In creating her hundreds of drawings, Salomon was choosing life over the self-destruction that seemed to be her family heritage. Some characters in her work share the first names of her relatives and herself. She, for example, is named Charlotte Kahn (which in German,

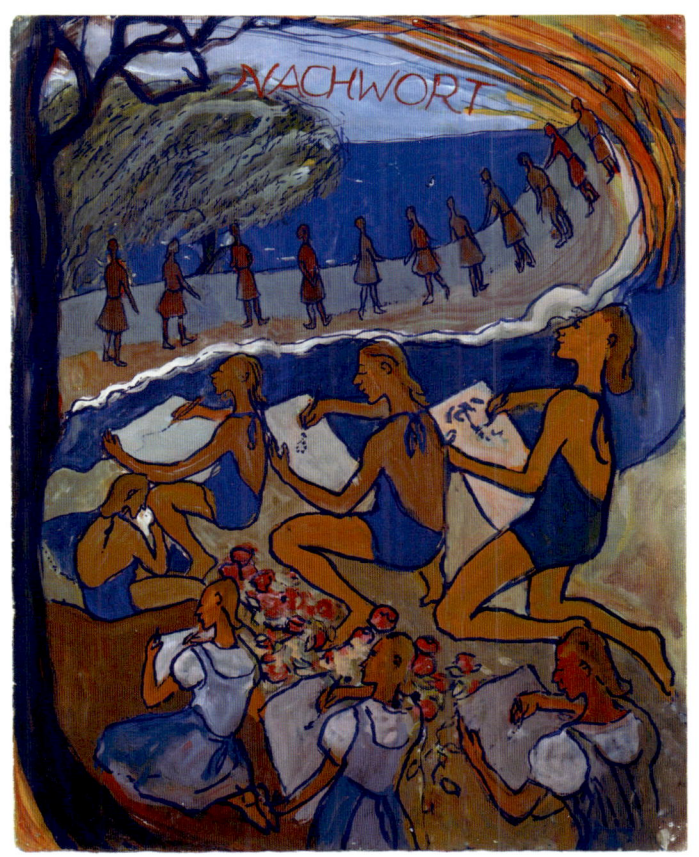

as in English, makes an optimistically declarative sentence: "Charlotte *can*."). Her biographer eloquently wrote of this endeavor:

> The aloneness of Lotte Salomon in 1942—the worst year in Jewish history—so matched the silence and suicide in her family that she had to break through it or give in. She had to conceive inconceivable spectators, draw back the curtains, and enact what threatened her: the absence of an audience to speak to, the vanishing of an identity. Any creative use of these conditions—and this three-color opera was ingenious—pushed the fear of nonbeing a little farther away.[48]

The work illustrated here is one of the last in the complex visual saga, and one of the most hopeful. The word *Nachwort* (epilogue) is painted at the top of the image. Seven young women who are drawing overlook the sea. Three are dressed as young girls; four seem older and wear bathing suits. It is tempting to see them as various incarnations of the artist/author herself, "always drawing, always humming," finishing her epic work in the summer of 1942 by the Mediterranean. On the shore Salomon has painted more than a dozen figures receding into the swirling orange gestural strokes of paint at the upper right. At left, a large tree frames and anchors all of these figures.

Life? or Theatre? is no simple visual autobiography. Salomon moves through time and space, presenting aspects of the lives of three generations of women in her family. As feminist art historian Griselda Pollock has written, the work is

> not only cinematic in its use of flashback, but hypertextual in its transitions. Every so often we hit an image that opens up a passageway to the life story of yet another woman, imagined, of course, and represented by the daughter, granddaughter, stepdaughter whose lineaments of being were gathered from the derelict remnants of these feminine m/others.[49]

This observation leads me to ponder the identities of the various women in Tota's *oeuvre*. In a tripartite scene, three women in long dark dresses face the viewer (cat. 57). Are all meant to stand for Tota herself? The figures at left and right clutch scarves with weeping eyes, and each has a tack beneath her bare foot (Tota's emblem for her painful fallen arches). Each shoulders another head, while partial faces weeping tears of blood peer in from the upper margin of the image. The viewer longs for a tracing-paper overlay with explanatory text, as in Salomon's work, to unlock the meanings of so many of Tota's complex narratives. In the quote that opens this section and that accompanies page 49, Salomon asks of her dreams, "What makes you shape and reshape yourselves so brightly from so much pain and suffering?" Are the many women in Tota's works aspects of her own persona, shaped and reshaped from her own pain and suffering?

In both Salomon's and Tota's paintings, one feels the threat of nonbeing as an urgent motivator for the work. Salomon's threat was twofold. Suicide may have seemed inevitable to her, given that so many of her female forebears had killed themselves. Moreover, there was the urgent external threat of deportation and incarceration as a Jew.[50] Tota's ever-increasing pain and disability, as well as old age itself, may have lent urgency to her task of recording her experiences in these private but highly charged visual narratives.

Since Salomon's first public exhibition in Amsterdam in 1961, her work has been seen by millions of people in Israel, Western Europe, and North America.[51] In the spring of 2016, it was exhibited at a museum in Nice, where it had been created three-quarters of a century earlier.[52] Of the artists examined here, only Salomon's work was completely unknown to outsiders while she was alive. Tota, compared to Kahlo, Hamblett, and Evans, had only modest acknowledgment during her lifetime—a 1990 exhibit at the Creative Workshop at the Memorial Art Gallery when she was seventy-nine. As Marten notes, she was reluctant to have even this much public attention. Perhaps the exhibition and publication of her work in 2018 will mark the beginning of greater interest in this unusual Rochester artist.

CONCLUSION

All the artists considered here share an affinity for what art historians call the *Gesamtkunstwerk*—the all-encompassing work of art.[53] Hildegard's *Scivias* incorporated text, imagery, music, and drama. Kahlo, who often wore the garb of indigenous Tehuana women, was as well known for her presentation of *herself* as a work of art as for her paintings. Hamblett, despairing of portraying her visions vividly enough in paint, confided to her dealer that she had written to Cecil B. DeMille suggesting they would make great material for a movie.[54] And by the end of her life, Hamblett's home, thickly hung with her works in stained glass as well as her paintings, was both art gallery and *Gesamtkunstwerk*. Minnie Evans labored for twenty-seven years in the lush botanical environment of Airlie Gardens, which provided the stage set (and additional inspiration beyond that of her visions) for the drawings she sold in the gatehouse. Charlotte Salomon's *Life? or Theatre?*, though set down on paper, was conceived by its maker as a multimedia performance, with music providing the thrumming pulse behind the visual and written narratives. And Josephine Tota extended her artistry into three dimensions: garment-making, needlepoint, ceramics, and painting her dressmaker's mannequin in a manner akin to her two-dimensional works of art (page 15 and cat. 23). The creative drive of each one of these women was truly remarkable.

Except for the paintings of Frida Kahlo, who was too firmly lodged in the modern art world to be ignored, all of the works discussed here could easily have been overlooked or lost—a fate surely encountered by many other extraordinary but unsung women. If Theora Hamblett had never met Betty Parsons, or if Minnie Evans had never encountered Nina Howell Starr, their work might have enjoyed a minor reputation in the South. Charlotte Salomon's masterwork might easily have been lost in the upheavals of post–World War II life

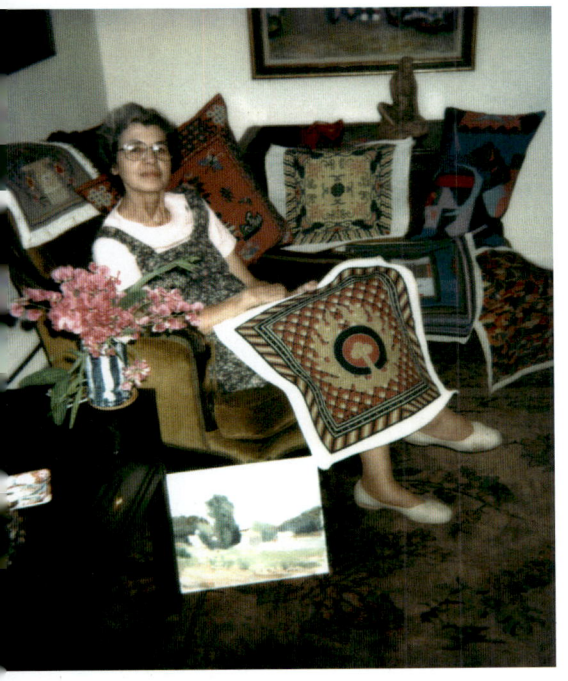

Josephine Tota at home, ca. 1980s
Photo courtesy of Rosamond Tota

in Nice. Similarly, if Josephine Tota had not had a daughter and niece who valued her work, Larry Merrill as her advocate, and a local art museum that found her paintings worthy of collection, she, too, would be unknown. The serendipity of these histories makes us wonder how many other bodies of astonishing work by singular and remarkable woman may have perished in the last century. Such a thought should make us value even more highly those that have survived.

The Surrealist artists discussed by Jessica Marten and the self-taught artists I have examined here may well be the best prospects we have for further illuminating the work of Josephine Tota. But in thinking about this vexingly elusive artist over the last months, I have often been reminded of two heroines of classic British children's literature who have long inspired females young and old to be adventuresome. Alice, of *Alice in Wonderland* and *Through the Looking Glass*, first tumbles down a rabbit hole and later passes through a mirror to discover lands disquietingly different but puzzlingly similar to those she inhabits at home. Lucy, of *The Lion, the Witch and the Wardrobe*, thinks creatively and discovers within an ordinary piece of furniture a magic portal to a land called Narnia.[55] As I look at Josephine Tota's painting that depicts a little girl who has opened three successive sets of large doors and is intent upon discovering what is behind the fourth (cat. 16), I think of the artist's courage in examining her demons, her disappointments, her trials by sewing needle, operating scalpel, and radiation. She recorded them in tempera on panel, in all their terrible beauty.

We endeavor to follow her through these doors, to understand her own rich emotional and cerebral terrain, one far more harrowing than either Wonderland or Narnia. Yet we are stymied in this; in fact, one of her paintings seems to foreclose the possibility of our ever following her there (cat. 27). A painted door sports an oversized hasp and padlock (the lock mysteriously labeled "82" though the painting itself is otherwise undated). Behind the door is a large yellow bilobed form. Two green-stockinged feet emerge from behind the yellow form, and two hands appear above the doors. It is as if the artist herself is flattened behind these definitively locked doors. Perhaps she is even dismembered, for the oddly facing feet don't really match up with the hands. The reclusive and laconic Josephine Tota has painted her inner reality in dozens of works of art that all can marvel at, but she has reserved their deepest meanings for herself.

ACKNOWLEDGMENTS

I am grateful to Jessica Marten for inviting me to collaborate with her on this project, and for being a good sounding board for my ideas. Paul D. Weiss and Mary M. Fox provided careful readings of the first draft of this essay.

NOTES

1   Jessica Marten, "At the Margins: The Art of Josephine Tota," *Panorama: Journal of the Association of Historians of American Art* 2, no. 2 (Fall 2016).

2   Among the most notable exceptions are Georg a O'Keeffe (1887–1986), Louise Nevelson (1899–1988), and Louise Bourgeois (1911–2010). All were serious artists in their youth and achieved some early success. All achieved their greatest fame in old age. See, for example, Barbara Haskell, ed., *Georgia O'Keeffe: Abstraction* (New York: Whitney Museum of American Art, 2009); Brooke Rapaport, *The Sculpture of Louise Nevelson* (New York: The Jewish Museum, 2007); and Robert Storr, Paulo Herkenhoff, and Allen Schwartzman, *Louise Bourgeois* (London: Phaidon, 2003).

3   On Moses, see Otto Kallir, *Grandma Moses: American Primitive* (New York: Dryden Press, 1946); and *Grandma Moses: My Life's History*, ed. Otto Kallir (New York: Harper & Brothers, 1952); Jane Kallir, *Grandma Moses: The Artist Behind the Myth* (New York: Clarkson Potter, 1982). More recent reframings of Moses that have been more discerning include Karal Ann Marling, *Designs on the Heart: The Homemade Art of Grandma Moses* (Cambridge: Harvard University Press, 2006); and Thomas Denenberg et al., *Grandma Moses: American Modern* (New York: Skira Rizzoli, 2016).

4   Hildegard of Bingen, preface to *Scivias*, as quoted in Sabina Flanagan, *Hildegard of Bingen, 1098–1179: A Visionary Life*, 2nd ed. (London: Routledge, 1998), 40.

5   Flanagan, *Hildegard of Bingen,* 52–54.

6   Madeline Caviness, "To See, Hear, and Know All at Once," in *Voice of the Living Light: Hildegard of Bingen and Her World*, ed. Barbara Newman (Berkeley: University of California Press, 1998), 115. There is much scholarly debate about which images may have been painted by Hildegard herself and which were created in subsequent generations, either after her designs or based on her writings rather than her own images. See Madeline Caviness, "Hildegard as Designer of the Illustrations to her Works," in Char es Burnett and Peter Dronke, *Hildegard of Bingen: The Context of Her Thought and Art* (London: The Warburg Institute, 1998), 29–63. According to Caviness, the paintings in *Scivias* are undoubtedly by Hildegard's hand. Moreover, in the preface to that work, Hildegard painted a self-portrait in which she is writing or drawing. (Caviness, fig. 19.) Though later copies by others are extant, the *Scivias* that Hildegard wrote at Rupertsberg was lost in the bombing of Dresden in 1945. A facsimile made in the late 1920s by German nuns provides the images that scholars study today. Hildegard von Bingen, *Scivias,* trans. Columba Hart and Jane Bishop, introduction by Barbara J. Newman (New York: Paulist Press, 1990), 25–26.

7   Hildegard, *Scivias*, 201.

8   Judy Chicago, *The Dinner Party: A Symbol of Our Heritage* (New York: Anchor Books, 1979); and *Embroidering Our Heritage: The Dinner Party's Needlework* (New York: Anchor Books, 1980).

9   The publisher George Braziller was the first to make this formerly arcane imagery widely available. See for example, John Plummer, *The Hours of Catherine of Cleves* (New York: George Braziller, 1966); Millard Meiss and Elizabeth Beatson, *The Belles Heures of Jean, Duke of Berry* (New York: George Braziller, 1974); and Roger Wieck, ed., *Time Sanctified:*

The Book of Hours in Medieval Art and Life (New York: George Braziller, 1988)—all of which were available in Rochester libraries when Tota was working.

10   "Mexican Autobiography," *Time Magazine*, April 27, 1953, quoted in Hayden Herrera, *Frida: A Biography of Frida Kahlo* (NY: Harper & Row, 1983), 266.

11   During her own lifetime, Kahlo was better known as the wife of the famous Mexican muralist Diego Rivera (1886–1957). She was discussed in the press and photographed more for her colorful personality and unusual indigenous garb than for her painterly accomplishments. Hayden Herrera started publishing on Kahlo in 1976. See for example, Hayden Herrera, "Frida Kahlo," in *Women Artists 1550–1950*, eds. Ann Sutherland Harris and Linda Nochlin, exh. cat. (Los Angeles County Museum of Art, 1976), 335–337; and "Frida Kahlo: Her Life, Her Art," *Art Forum* 14 (May 1976): 38–44. Her best-selling and well-illustrated biography *Frida* was published in 1983. Numerous publications by others have followed.

12   Herrera, *Frida*, 223.

13   Geoffrey T. Hellman and Harold Ross, "Ribbon Around Bomb," Talk of the Town, *New Yorker*, November 12, 1938.

14   In the years between the New York and Philadelphia exhibitions, Kahlo's work was exhibited in Paris, where it was lauded by Duchamp, Miró, Picasso, Kandinsky, and others. It was included in group shows of the new Mexican painting in San Francisco, Boston, New York, Mexico City, and elsewhere. See Herrera, *Frida*, chapters 17 and 19.

15   Many of Kahlo's Tehuana outfits were displayed in a 2013 exhibit entitled *Appearances Can Be Deceiving*, at La Casa Azul/Museo Frida Kahlo, the artist's former home in Mexico City. See "Appearances Can Be Deceiving," accessed November 22, 2016, http://grey-magazine.com/appearances-can-be-deceiving-the-dresses-of-frida-kahlo.

16   Theora Hamblett to Betty Parsons, January 16, 1957, Betty Parsons Papers, Archives of American Art, Washington, DC (hereafter cited by the correspondents' initials).

17   See Theora Hamblett in collaboration with Ed Meek and William Haynie, *Theora Hamblett Paintings* (Jackson: University Press of Mississippi, 1975), 27.

18   William Thomas, "The Artist as a Dreamer," *Mid-South* (Memphis, TN), July 26, 1970, 5. Theora Hamblett clipping files, Betty Parsons Papers.

19   Parsons (1900–1982) was an influential New York City gallerist. The Betty Parsons Gallery, operating from 1946–1981, represented and promoted the work of the most famous Abstract Expressionists, including Jackson Pollock and Barnett Newman. See Lee Hall, *Betty Parsons: Artist, Dealer, Collector* (New York: Harry N. Abrams, 1991).

20   Hamblett, Meek, and Haynie, *Theora Hamblett Paintings*, 77. The artist always referred to this work as *The Golden Gate*, though the Museum of Modern Art calls it *The Vision*. But Hamblett had many visions, so she preferred to be more specific.

21   The other, which she repainted several times in an effort to perfect it, was *Heaven's Descent to Earth,* where she stands in the same location with four children, watching two rows of golden chariots descend from heaven to reveal several luminous child-spirits. Two versions are depicted in Hamblett, Meek, and Haynie, *Theora Hamblett Paintings*, 54–55.

22   For an excellent exploration of the place of religion in the work of southern self-taught artists, see Alice Rae Yelen, ed., *Passionate Visions of the American South* (New Orleans: New Orleans Museum of Art, 1993).

23   Parsons already represented the visionary Texas painter Forrest Bess (1911–1977), whom she took on the year before she met Hamblett, though she had not yet given him a show. See Clare Elliott, *Forrest Bess: Seeing Things Invisible* (New Haven: Yale University Press, 2013). While Parsons championed the work of many more women and lesser-known artists than her male peers, to my knowledge Hamblett and Bess were the only visionary or self-taught painters she represented.

24 Sidney Janis, whose eponymous gallery shared the fourth floor at 15 East 57th St. with the Parsons Gallery, had curated *Contemporary Unknown American Painters* at MoMA in the fall of 1939, an exhibit of eighteen nonprofessionals, including the newly discovered Morris Hirshfield, and Anna Maria Robertson Moses, "Grandma Moses." In 1942, Janis's book *They Taught Themselves: American Primitive Painters of the 20th Century* was published, the first serious exploration of this category of art. Across the street from Betty Parsons Gallery was Galerie St. Etienne, where Otto Kallir gave Grandma Moses her first one-person show in New York City in 1940 and where Moses's works were often on display.

25 Holger Cahill et al., *Masters of Popular Painting: Modern Primitives of Europe and America* (New York: Museum of Modern Art, 1938), 105. Notably, no women were included among the American artists and only one among the European artists in this exhibit.

26 See, for example, Hamblett, Meek, and Haynie, *Theora Hamblett Paintings*, 30, 38, 67 passim.

27 Dorothy Adlow, "Miss Hamblett's Paintings," *Christian Science Monitor*, June 27, 1962; Margaret McKee, "Profile on Art: Theora Hamblett, 'Will There Be Any Stars in My Crown,'" *Memphis Press-Scimitar*, May 19, 1967, 19.

28 Founded in 1948 by illustrator Albert Dorne with the help of Norman Rockwell and other illustrators, the Famous Artists School was located in Westport, Connecticut. A twenty-four-lesson correspondence course that promised instructor critique by mail, it was well known for its ubiquitous ads in popular magazines. Though its heyday was in the 1950s and 1960s, it only closed in 2016. Its archives are held by the Norman Rockwell Museum in Massachusetts. See Rena Tobey, "Instruction by Mail: The Famous Artists School," *Connecticut History*, accessed January 12, 2017, http://connecticuthistory.org/instruction-by-mail-the-famous-artists-school/.

29 Most of the visionary works remained in Hamblett's collection until her death. See Hamblett, Meek, and Haynie, *Theora Hamblett Paintings*, 53–96. In letters to Parsons, she repeatedly cautions her not to sell the visionary work, or "only to museums." See, for example, TH to BP, January 5, 1956; and Gene Derr (Parsons's assistant) to TH, October 8, 1970: "King Saul and his Harps was marked for sale to museums only." Less than a year before she died, Hamblett wrote to Parsons, "I am putting my Dreams and Visions in a Trust when I am gone. I have a bunch of half neices [*sic*] and nephews who think they should get them. I prefer for them to stay together. . . . I dedicated them to my Maker several years ago. University gets first choice, and if she does not wish them, some other place in Mississippi." TH to BP, May 17, 1976.

30 TH to BP, June 24, 1960.

31 In 1956, Hamblett was planning to enter shows in New Orleans and Memphis: "I am anxious to win some prizes or sell some pictures." TH to BP, January 13, 1956. In the South, her work usually sold for $50 to $100, but in the 1950s and 1960s, Parsons priced Hamblett paintings between $100 and $1200, depending on size and subject matter. Astonishingly, this was similar to the prices for most of the New York artists Parsons represented.

32 TH to BP, April 6, 1959.

33 Barbara Rogers, "'Something Told Me to Draw or Die,'" *Wilmington Morning Star*, January 19, 1969.

34 As she stated in the film *The Angel That Stands by Me: Minnie Evans' Paintings* (San Francisco: Light-Saraf Films, 1983).

35 Nina Howell Starr, "Minnie Evans and Me," *Folk Art* 19, no. 4 (Winter 1994-95): 56.

36 Mitchell D. Kahan, *Heavenly Visions: The Art of Minnie Evans* (Raleigh: North Carolina Museum of Art, 1986), 43.

37 Charles M. Lovell, *Minnie Evans: Artist* (Greenville, NC: Gray Gallery, East Carolina University, 1993), 11.

38 See Lovell, *Minnie Evans*, plates 17–21, for example.

39   As she stated in the film *The Angel That Stands by Me*. Hildegard of Bingen extended the Latin word *viriditas* (greenery or greening) to mean not only nature's greenery but "all natural and spiritual life as quickened by the Holy Spirit." Barbara J. Newman, introduction to Hildegard, *Scivias,* 25.

40   Starr, "Minnie Evans and Me," 52.

41   Nina Howell Starr (1903–2000) graduated from Barnard College in 1926, studied architecture briefly in the 1930s, and earned an MFA in photography in 1963. From 1964 until her death, she lived in New York City. Nathan Kernan, "Nina Howell Starr: The New Yorker Project" (Lexington, KY: Institute 193), http://institute193.org/nina-howell-starr.

42   Nathan Kernan, "Aspects of Minnie Evans," *On Paper* 1, no. 6, 15; Charles M. Lovell, *Minnie Evans: Artist* (Greenville, NC: Gray Gallery, East Carolina University, 1993), 15-16.

43   Nina Howell Starr, "Innocent Surrealist," *Newsweek*, September 1, 1969, 4A; "Minnie Evans– Innocent Surrealist," in Lovell, *Minnie Evans*, 27-29.

44   Charlotte Salomon's words that accompany the image reproduced here in fig. 5. Norman Rosenthal et al., *Charlotte Salomon: Life? or Theatre?* (Amsterdam: Jewish Historical Museum, 1998), 722.

45   Mary Lowenthal Felstiner, *To Paint Her Life: Charlotte Salomon in the Nazi Era* (New York: HarperCollins, 1994), 144, points out that three-color opera was surely an homage to Bertolt Brecht's *Threepenny Opera*.

46   Felstiner, *To Paint Her Life,* 130, 142, 146. Unless otherwise noted, all details of Salomon's biography are drawn from Felstiner's account.

47   Felstiner, *To Paint Her Life*, 236.

48   Felstiner, *To Paint Her Life,*152.

49   Griselda Pollock, "Theatre of Memory: Trauma and Cure in Charlotte Salomon's Modernist Fairytale," in *Reading Charlotte Salomon*, eds. Michael P. Steinberg and Monica Bohm-Duchen (Ithaca: Cornell University Press, 2006), 57.

50   In 1940, Salomon and her grandfather had been interned (along with the other German nationals living in Nice) for some six weeks in Gurs, a camp in the French Pyrenees. Her biographer posits that the art-making program at Gurs may have inspired Salomon to begin her own epic pictorial history a year later. Felstiner, *To Paint Her Life*, 111–124.

51   Felstiner, *To Paint Her Life*, discusses Salomon's early exhibition history, 223–230. Several recent exhibitions have been analyzed by Reesa Greenberg, "The Aesthetics of Trauma: Five Installations of Charlotte Salomon's *Life? or Theatre?*," in Steinberg and Bohm-Duchen, *Reading Charlotte Salomon,*148–166.

52   In the last four decades, *Life? or Theatre?* has also inspired films and plays. In 2014, a best-selling novel, *Charlotte*, was published in France, and an opera by French composer Marc-André Dalbavie, premiered at the Salzburg Music Festival. See David Foenkinos, *Charlotte* (Paris: Gallimard, 2014); and, in English, *Charlotte* (New York: The Overlook Press, 2016). At this writing, a feature film based on Salomon's drawings is in production with the cooperation of the Charlotte Salomon Foundation. See Elsa Keslassy, "Bibo Bergeron Set to Direct 'Charlotte Salomon' Animated Biopic," *Variety*, June 13, 2016.

53   This German term, espoused by the nineteenth-century composer Richard Wagner, has applications in art, drama, and architecture, as well as music. See Krisztina Lajosi, "Wagner and the (Re)mediation of Art: *Gesamtkunstwerk* and Nineteenth-Century Theories of Media," *Frame* 23, no. 2 (November, 2010): 42-60.

54   TH to BP, September 19, 1956. She added, "If I had not written to him, a blood vessel would have ruptured."

55   Lewis Carroll, *Alice's Adventures in Wonderland* (London: Macmillan, 1865); and *Through the Looking Glass* (London: Macmillan, 1871). C. S. Lewis, *The Lion, the Witch and the Wardrobe* (London: Geoffrey Bles, 1950).

CATALOGUE OF THE LATE PAINTINGS OF JOSEPHINE TOTA

Undated paintings are reproduced first, dated paintings follow in chronological order.

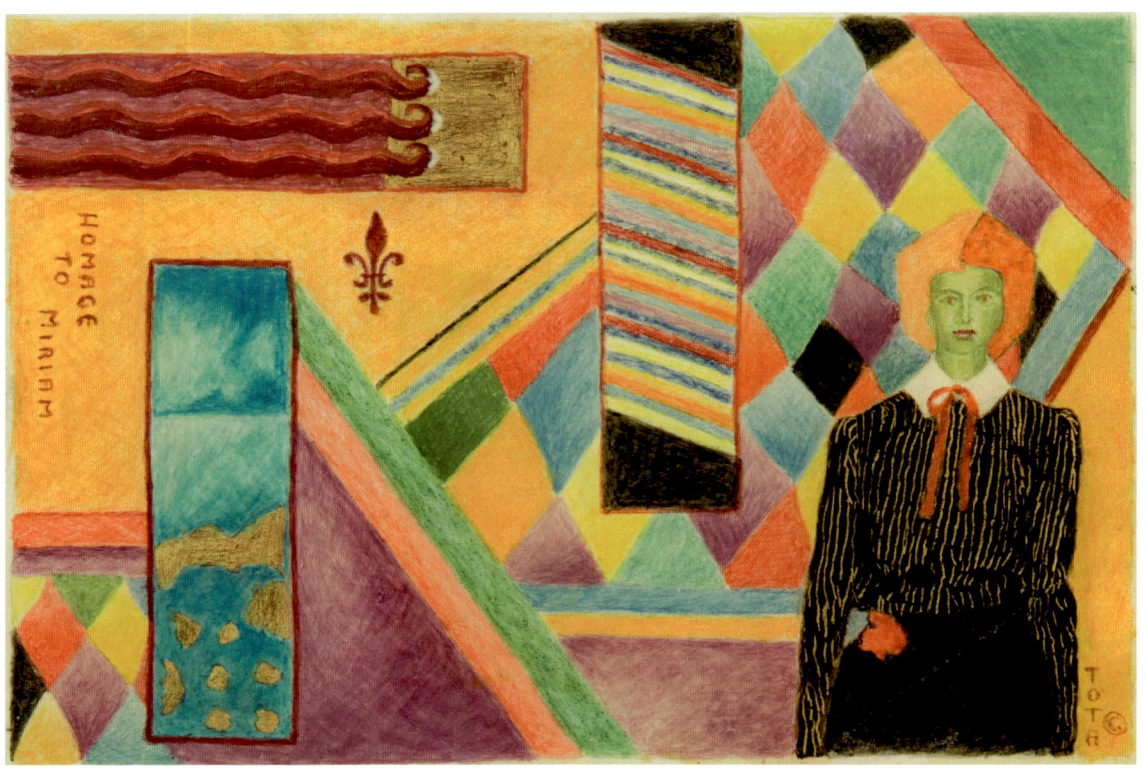

1

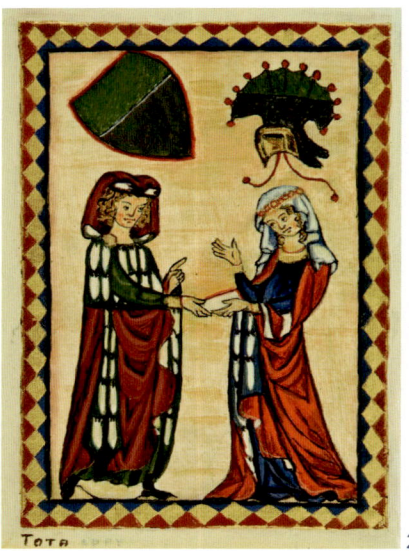

2

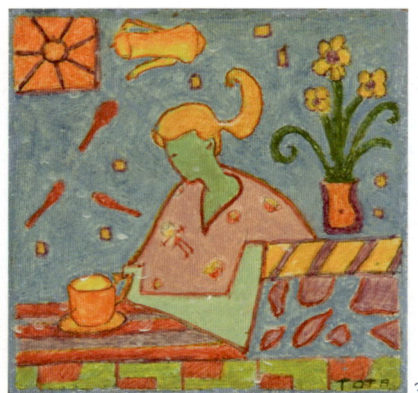

3

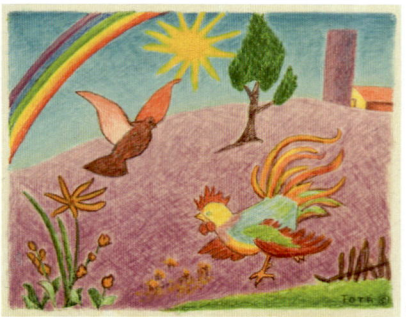

4

1. *Homage to Miriam*, undated, 1980s
Egg tempera and gold leaf on panel
6 ³⁄₁₆ x 8 ¹³⁄₁₆ in.
Private collection

2. Untitled, undated, 1980s
Egg tempera and gold leaf on panel
7 x 5 in.
Collection of Rosamond Tota, daughter

3. Untitled, undated, 1980s
Egg tempera on panel
4 x 4 in.
Private collection

4. Untitled, undated, 1980s
Egg tempera on panel
5 ½ x 6 ¾ in.
Private collection

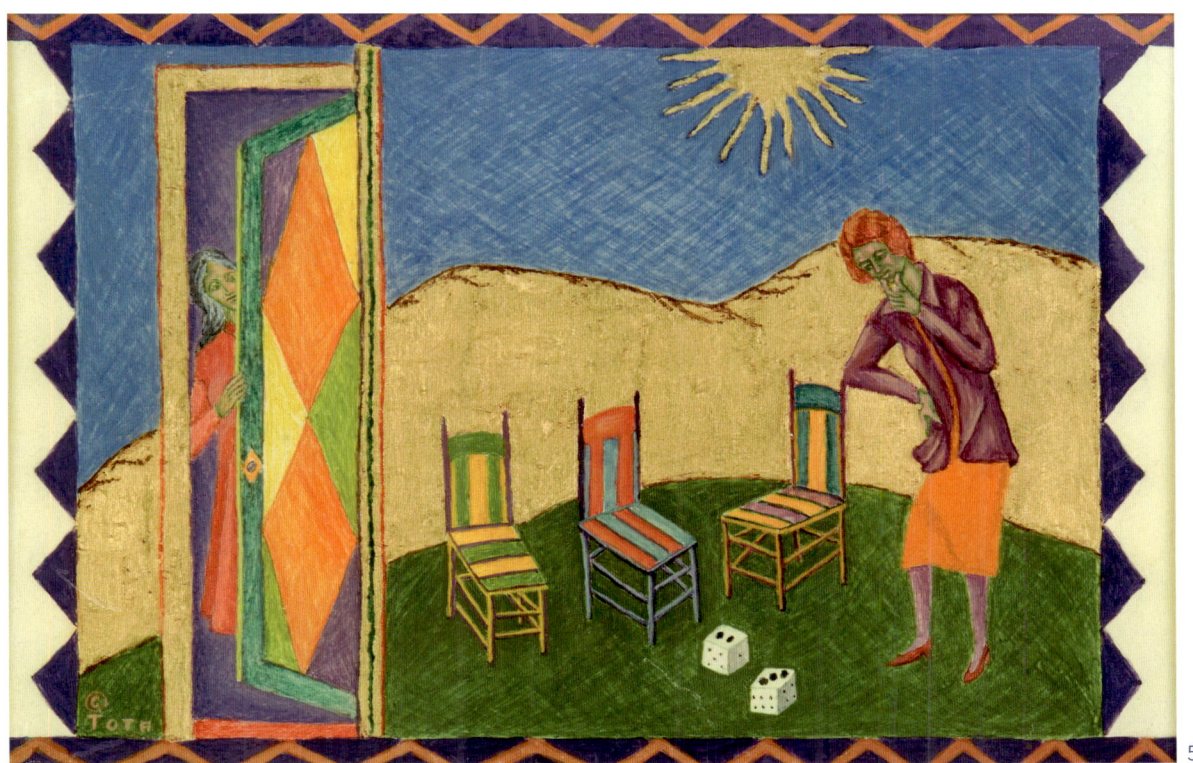

5

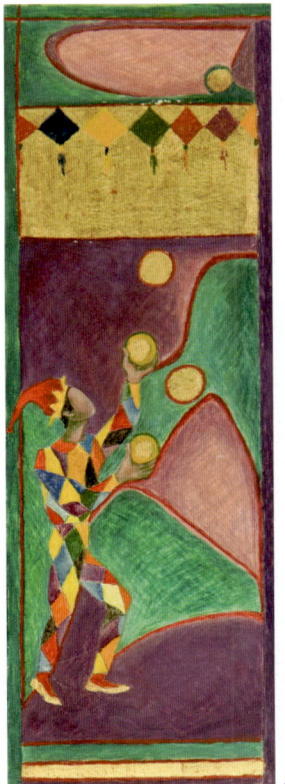

6

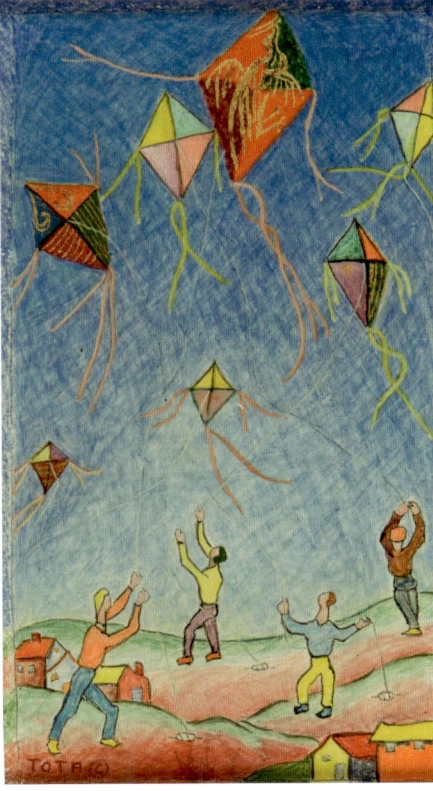

7

5. Untitled, undated, 1980s
Egg tempera and gold leaf on panel
7 ½ x 1 ³⁄₁₆ in.
Collection of Rosamond Tota, daughter

6. Untitled, undated, 1980s
Egg tempera and gold leaf on panel
12 ⁵⁄₁₆ x 4 ⅛ in.
Collection of Rosamond Tota, daughter

7. Untitled, undated, 1980s
Egg tempera on panel
8 ½ x 4 ¾ in.
Collection of Rosamond Tota, daughter

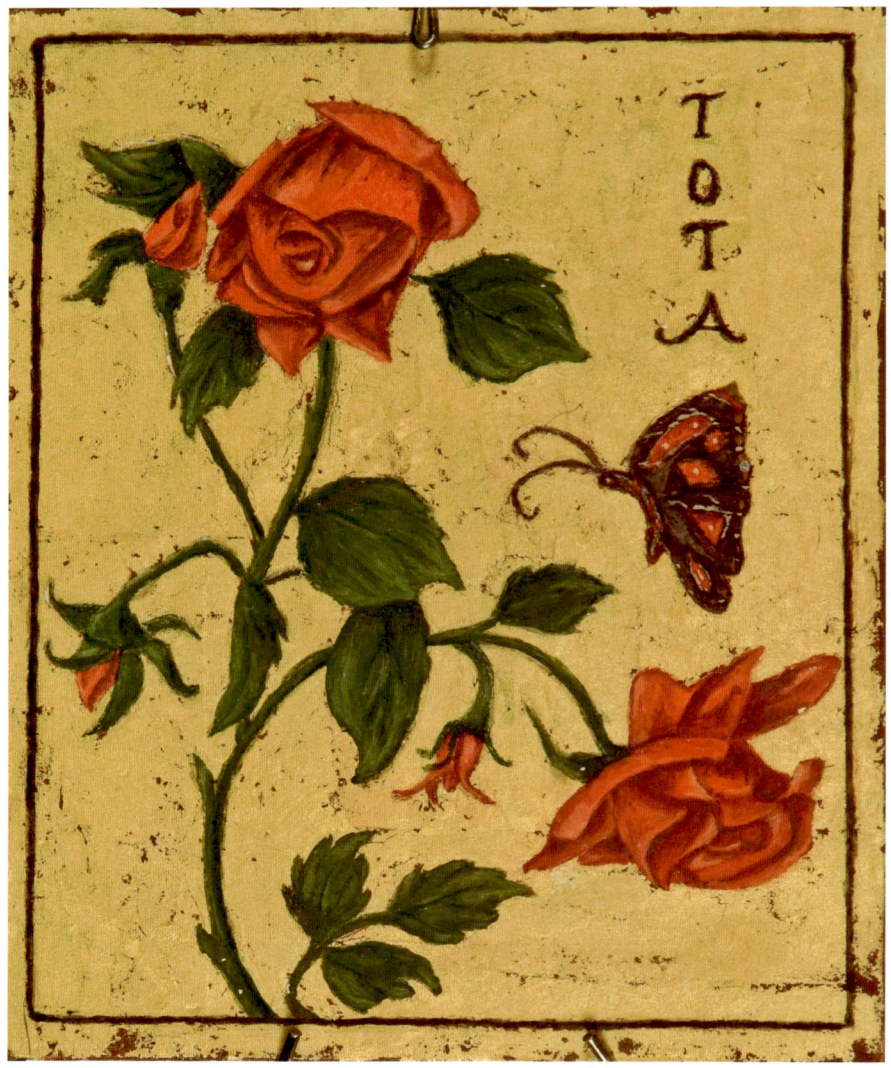

8. Untitled, undated, 1980s
Egg tempera and gold leaf on panel
6 ¾ x 5 ½ in.
Private collection

9. Untitled, undated, 1980s
Egg tempera and gold leaf on panel
7 x 8 ⅛ in.
Collection of Rosamond Tota,
daughter

10. Untitled, undated, 1980s
Egg tempera and gold leaf on panel
6 ½ x 8 ¾ in.
Collection of Rosamond Tota,
daughter

8

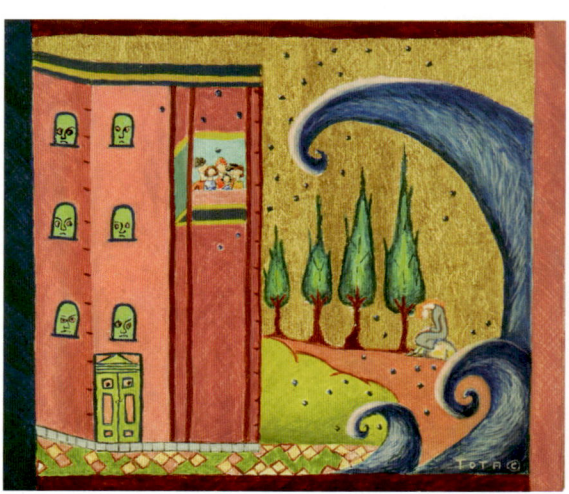

9

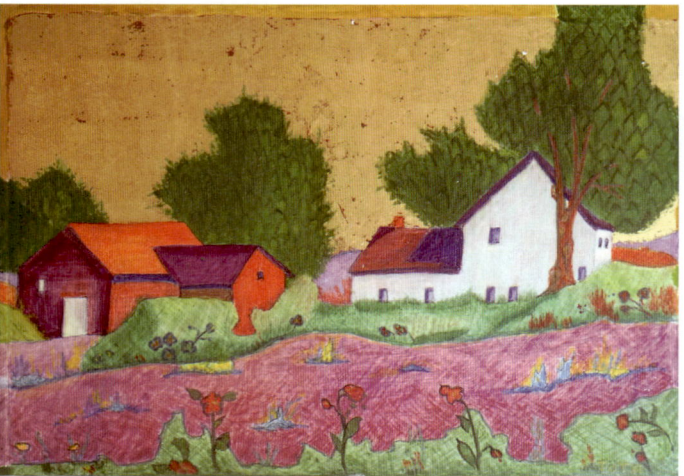

10

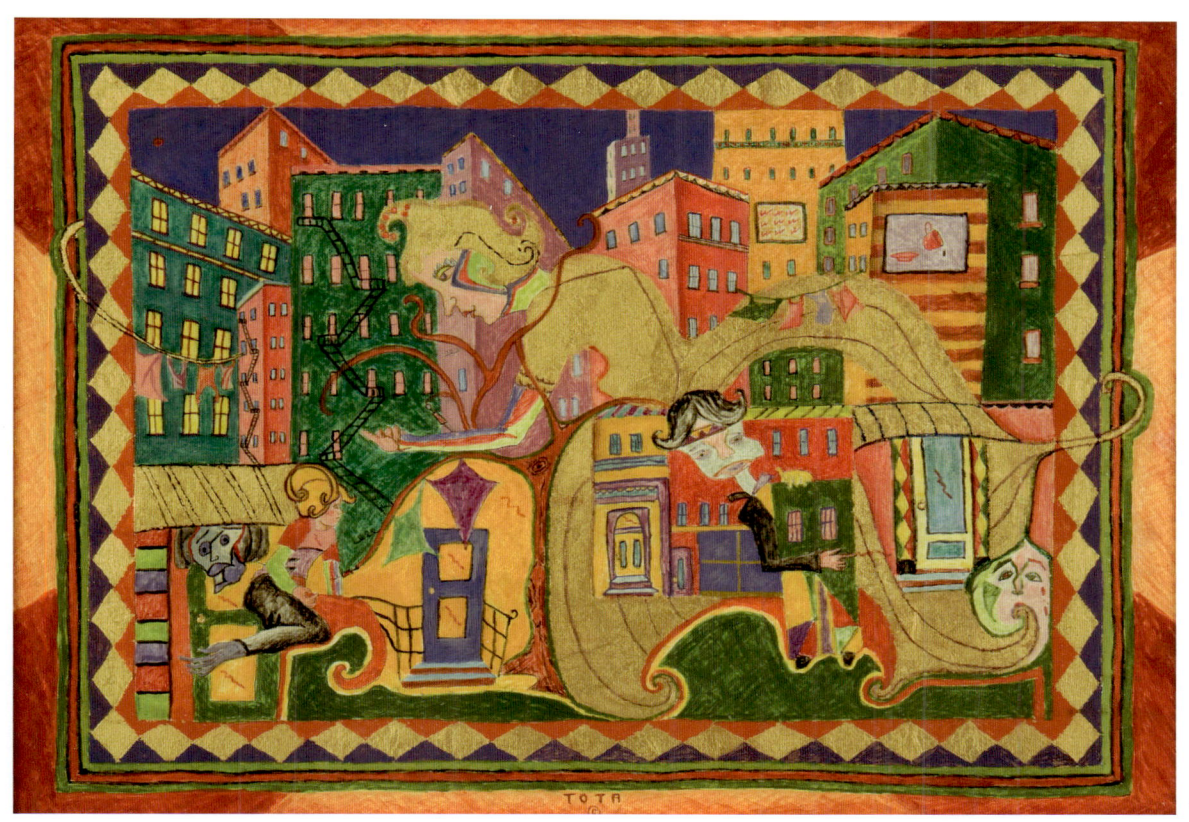

11

11. Untitled, undated, 1980s
Egg tempera and gold leaf on panel
10 ⅛ x 14 ¼ in.
Collection of Rosamond Tota, daughter

12. Untitled, undated, 1980s
Egg tempera and gold leaf on panel
6 ⅛ x 6 ⅛ in.
Collection of Rosamond Tota, daughter

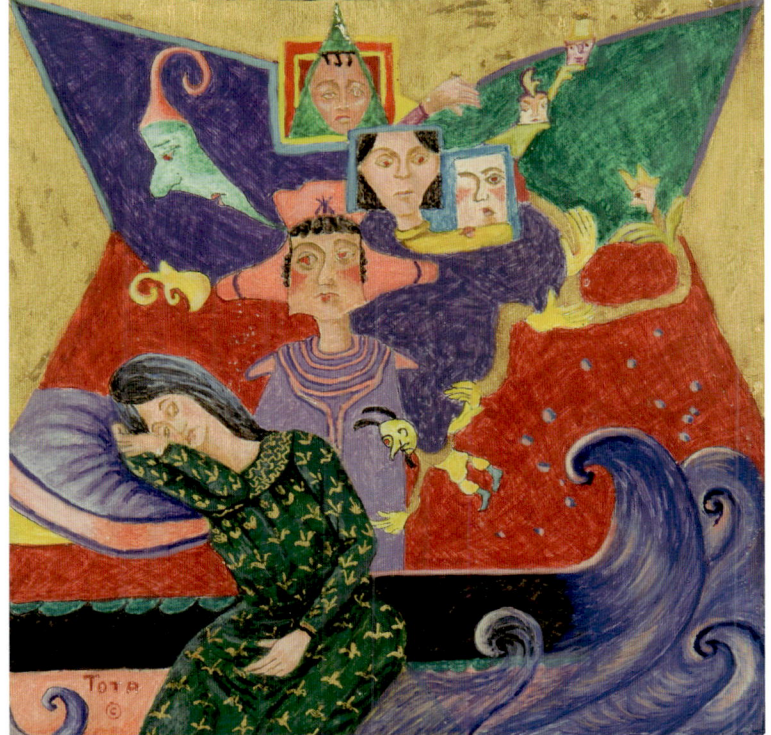

12

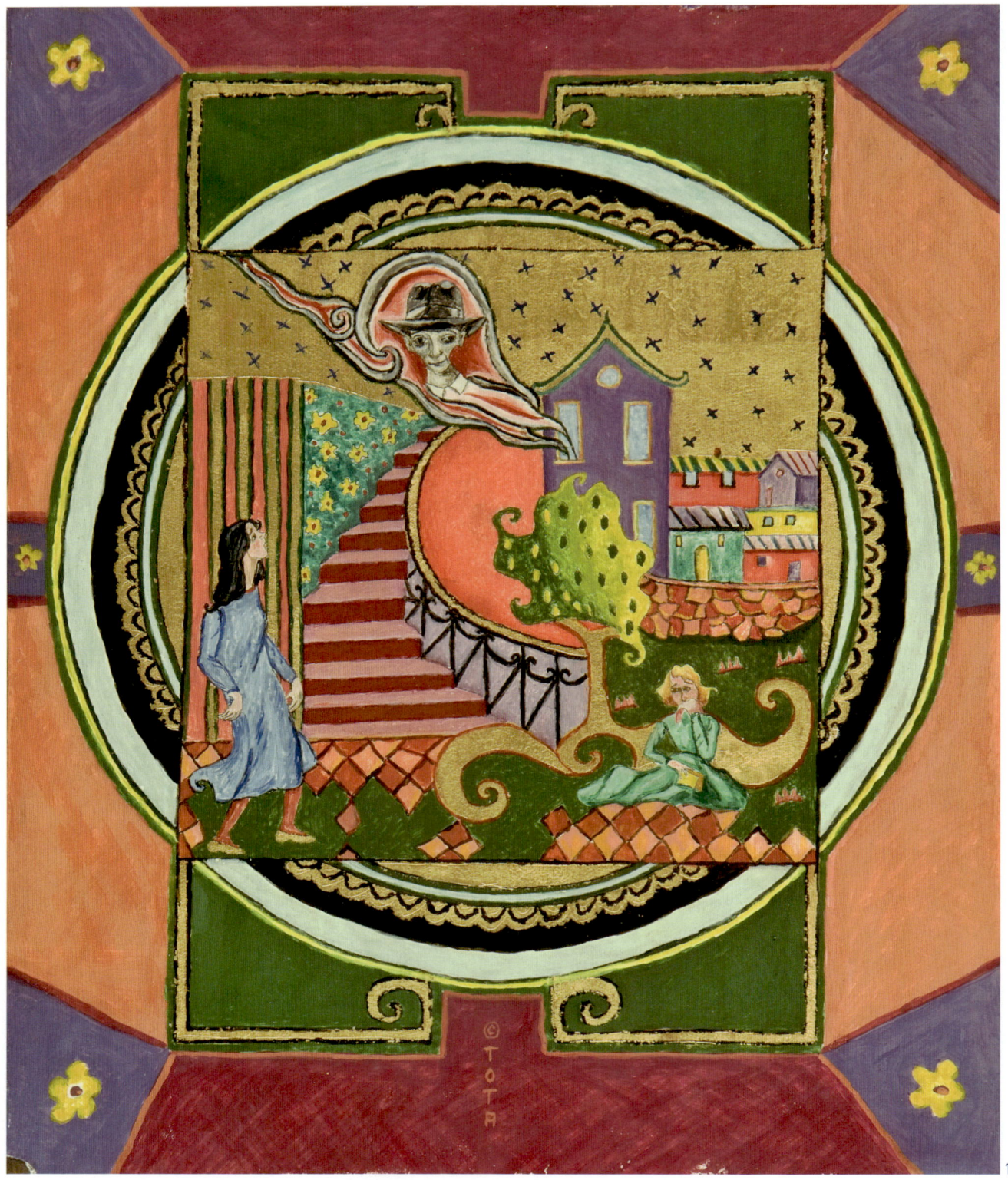

13

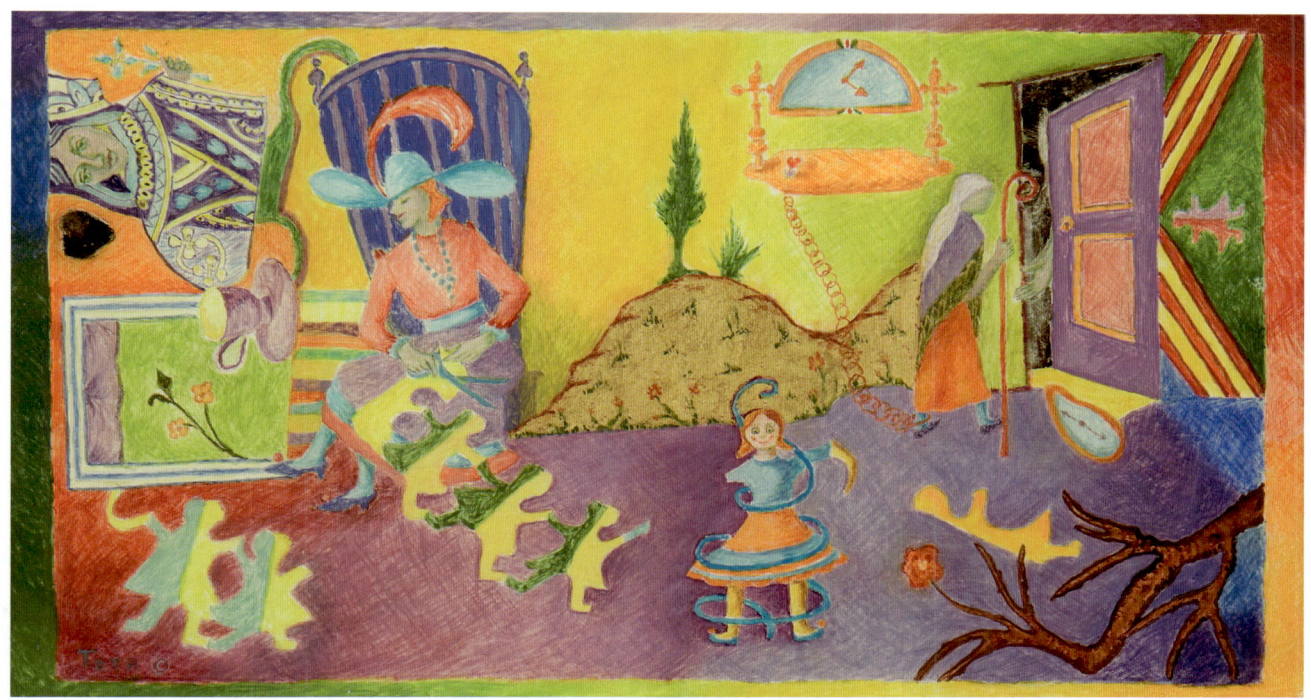

14

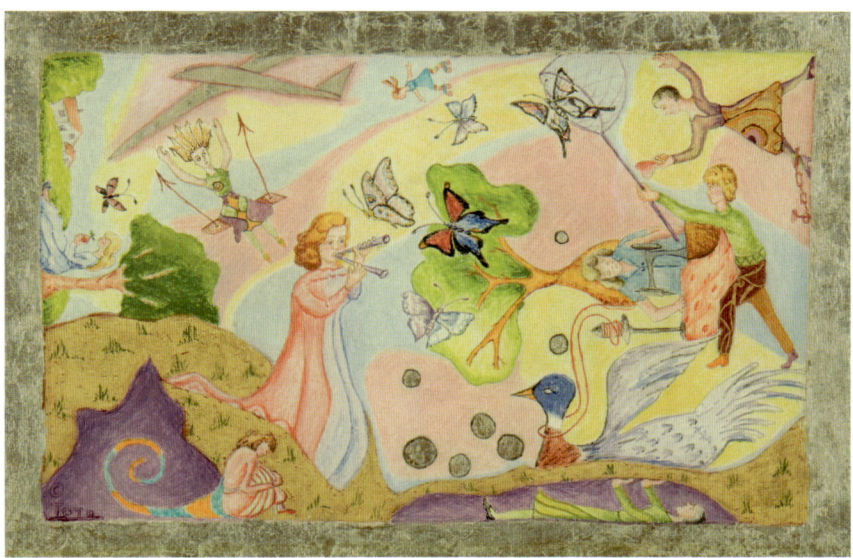

15

13. Untitled, undated, 1980s
Egg tempera and gold leaf on panel
11 ¾ x 9 ¾ in.
Collection of Rosamond Tota, daughter

14. Untitled, undated, 1980s
Egg tempera and gold leaf on panel
7 ½ x 13 ½ in.
Collection of Rosamond Tota, daughter

15. Untitled, undated, 1980s
Egg tempera and silver and gold leaf on
panel
7 ½ x 11 ¼ in.
Collection of Rosamond Tota, daughter

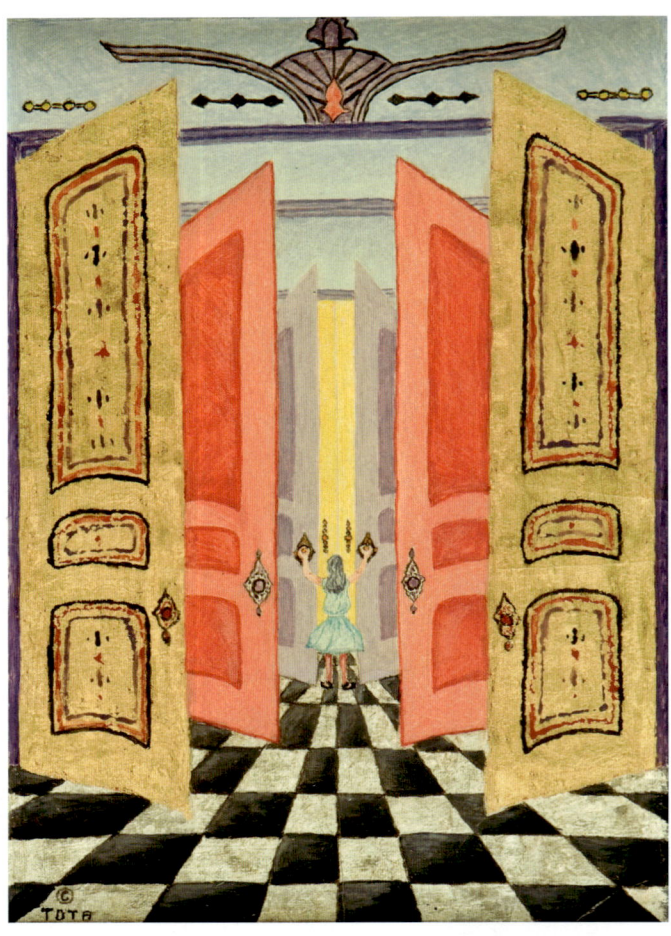

16

16. Untitled, undated, 1980s
Egg tempera and silver leaf on panel
10 %₁₆ x 7 %₁₆ in.
Private collection

17. Untitled, undated, 1980s
Egg tempera and gold leaf on panel
5 ⅞ x 5 ⅞ in.
Collection of Anthony F. Panzetta, MD

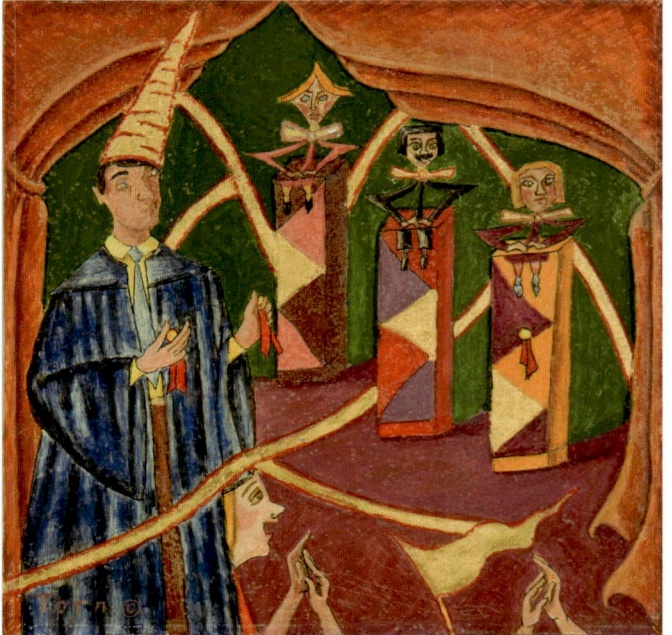

17

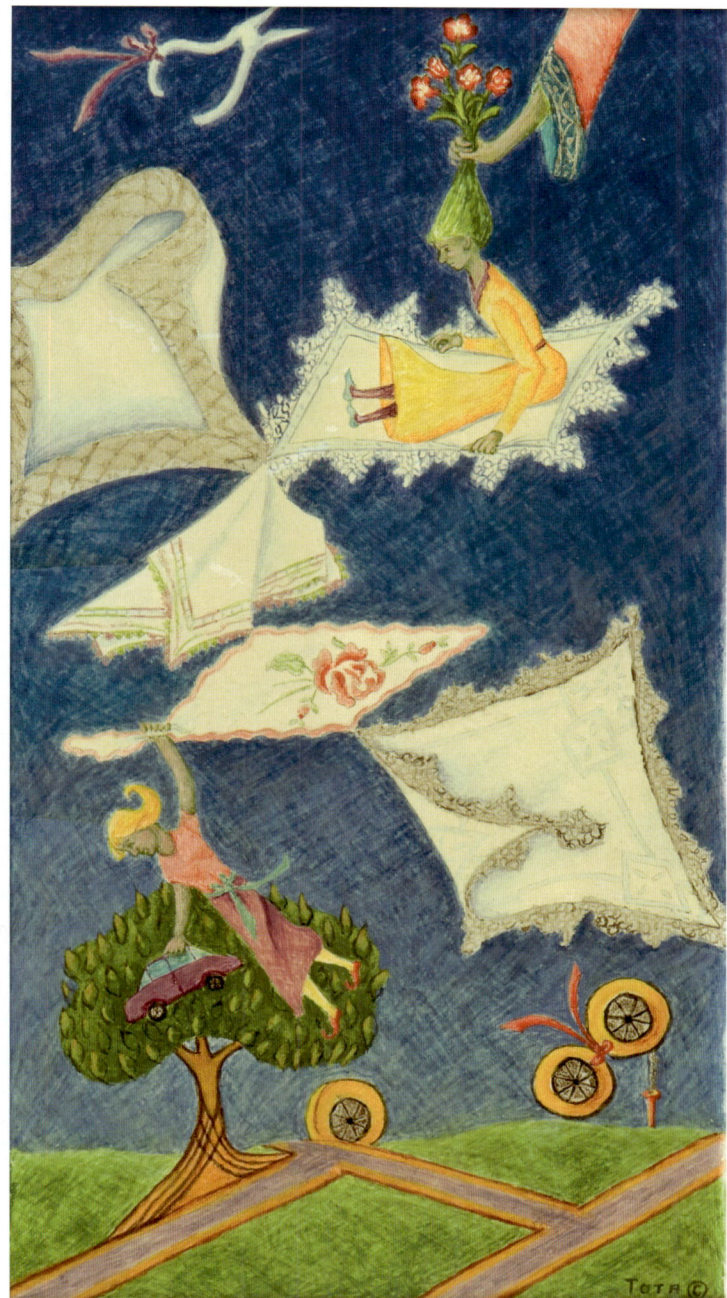

18. Untitled, undated, 1980s
Egg tempera on panel
13 ½ x 7 ½ in.
Private collection

19. Untitled, undated, 1980s
Egg tempera and gold leaf on panel
10 ⅝ x 8 ⅞ in.
Collection of Rosamond Tota, daughter

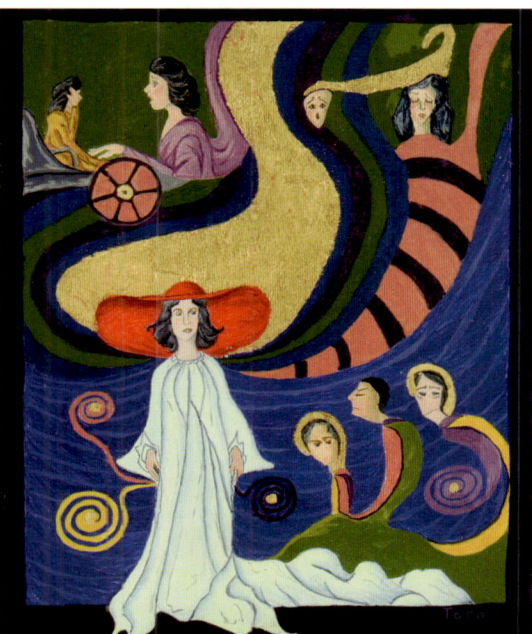

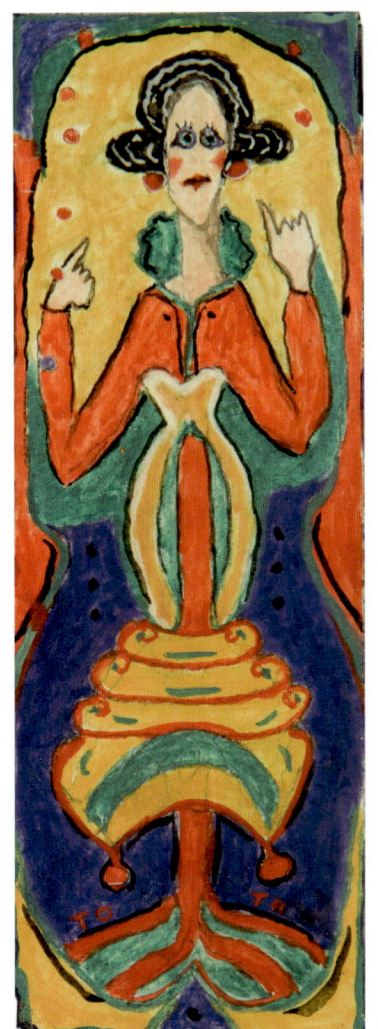

20

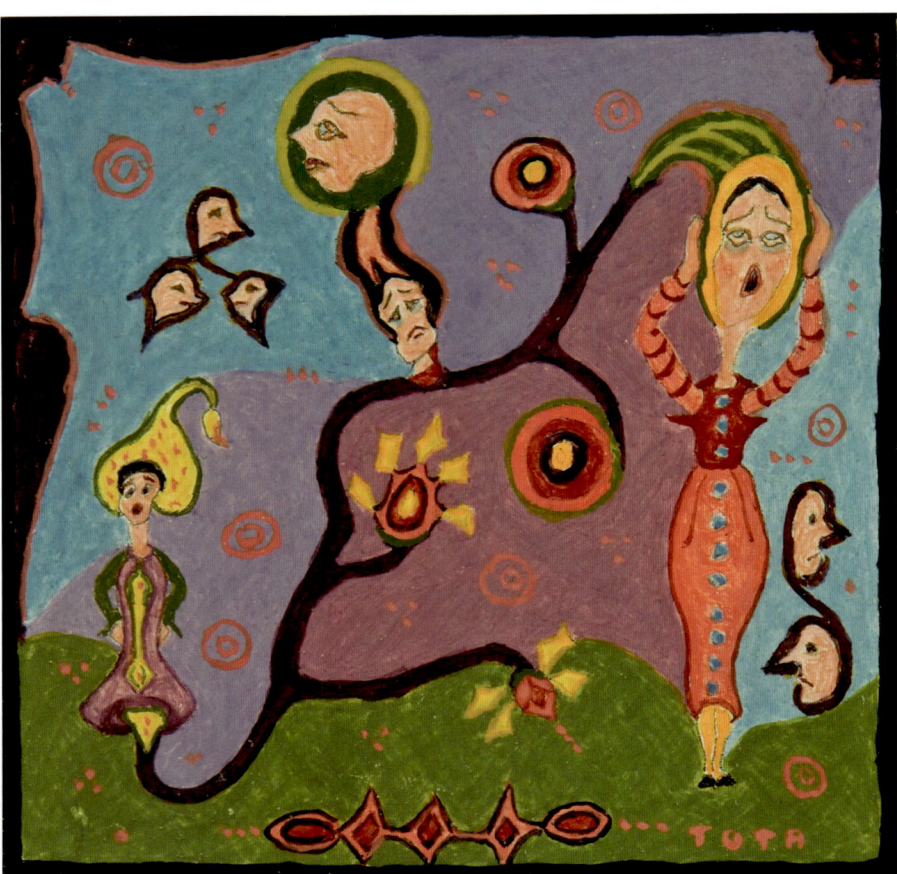

21

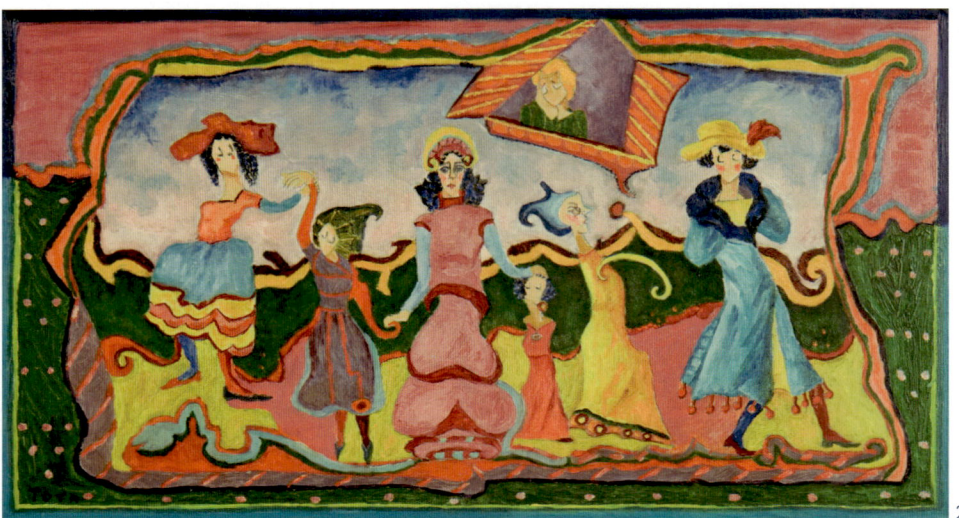

22

20. Untitled, undated, 1980s
Egg tempera on panel
5 x 1 ⅝ in.
Collection of Rosamond
Tota, daughter

21. Untitled, undated, 1980s
Egg tempera on panel
4 1/16 x 4 1/16 in.
Collection of Rosamond
Tota, daughter

22. Untitled, undated, 1980s
Oil on canvas panel
7 ⅞ x 14 1/16 in.
Collection of Rosamond
Tota, daughter

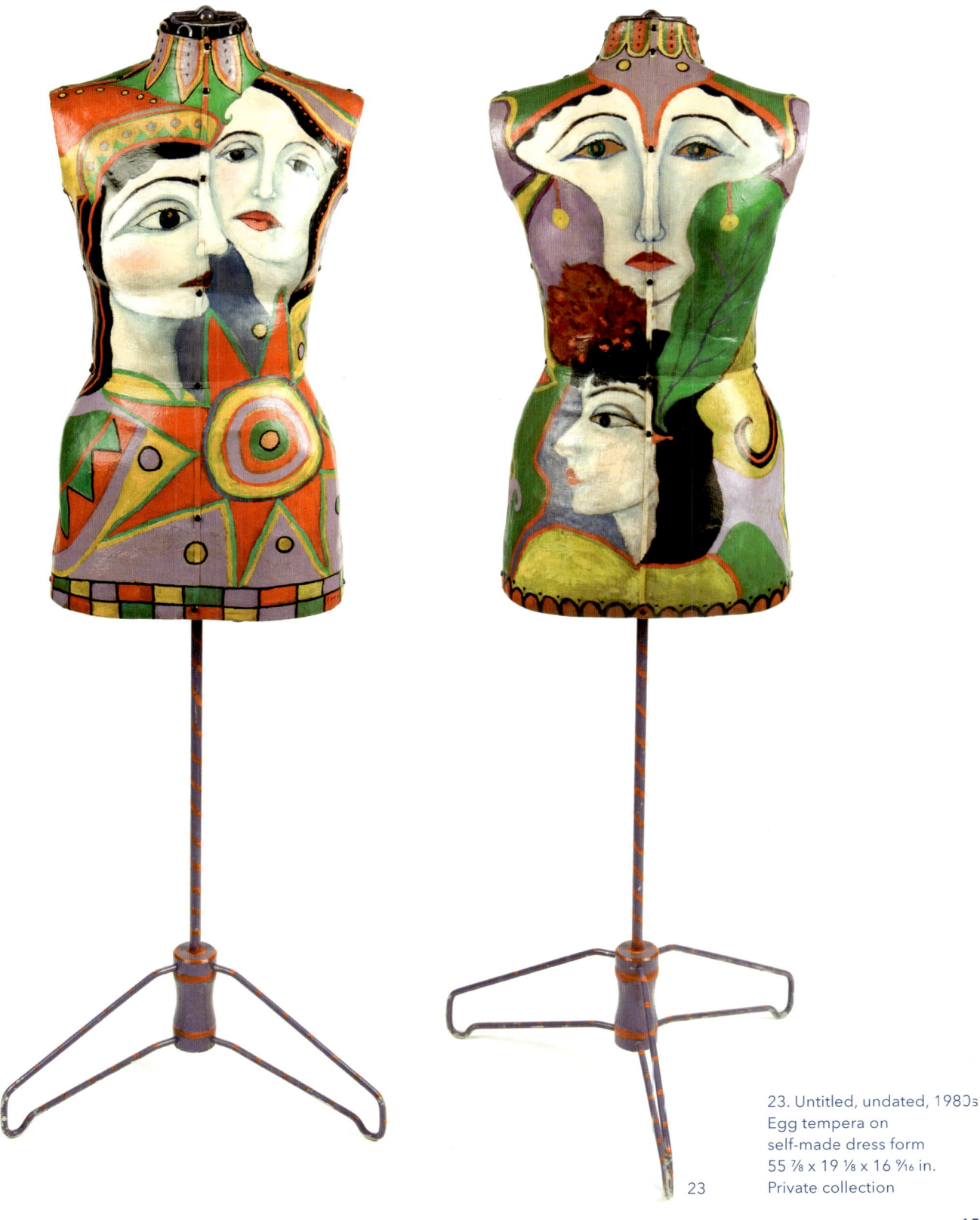

23. Untitled, undated, 1980s
Egg tempera on
self-made dress form
55 ⅞ x 19 ⅛ x 16 ⁹⁄₁₆ in.
Private collection

23

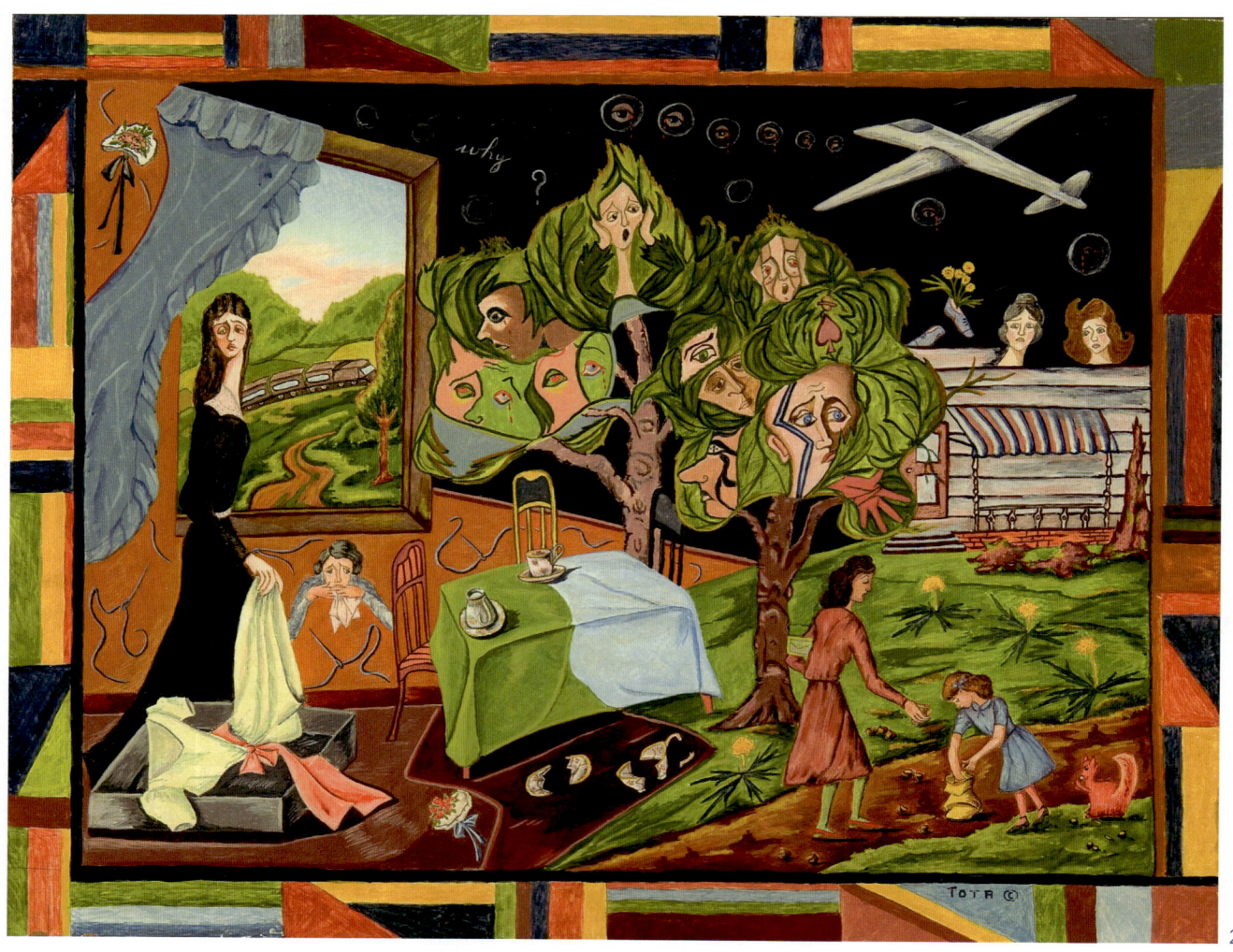

24. Untitled, undated, 1980s
Egg tempera on panel
16 x 20 ⅛ in.
Memorial Art Gallery of the University of
Rochester, Gift of Rosamond Tota, 97.3

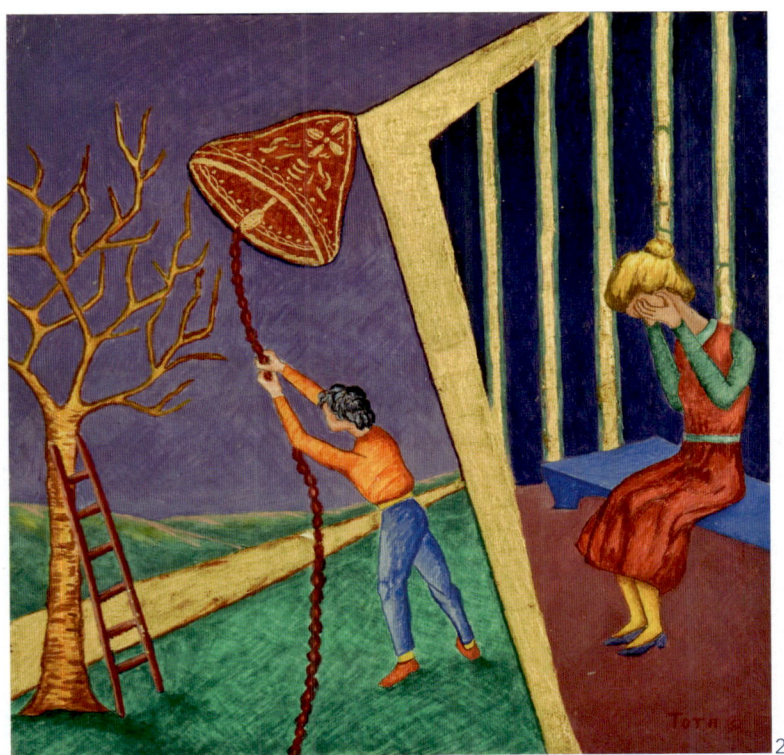
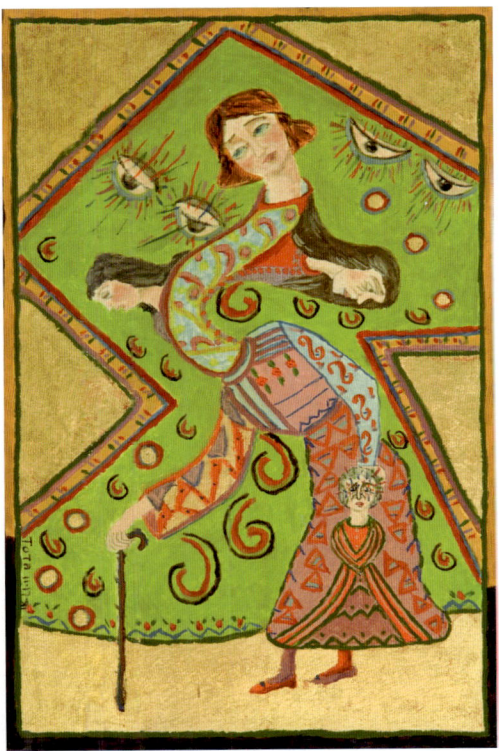

24

25. Untitled, completed May 19, 1981
Egg tempera and gold leaf on panel
9 x 9 in.
Collection of Judith G. Levy

26. Untitled, completed November 17,
1981
Egg tempera and gold leaf on panel
12 x 7 ¾ in.
Collection of Rosamond Tota, daughter

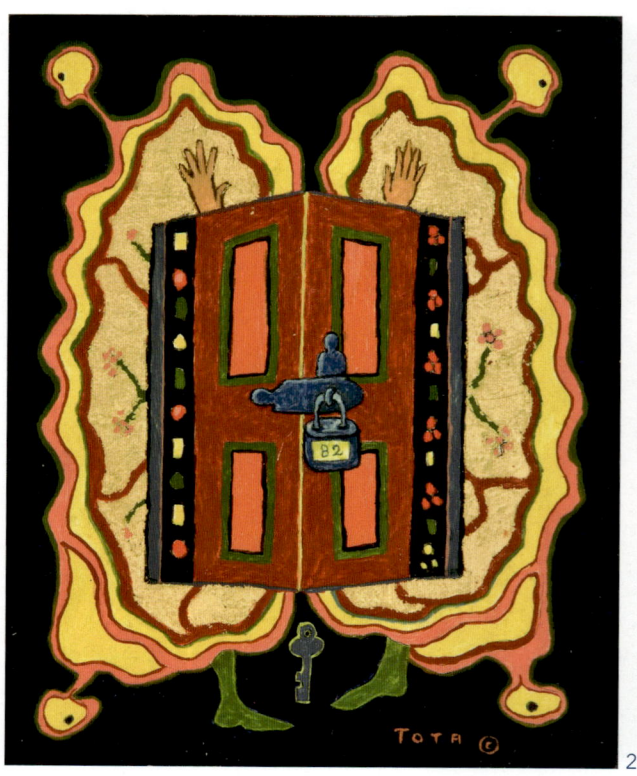

27

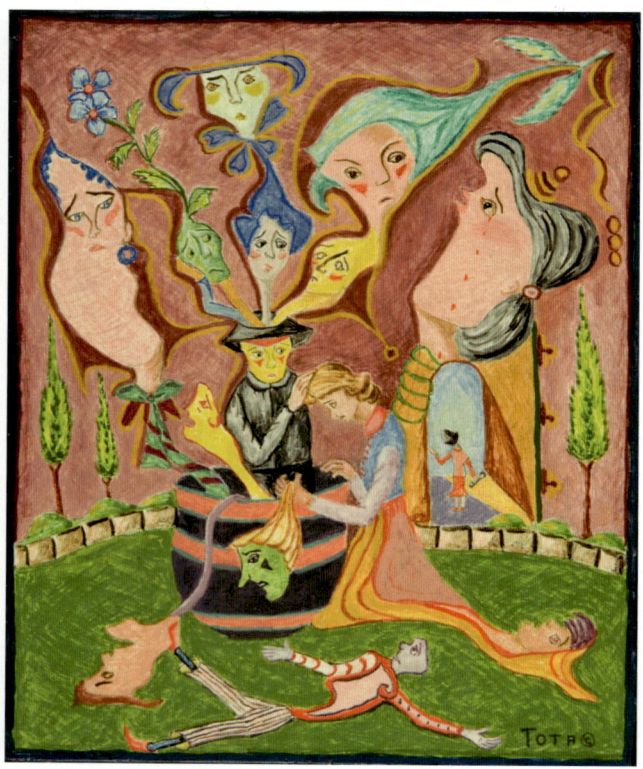

28

27. Untitled, 1982
Egg tempera and gold leaf on panel
7 1/16 x 5 5/8 in.
Private collection

28. Untitled, completed April 3, 1982
Egg tempera and gold leaf on panel
8 1/16 x 6 1/2 in.
Collection of Judith G. Levy

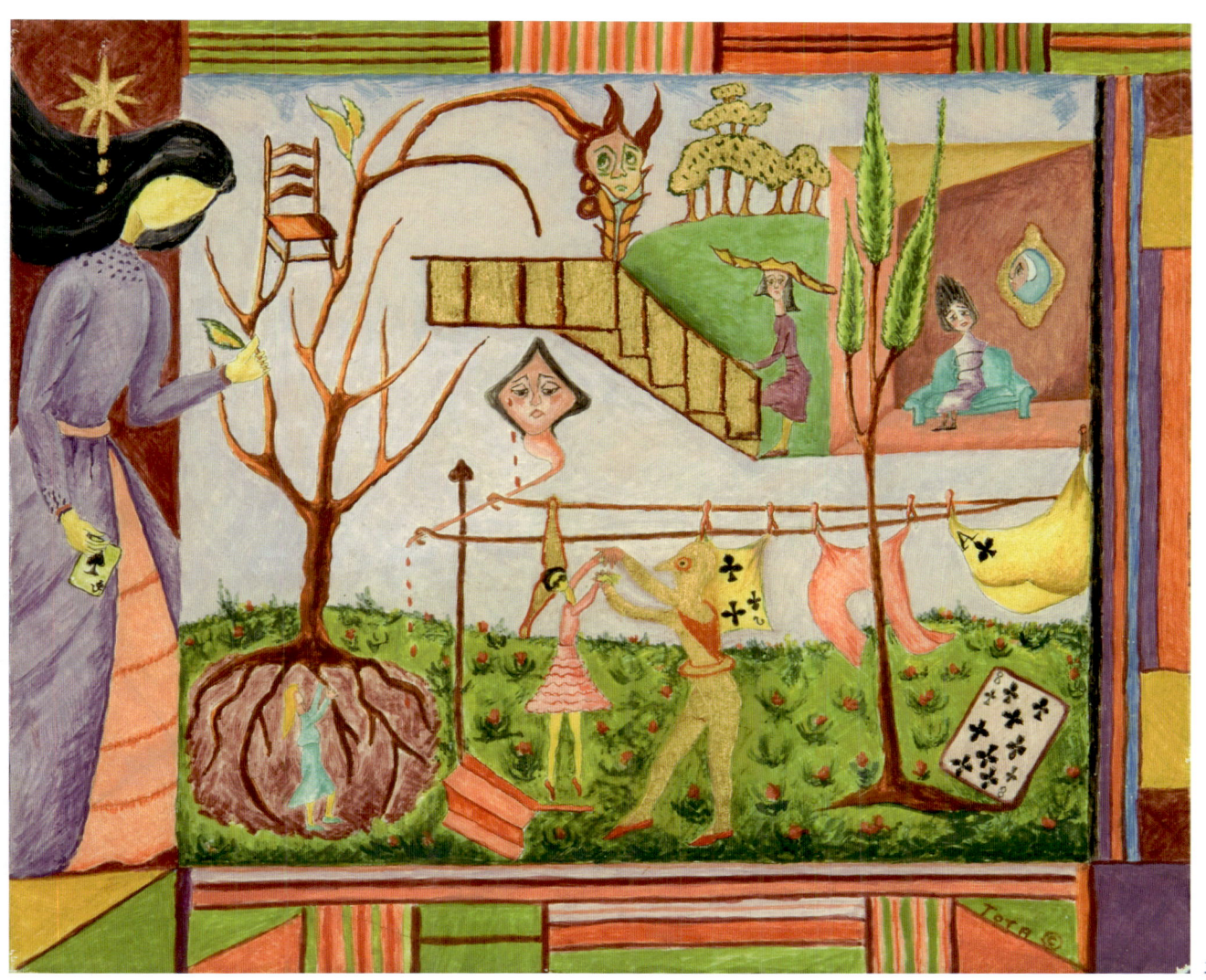

29. Untitled, completed March 20, 1982
Egg tempera and gold leaf on panel
8 7/16 x 10 in.
Memorial Art Gallery of the University
of Rochester, Gift of Rosamond Tota,
2011.61

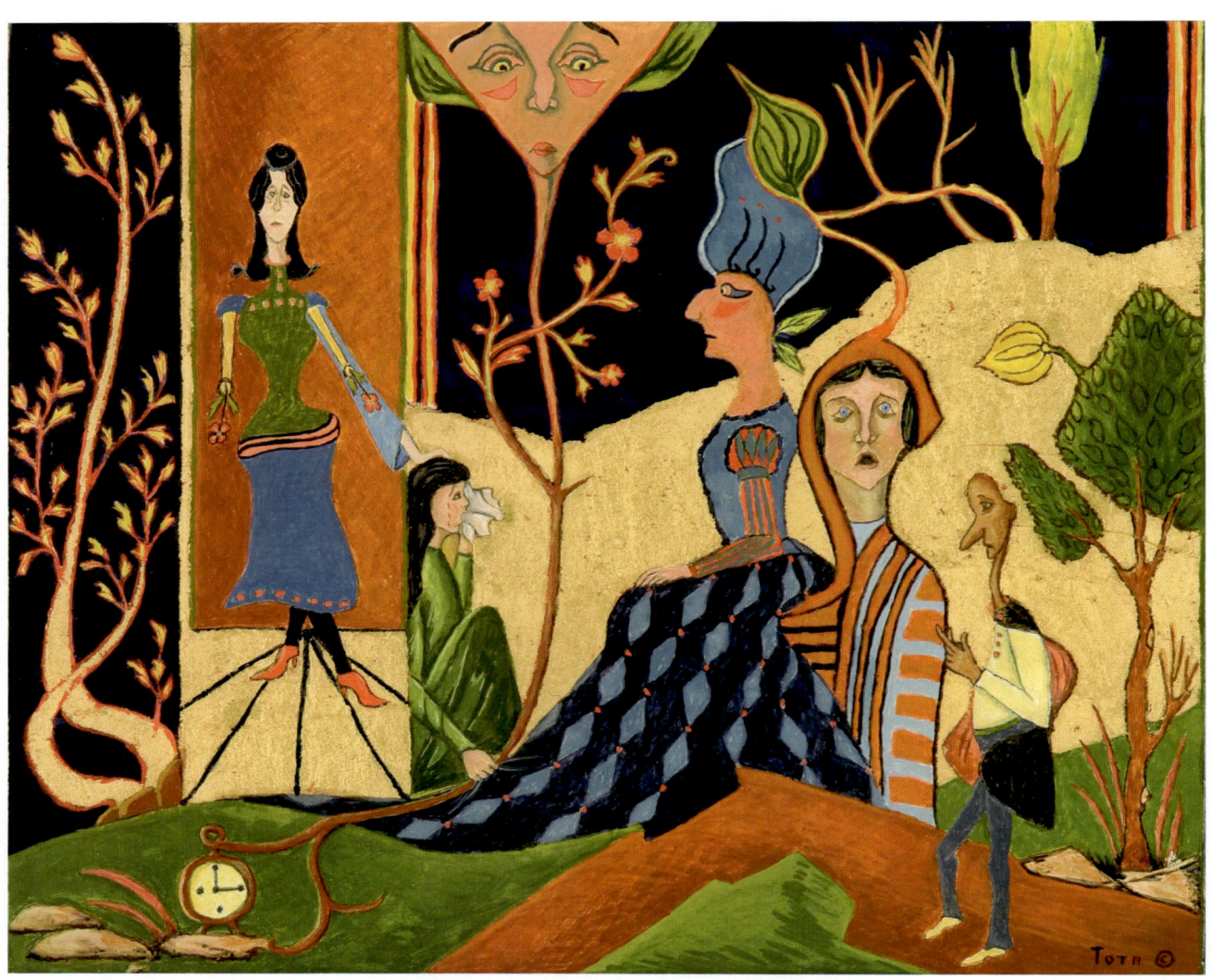

30. Untitled, completed May 16, 1982
Egg tempera and gold leaf on panel
9 9/16 x 11 3/16 in.
Memorial Art Gallery of the University
of Rochester, Gift of Rosamond Tota,
2011.59

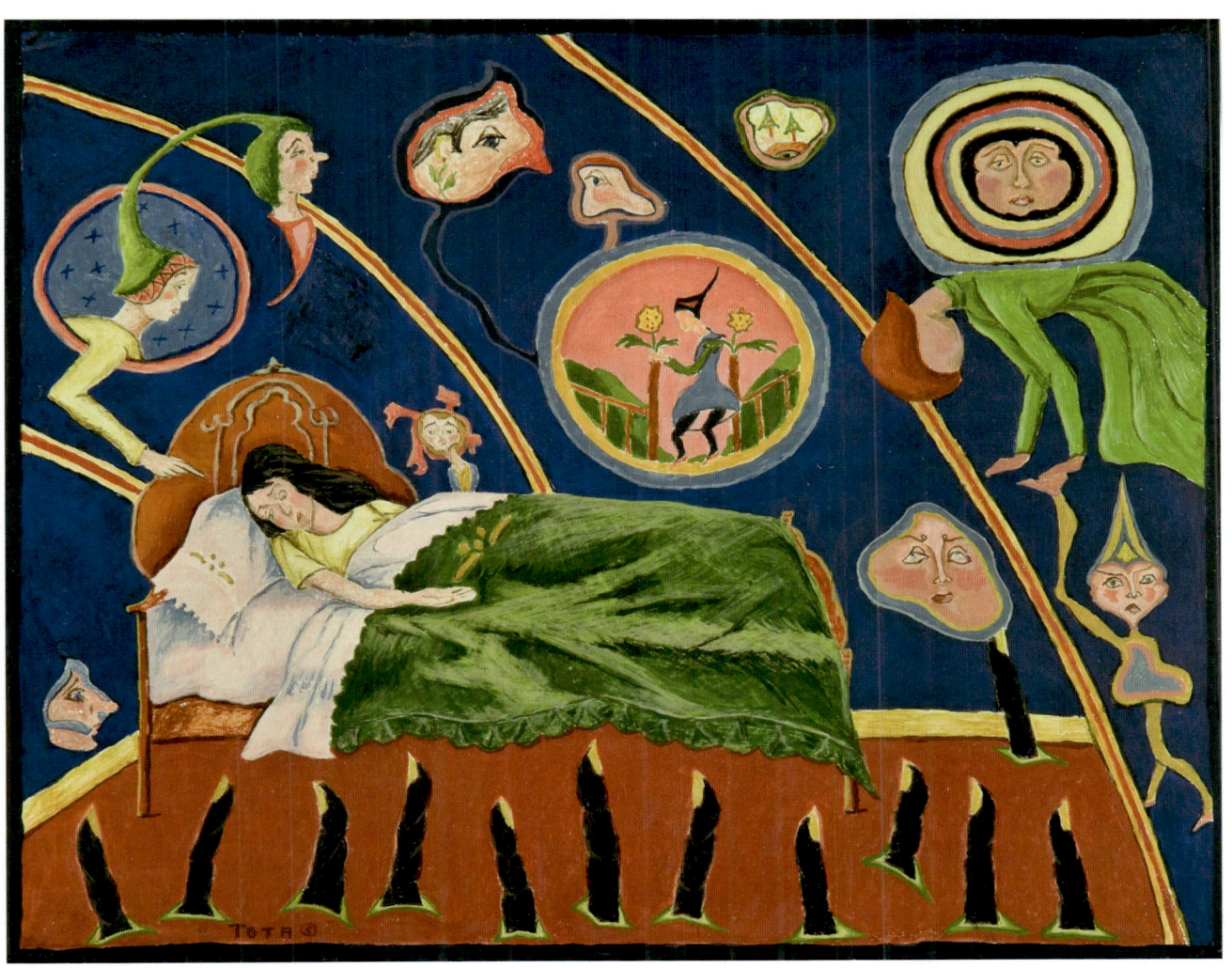

31. Untitled, completed July 20, 1982
Egg tempera on panel
8 ½ x 10 ½ in.
Collection of Rosamond Tota, daughter

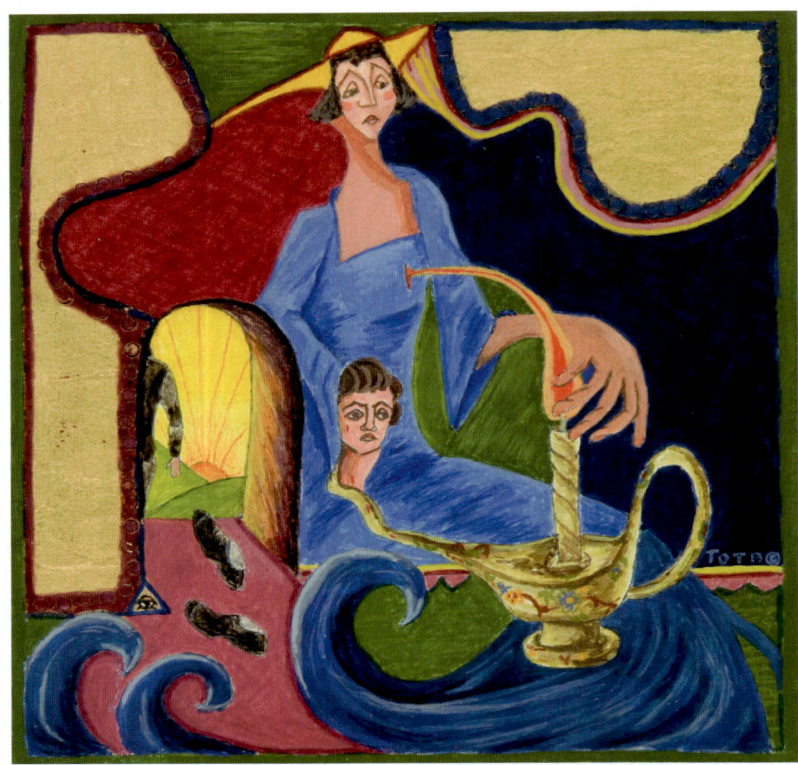

32. Untitled, completed July 21, 1982
Egg tempera and gold leaf on panel
6 1/16 x 6 1/8 in.
Collection of Rosamond Tota, daughter

33. Untitled, completed February 9, 1983
Egg tempera and gold leaf on panel
5 1/2 x 7 7/8 in.
Collection of Rosamond Tota, daughter

34. Untitled, completed February 23, 1983
Egg tempera and gold leaf on panel
6 7/8 x 8 1/4 in.
Collection of Desiree P. Rodriguez

35. Untitled, completed April 21, 1983
Egg tempera and gold leaf on panel
5 1/4 x 8 1/4 in.
Memorial Art Gallery of the University of
Rochester, Gift of Rosamond Tota, 2011.62

32

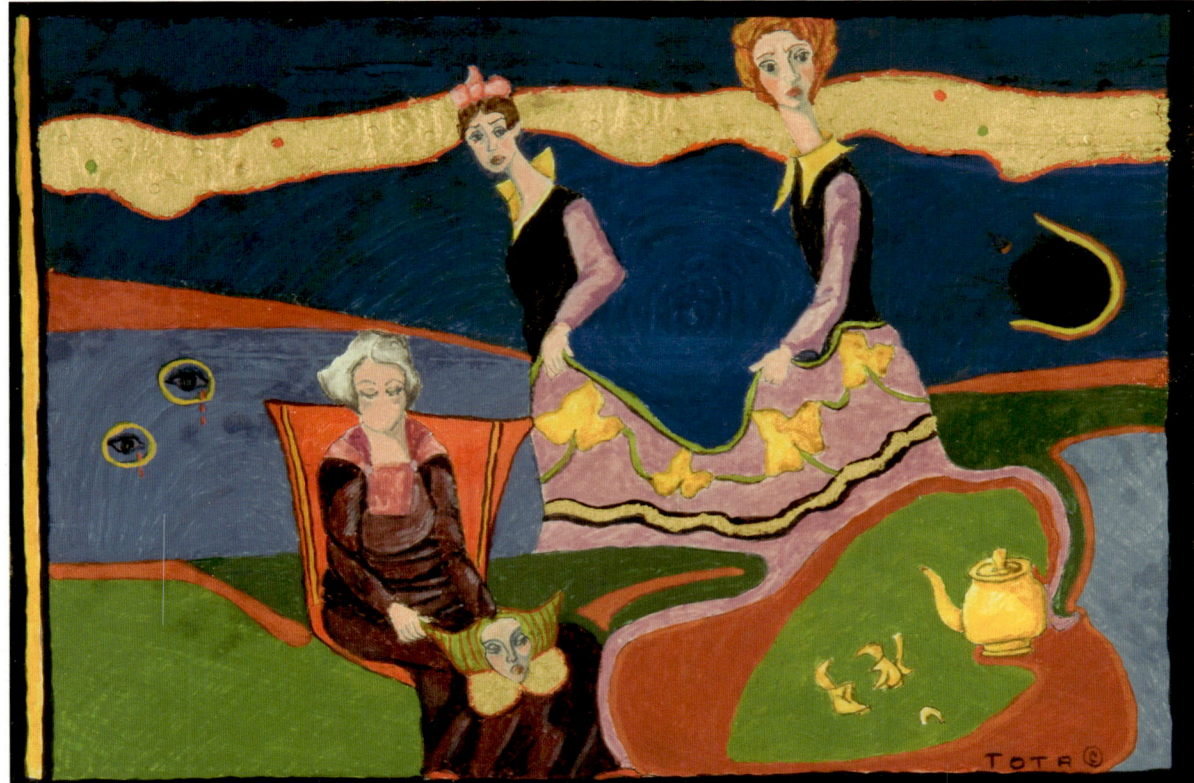

33

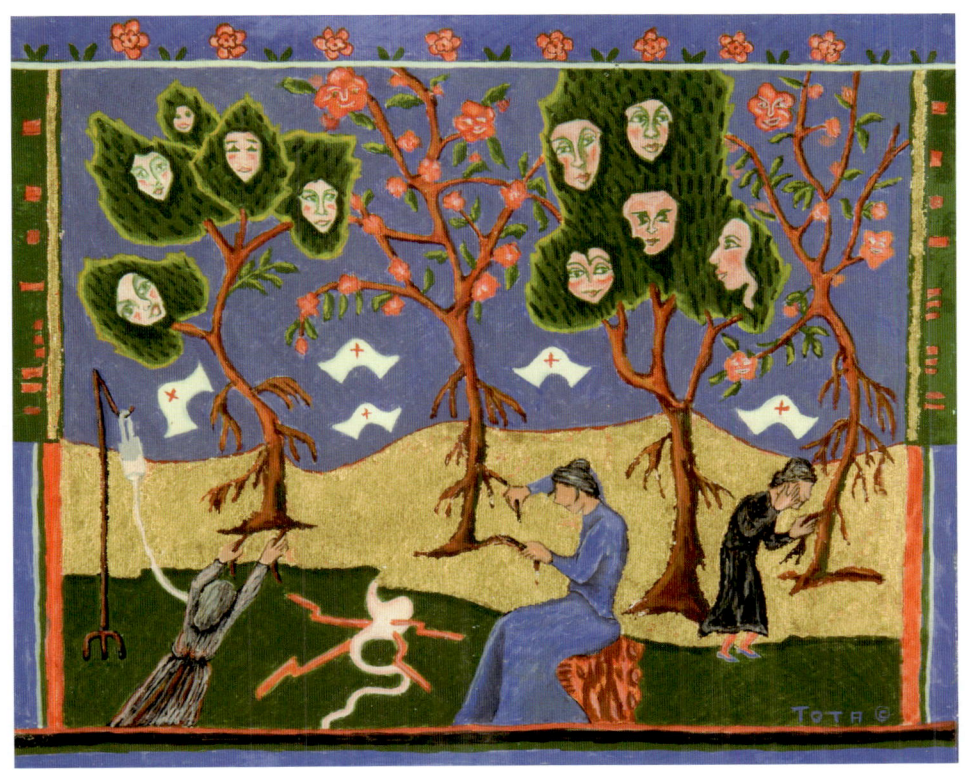

34

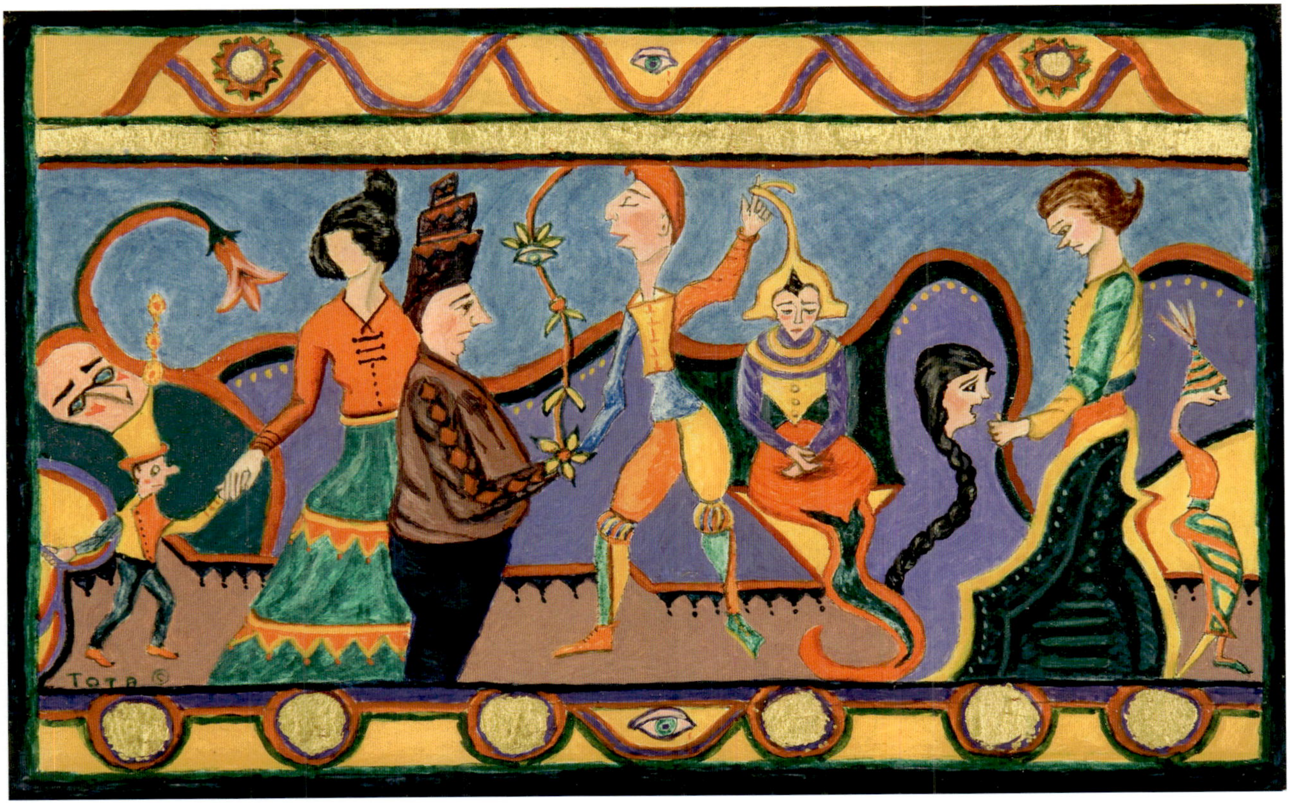

35

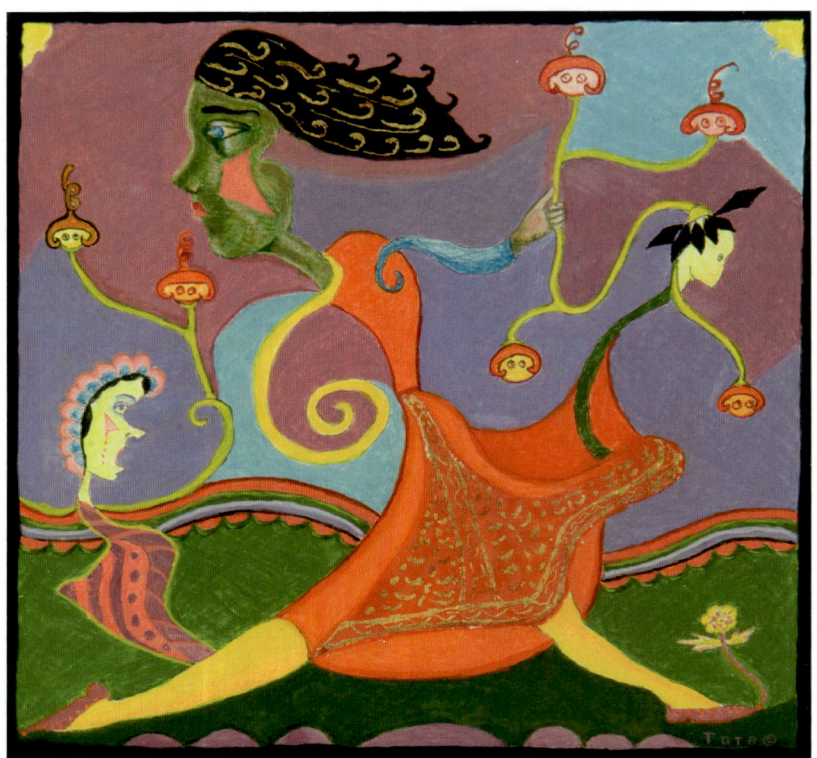

36. Untitled, completed May 14, 1983
Egg tempera on panel
6 ½ x 6 ¹¹⁄₁₆ in.
Collection of Margaret Manning Krug

37. Untitled, completed May 18, 1983
Egg tempera on panel
6 ⅛ x 6 ⅛ in.
Memorial Art Gallery of the University of
Rochester, Gift of Rosamond Tota, 2011.58

36

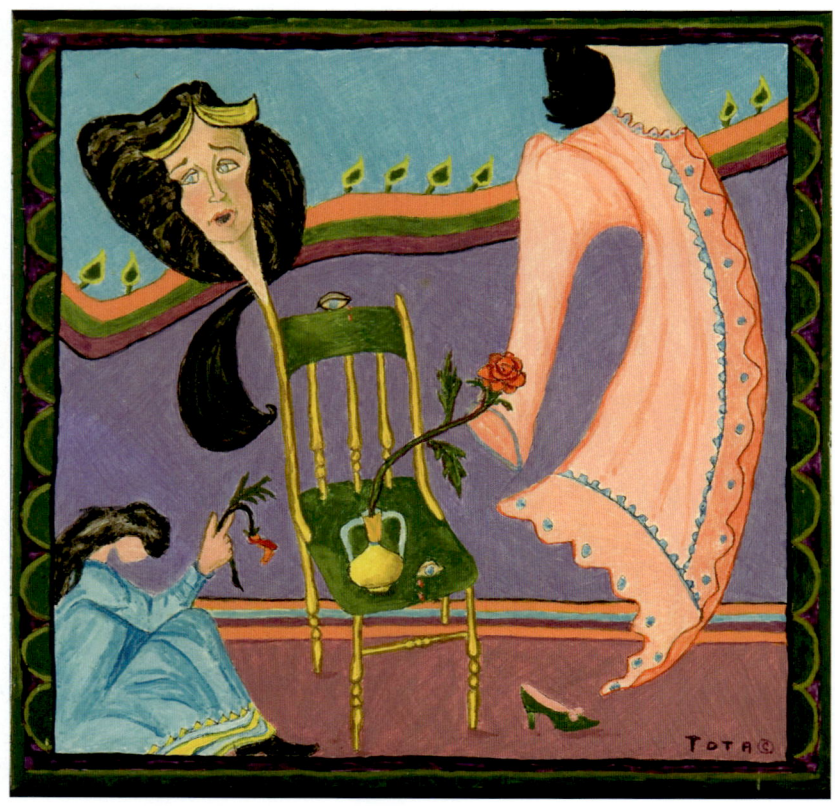

37

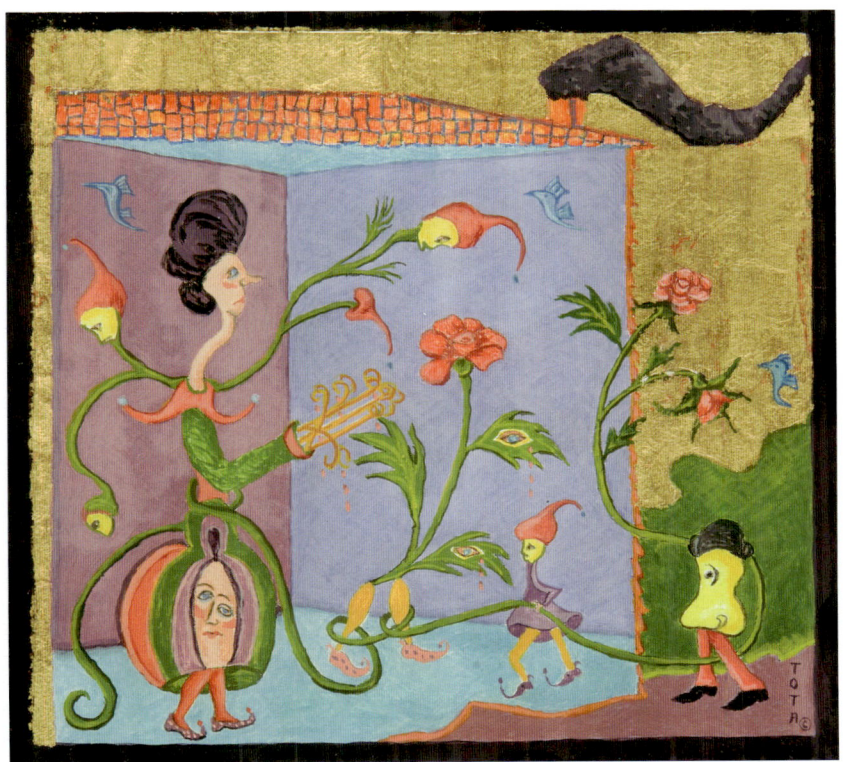

38. Untitled, completed May 26, 1983
Egg tempera and gold leaf on panel
6 ½ x 6 ¹⁵⁄₁₆ in.
Collection of Rosamond Tota, daughter

39. Untitled, completed July 19, 1983
Egg tempera and gold leaf on panel
6 ⁹⁄₁₆ x 16 in.
Memorial Art Gallery of the University of
Rochester, Gift of Rosamond Tota, 2011.55

38

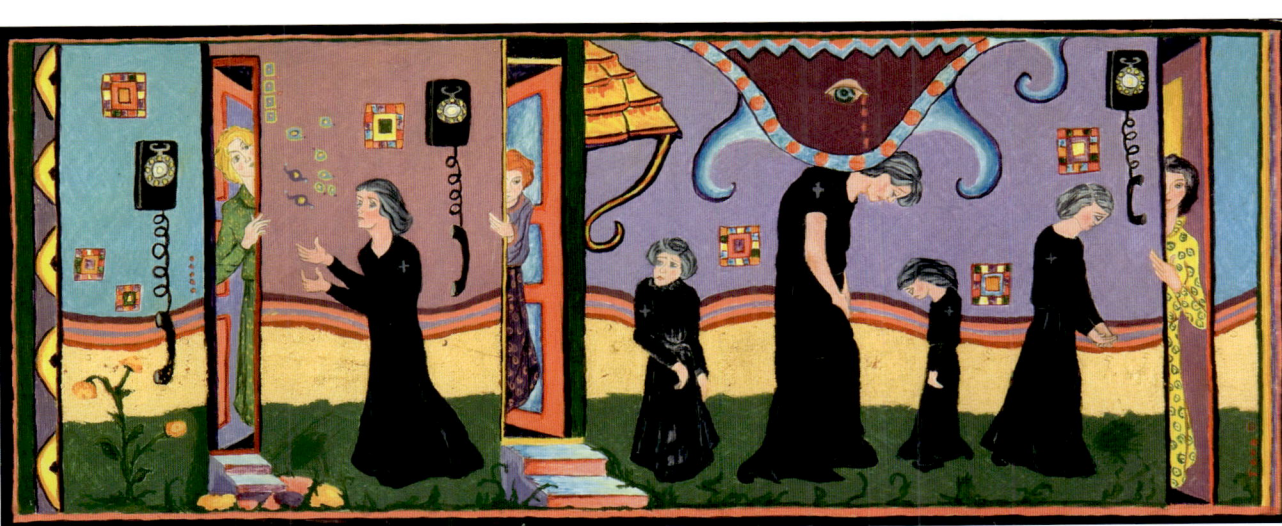

39

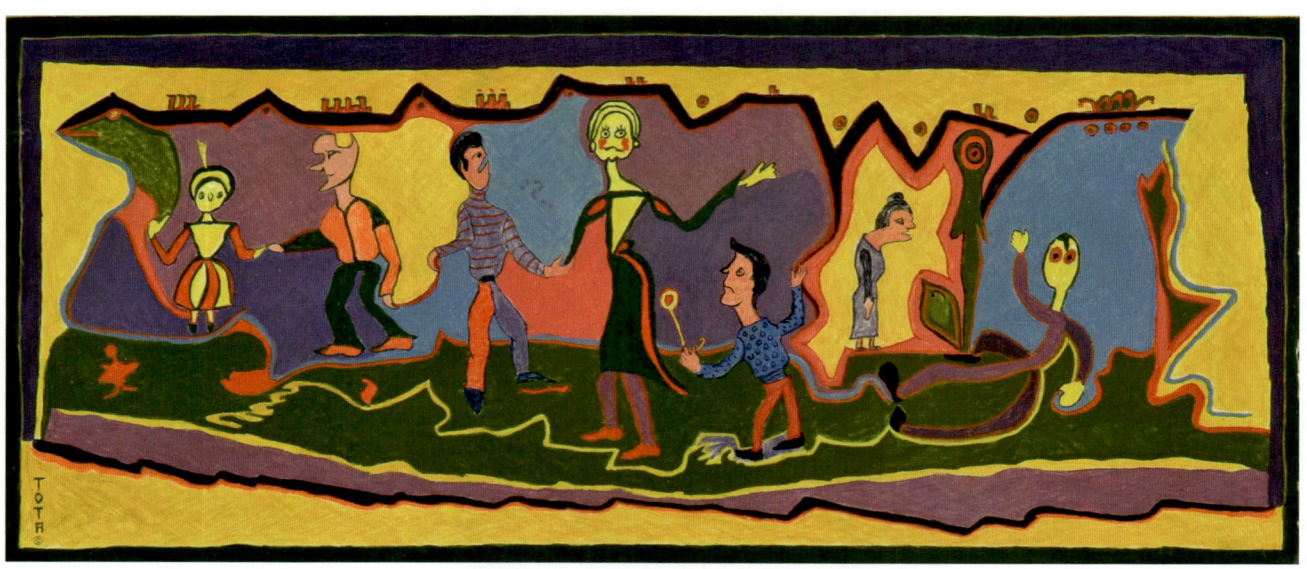

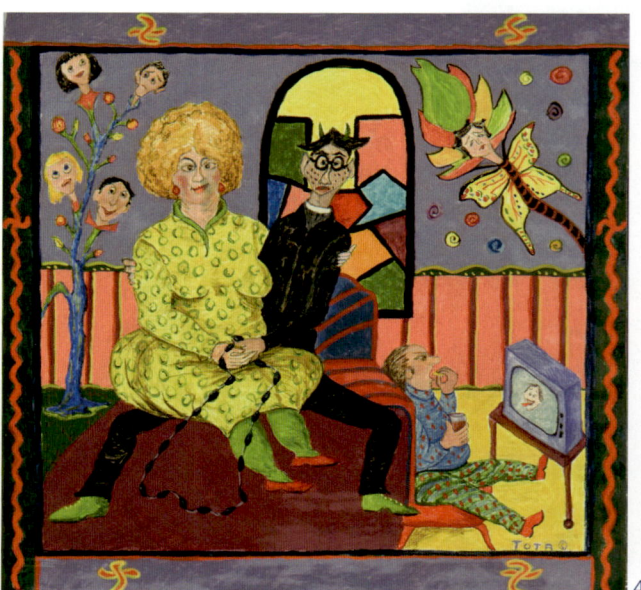

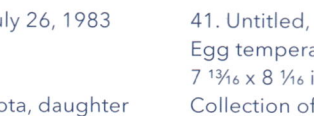

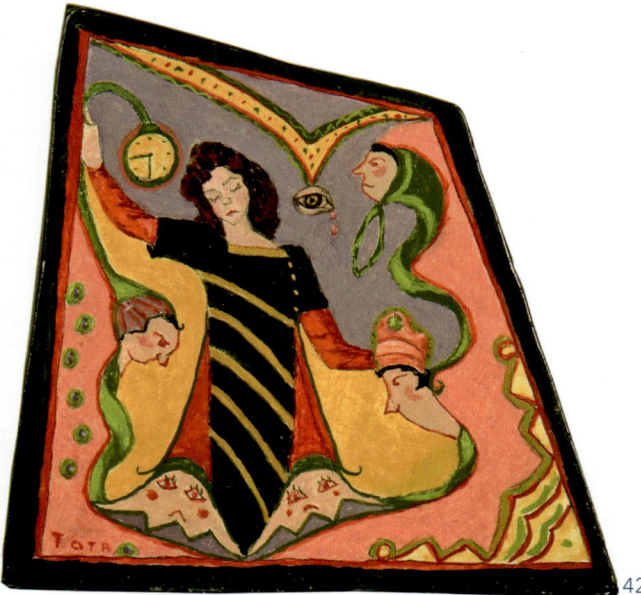

40. Untitled, completed July 26, 1983
Egg tempera on panel
7 x 16 in.
Collection of Rosamond Tota, daughter

41. Untitled, completed July 31, 1983
Egg tempera on panel
7 13/16 x 8 1/16 in.
Collection of Judith G. Levy

42. Untitled, completed August 3, 1983
Egg tempera on panel
4 1/8 x 4 1/4 in.
Collection of Rosamond Tota, daughter

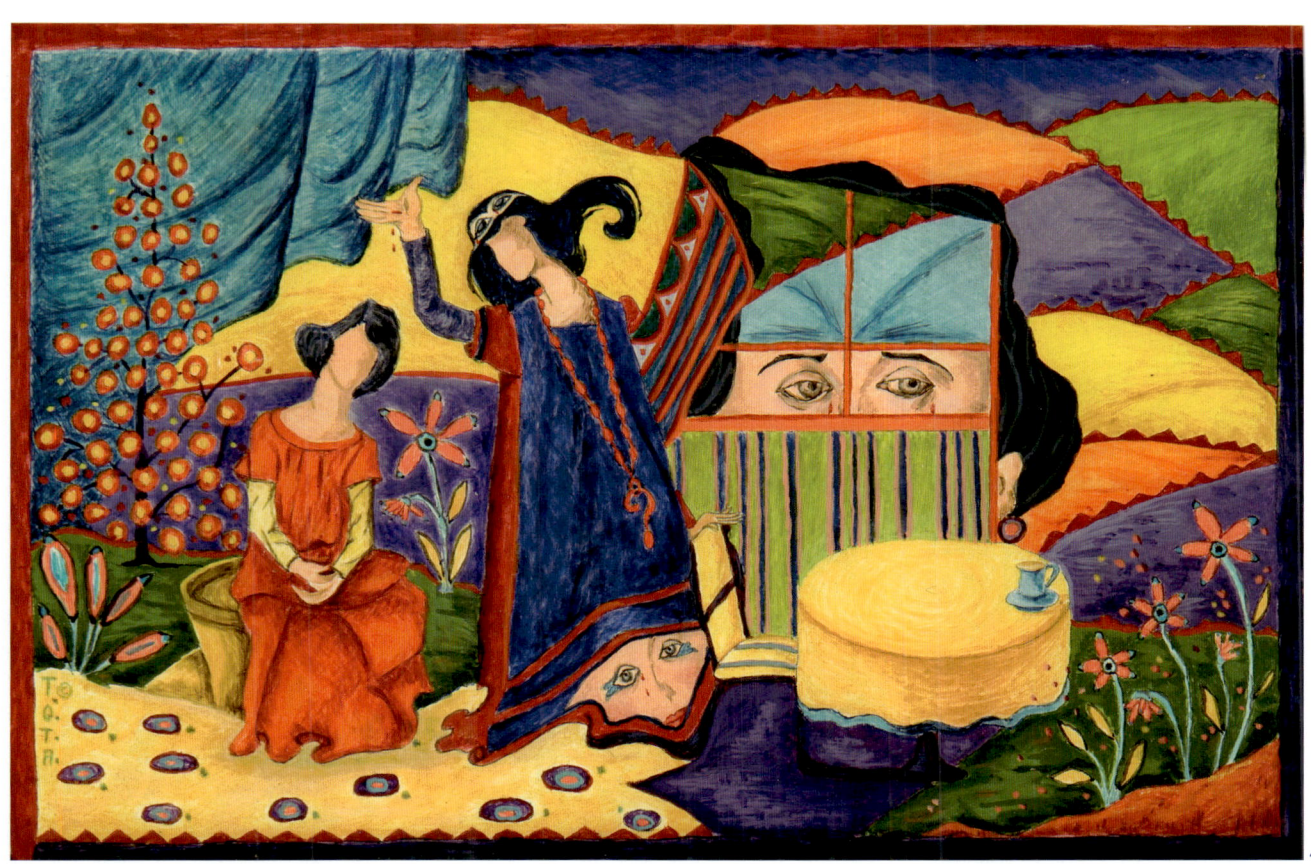

43

43. Untitled, completed August 6, 1983
Egg tempera on panel
7 x 10 ½ in.
Memorial Art Gallery of the University
of Rochester, Gift of Rosamond Tota,
2011.60

77

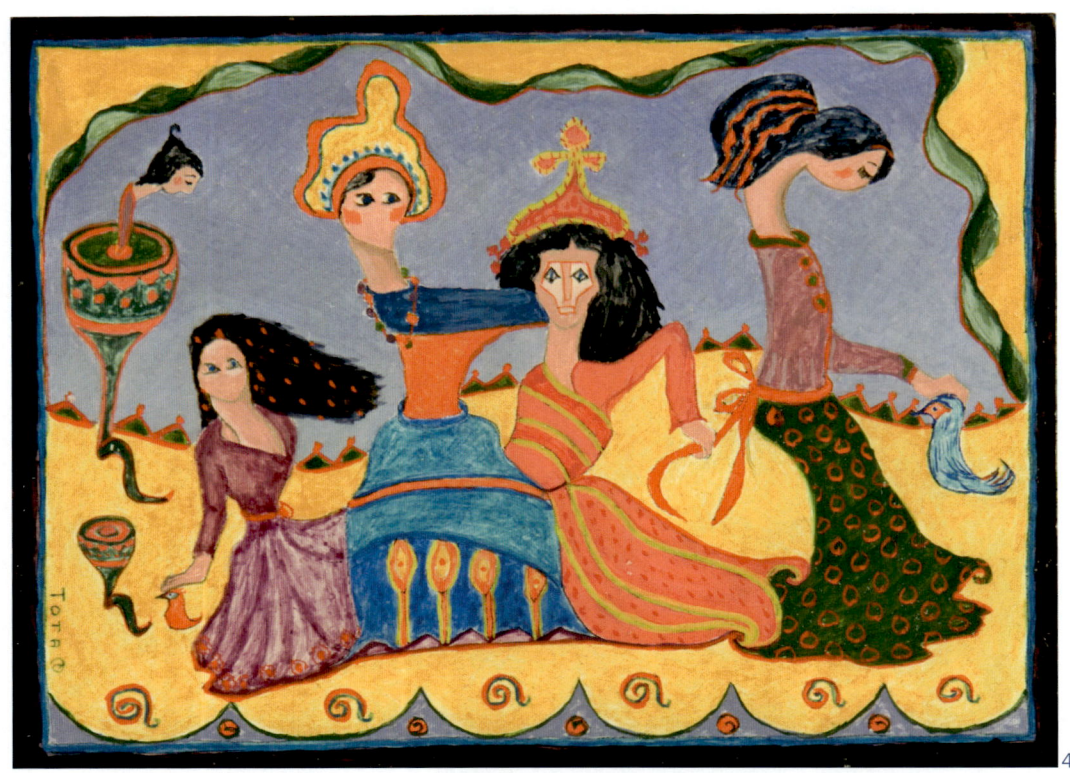

44

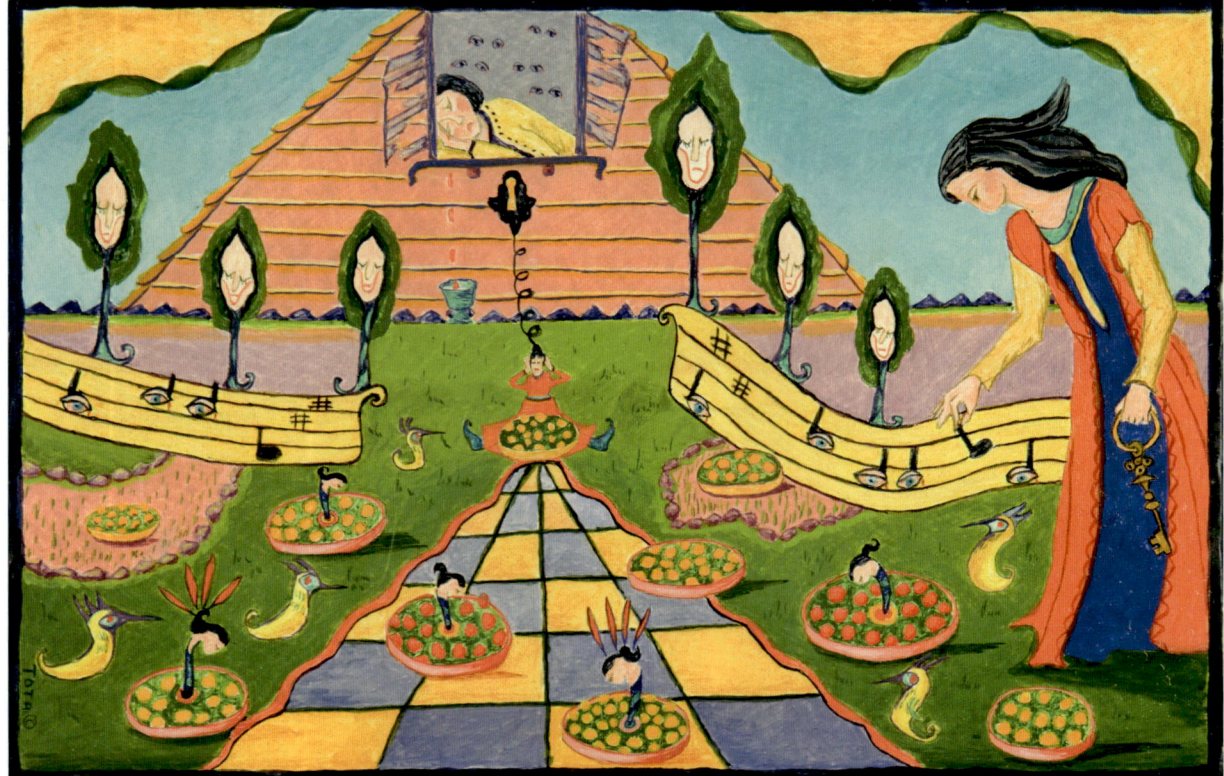

45

78

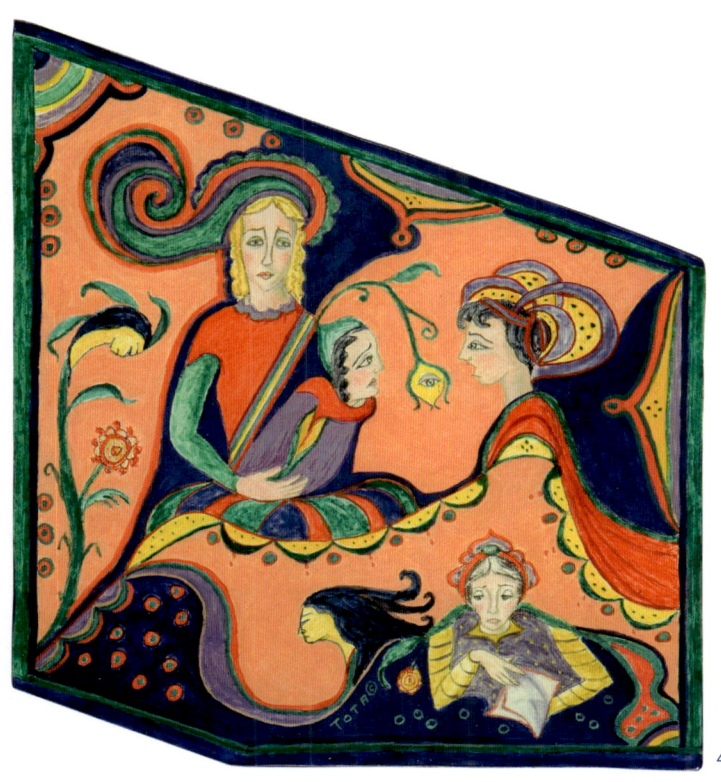

44. Untitled, completed August 17, 1983
Egg tempera on panel
5 3/8 x 7 1/16 in.
Private collection

45. Untitled, completed August 21, 1983
Egg tempera on panel
7 1/16 x 10 1/2 in.
Collection of Joseph Panzetta

46. Untitled, completed September 25, 1983
Egg tempera on panel
8 x 7 in.
Collection of Rosamond Tota, daughter

47. Untitled, completed September 3, 1983
Egg tempera on panel
7 x 8 3/16 in.
Memorial Art Gallery of the University of Rochester,
Gift of Rosamond Tota, 2011.57

46

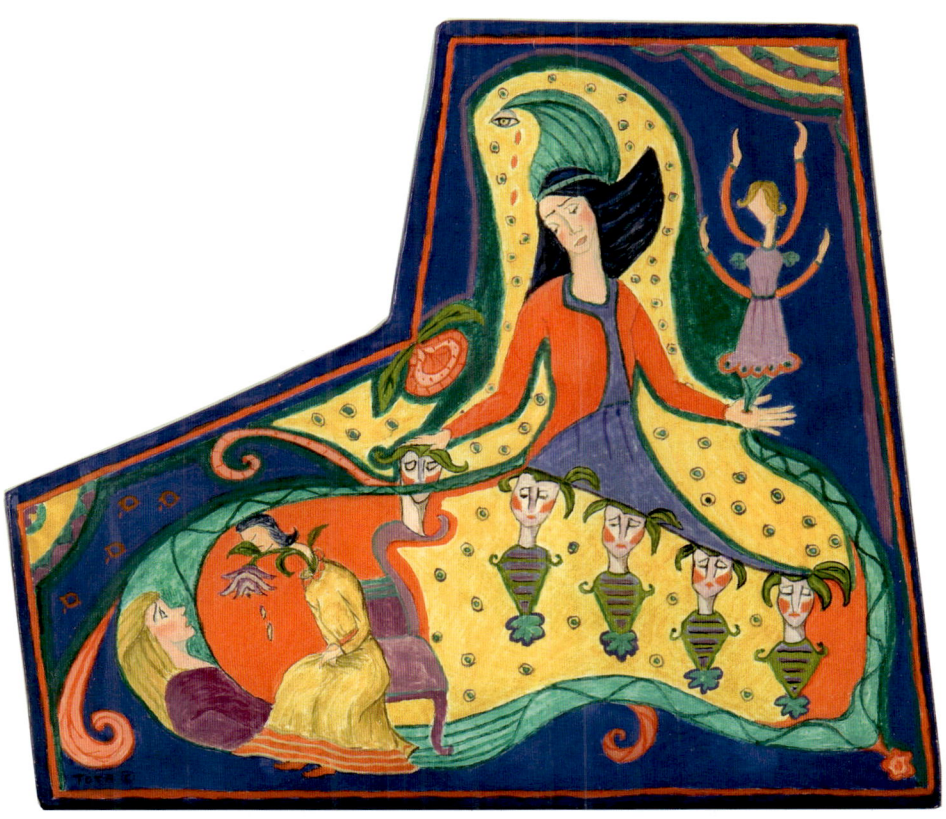

47

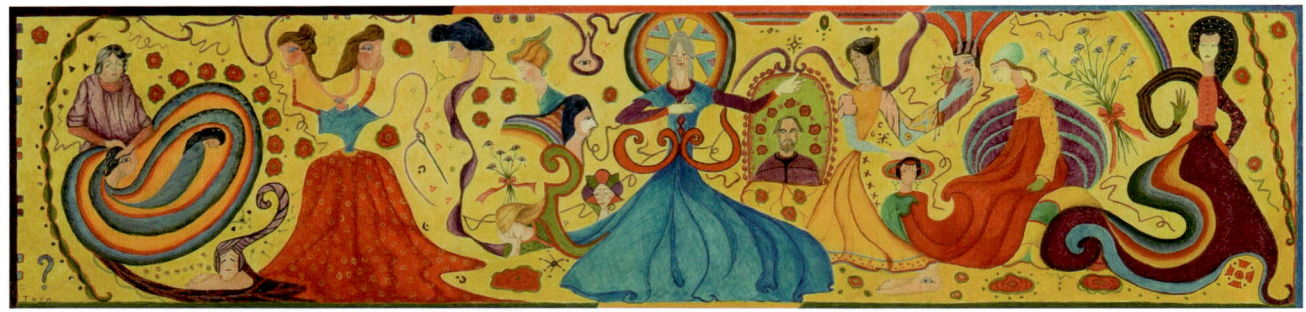

48. Untitled, completed March 12, 1984
Egg tempera on panel
7 1/16 x 28 13/16 in.
Collection of Rosamond Tota, daughter

49. Untitled, completed October 5, 1984
Egg tempera and gold leaf on panel
8 3/8 x 14 3/16 in.
Collection of Rosamond Tota, daughter

50. Untitled, completed May 6, 1984
Egg tempera and gold leaf on panel
5 x 8 ½ in.
Collection of Desiree P. Rodriguez

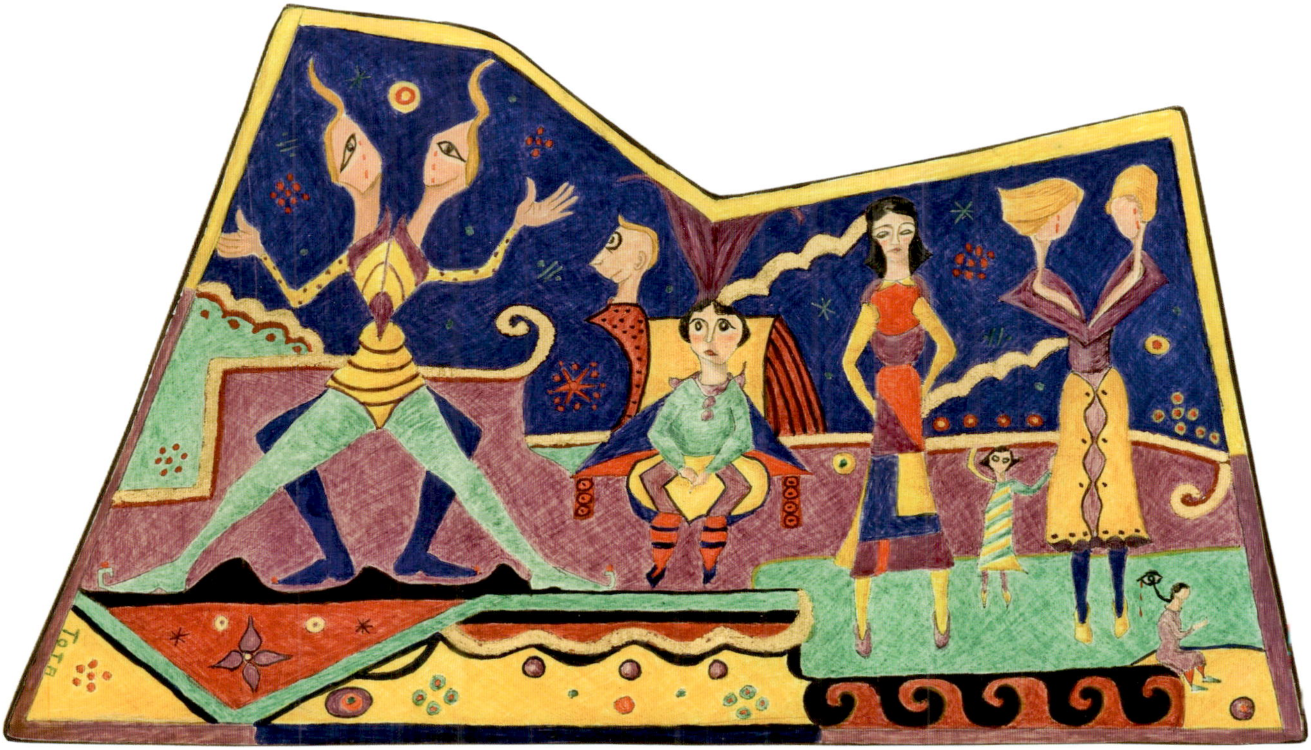

49

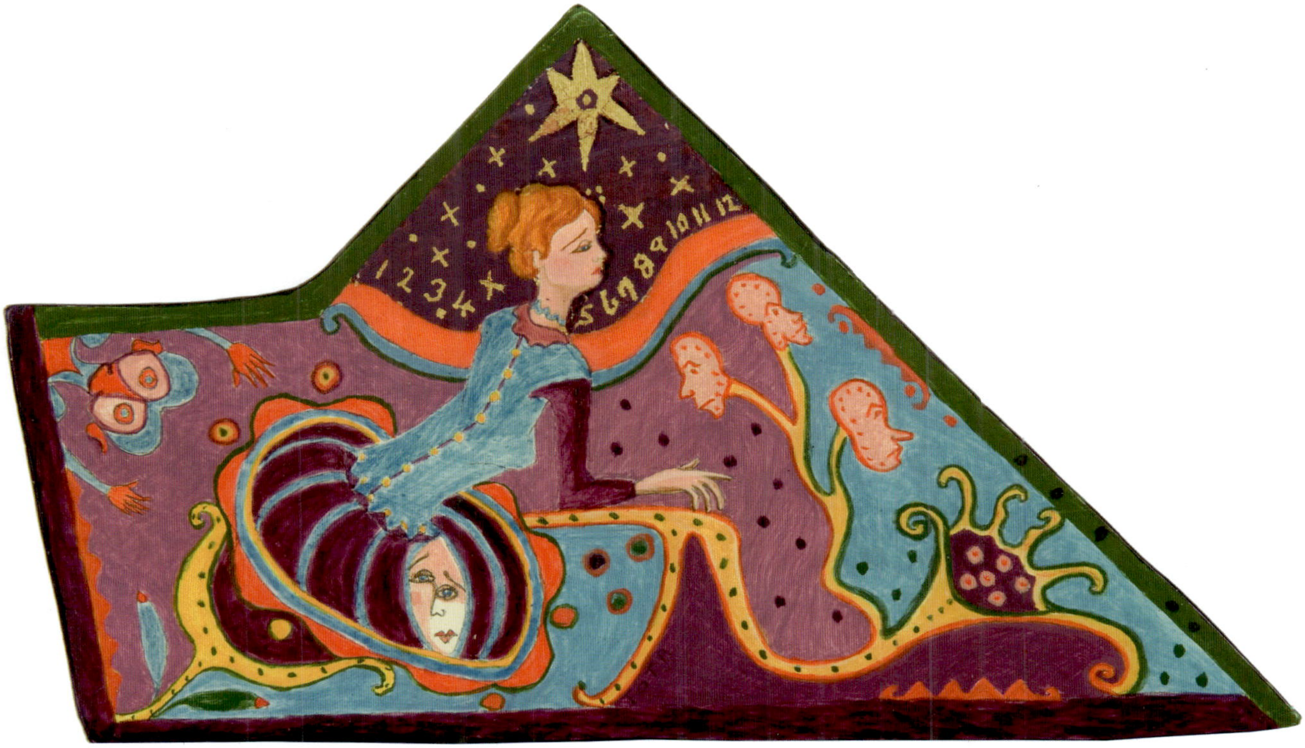

50

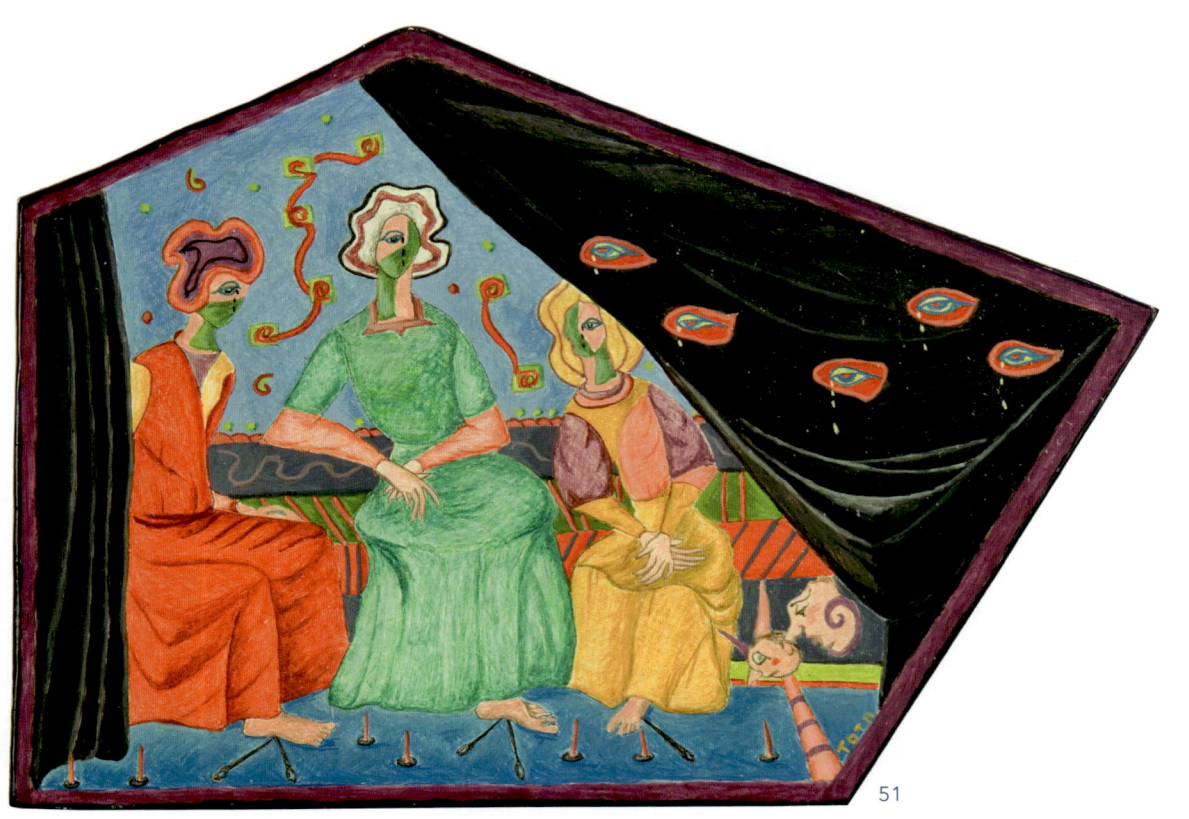

51

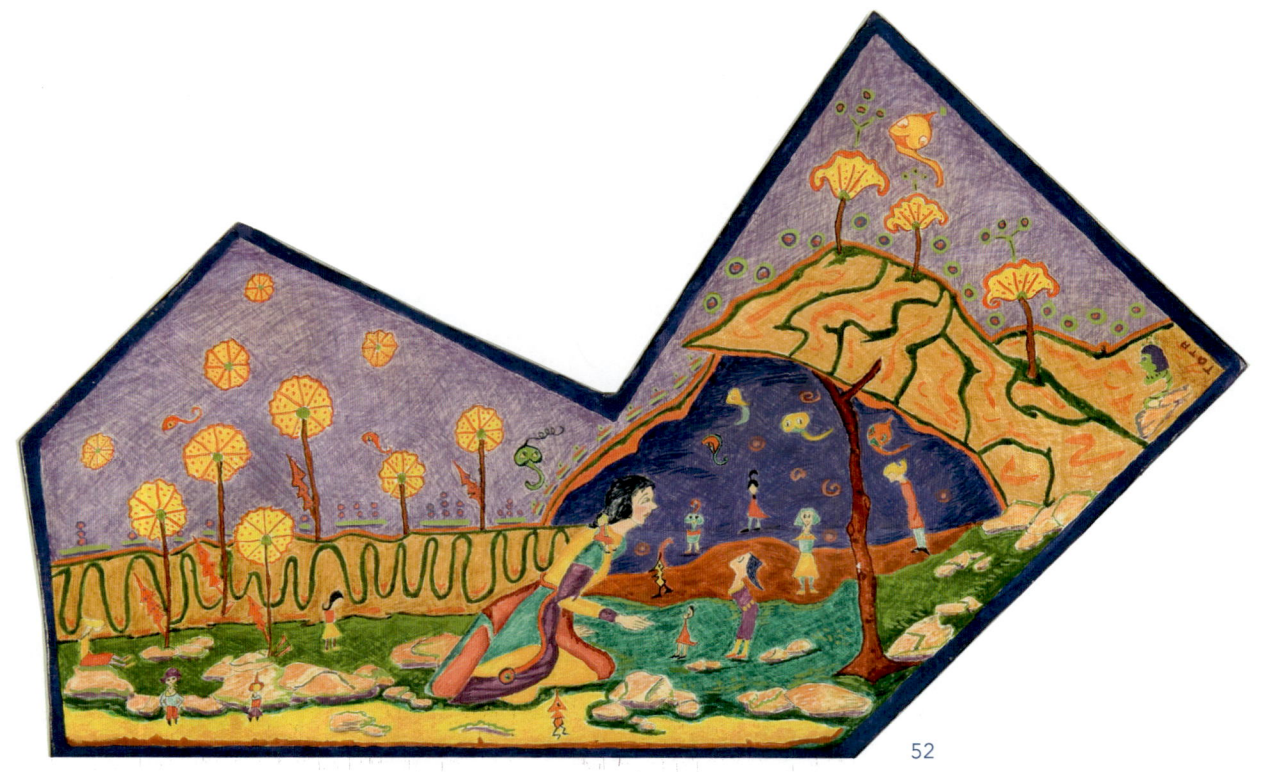

52

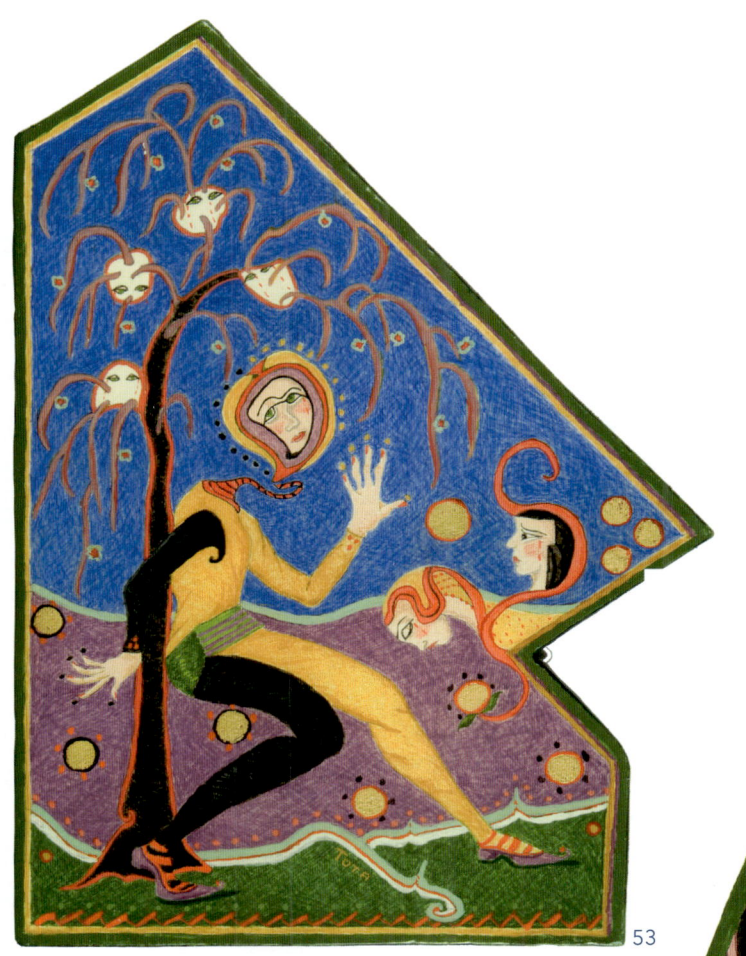

51. Untitled, completed October 29, 1984
Egg tempera on panel
7 ½ x 10 ⅝ in.
Collection of Judith G. Levy

52. Untitled, completed 1985
Egg tempera on panel
11 ⅝ x 18 ⅛ in.
Memorial Art Gallery of the University of
Rochester, Gift of Rosamond Tota, 2011.63

53. Untitled, completed January 26, 1985
Egg tempera and gold leaf on panel
13 ⅜ x 9 ¹³⁄₁₆ in.
Collection of Desiree P. Rodriguez

54. Untitled, completed February 15, 1985
Egg tempera on panel
14 ⅝ x 8 ¾ in.
Collection of Judith G. Levy

53

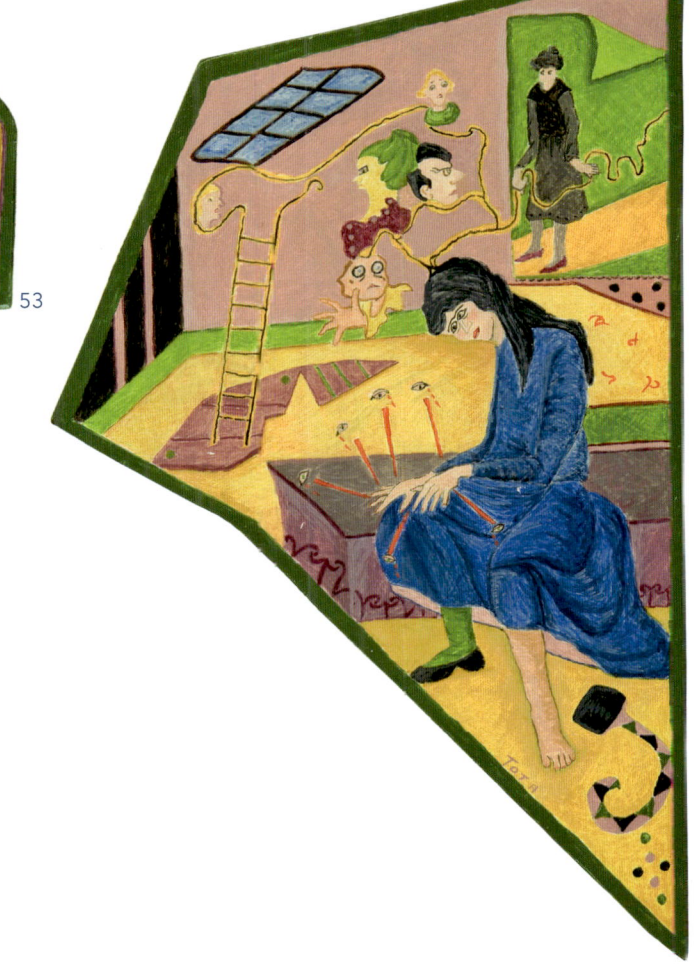

54

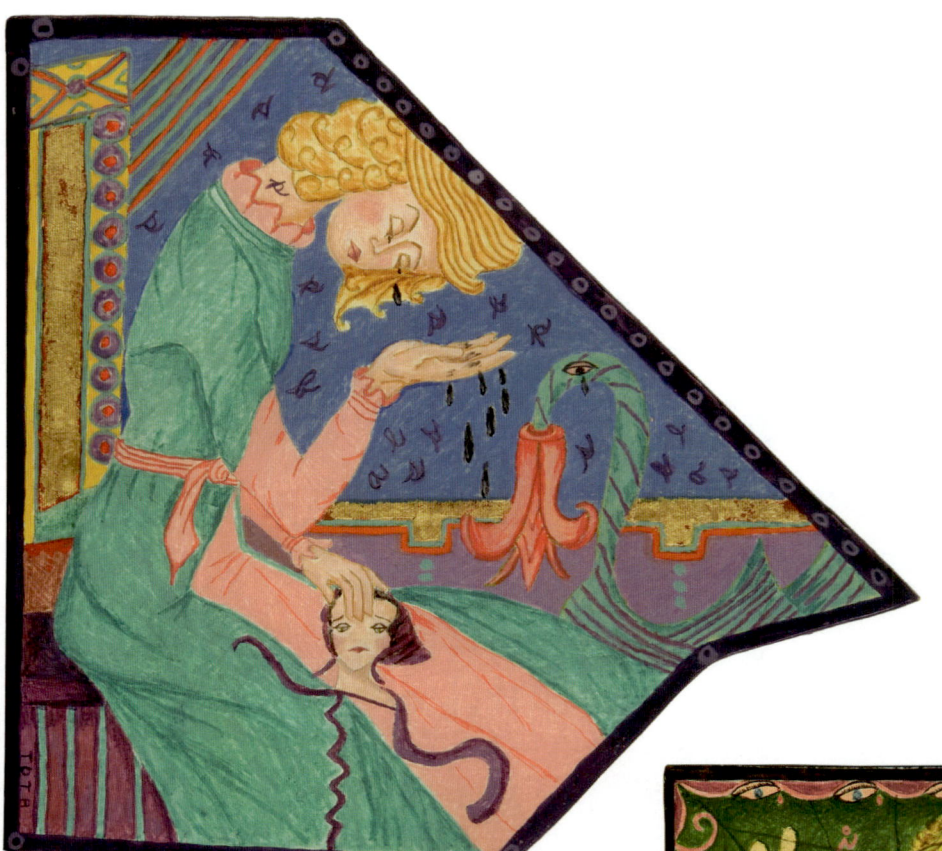

55

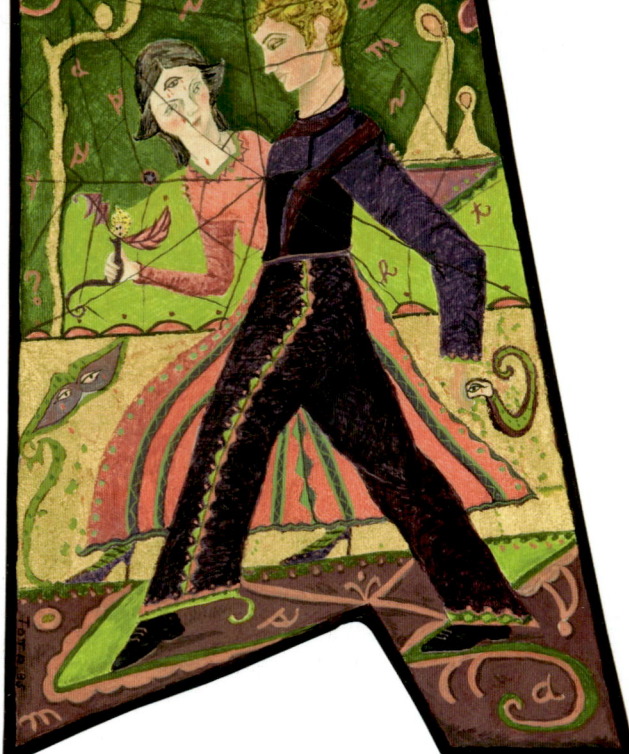

56

55. Untitled, completed February 24, 1985
Egg tempera and gold leaf on panel
9 1/16 x 9 3/8 in.
Collection of Desiree P. Rodriguez

56. Untitled, completed May 1, 1985
Egg tempera and gold leaf on panel
14 3/16 x 10 1/4 in.
Private collection

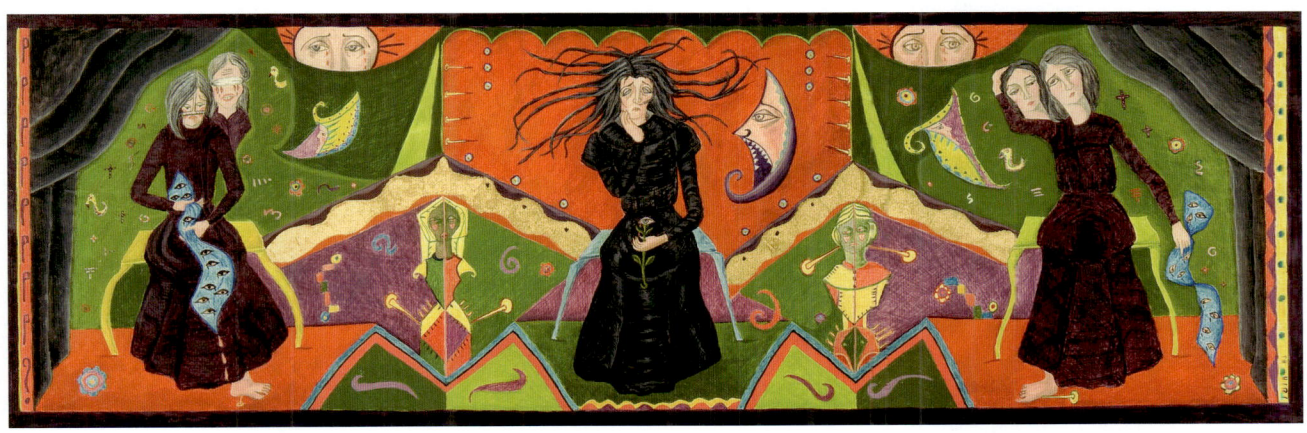

57. Untitled, completed June 2, 1985
Egg tempera and gold leaf on panel
10 ⅝ x 32 ¹⁵⁄₁₆ in.
Memorial Art Gallery of the University of
Rochester, Gift of Rosamond Tota, 2011.53

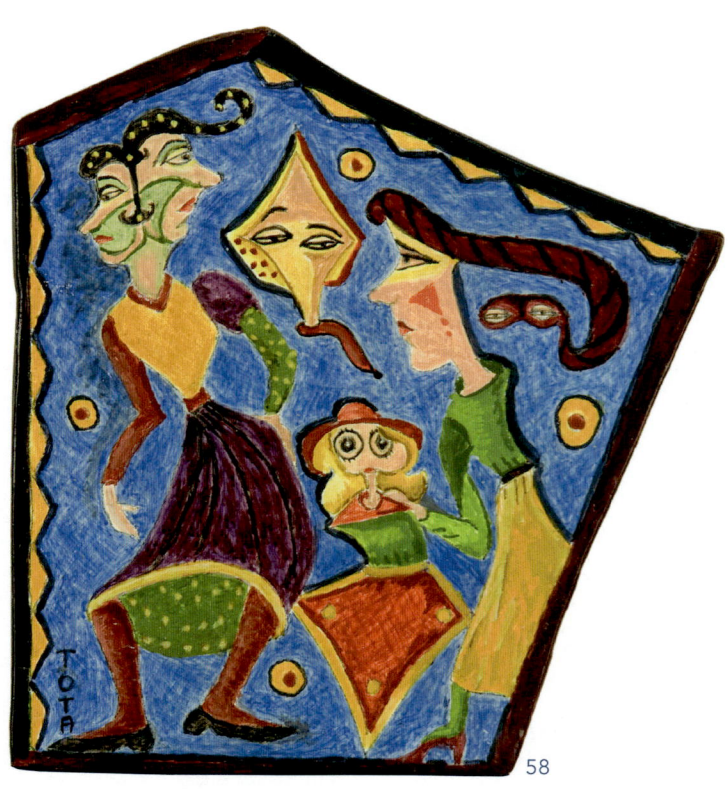

58. Untitled, completed January 13, 1986
Egg tempera on panel
6 ½ x 6 in.
Private collection

59. Untitled, completed January 23, 1986
Egg tempera on panel
11 ¹¹⁄₁₆ x 6 ⅝ in.
Collection of Margaret Manning Krug

60. Untitled, completed March 21, 1986
Egg tempera on panel
8 ¹³⁄₁₆ x 8 ¼ in.
Private collection

58

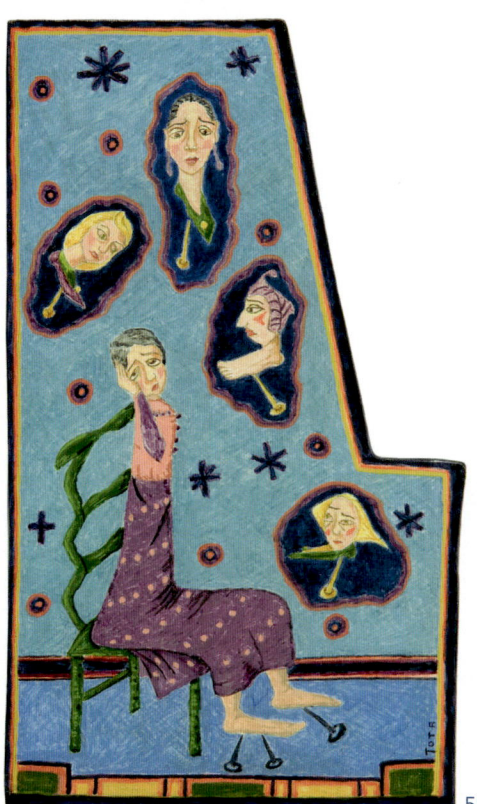

59

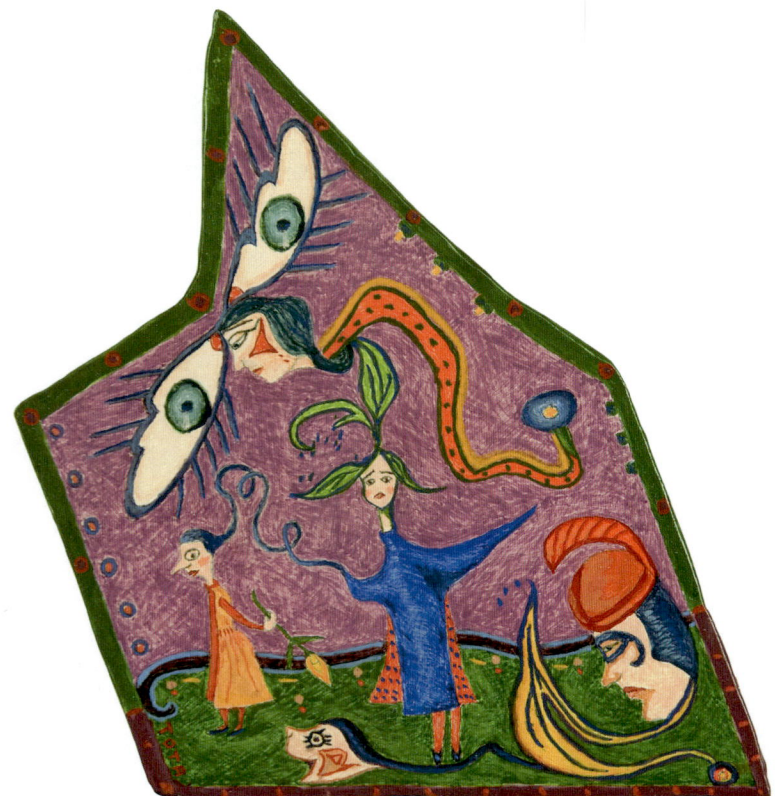

60

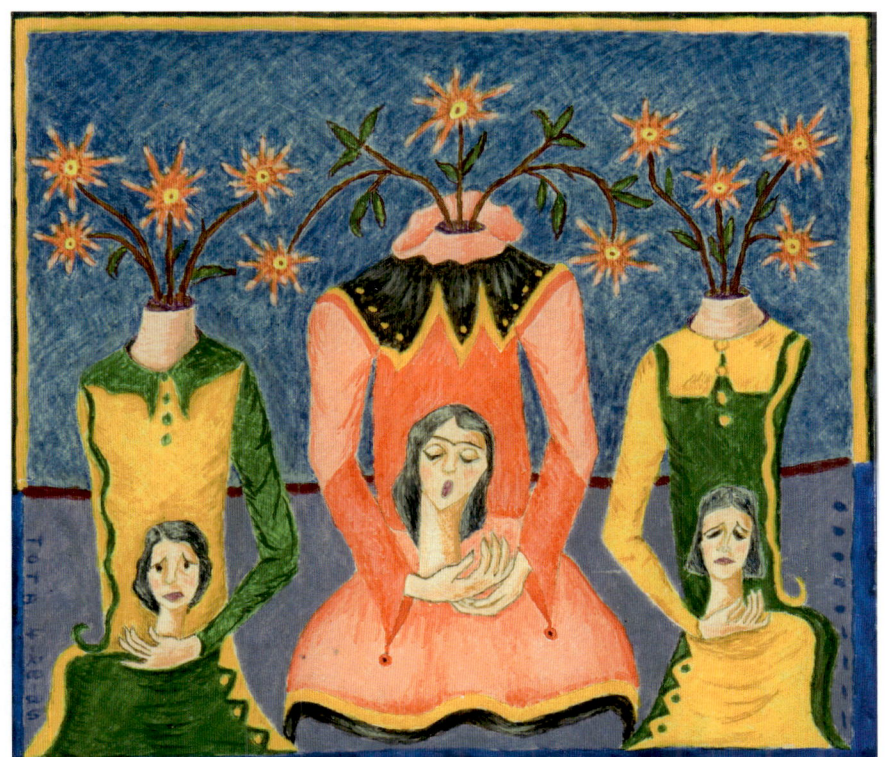

61. Untitled, completed April 28, 1986
Egg tempera on panel
8 x 8 11/16 in.
Collection of Rosamond Tota, daughter

62. Untitled, completed May 10, 1986
Egg tempera on panel
6 15/16 x 7 3/4 in.
Collection of Judith G. Levy

61

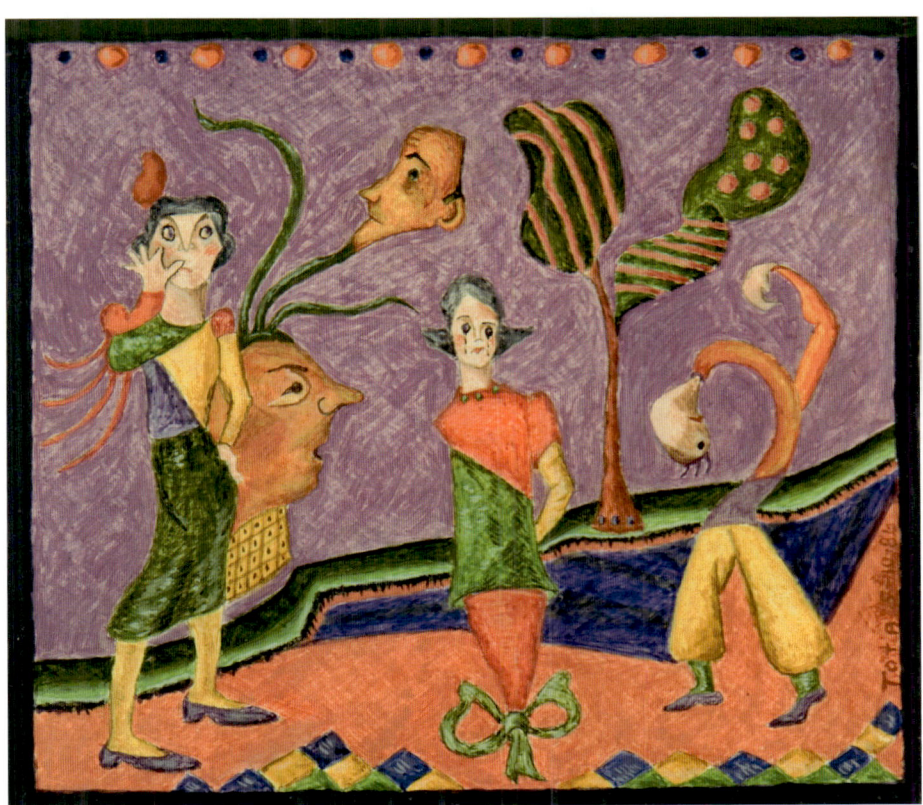

62

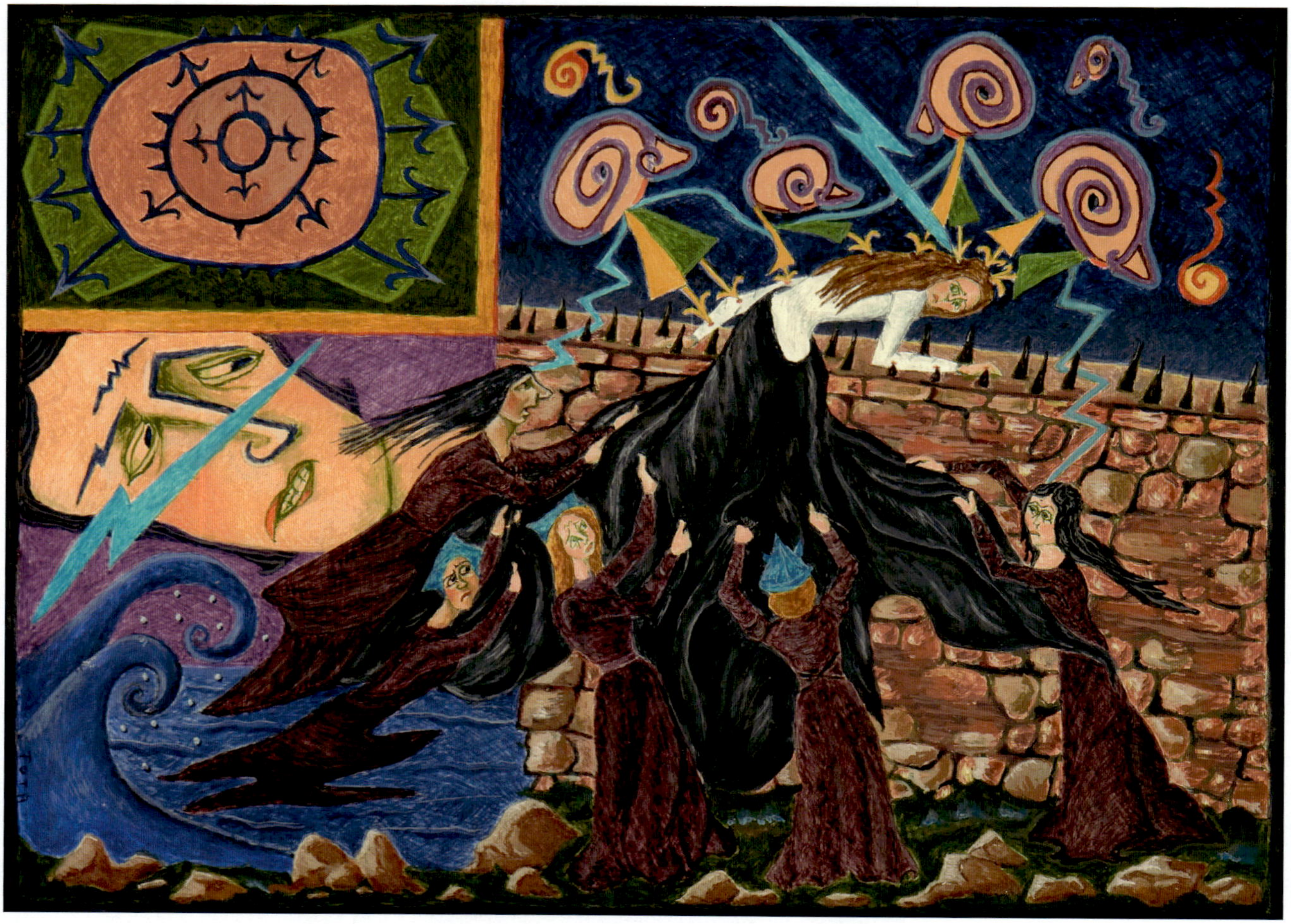

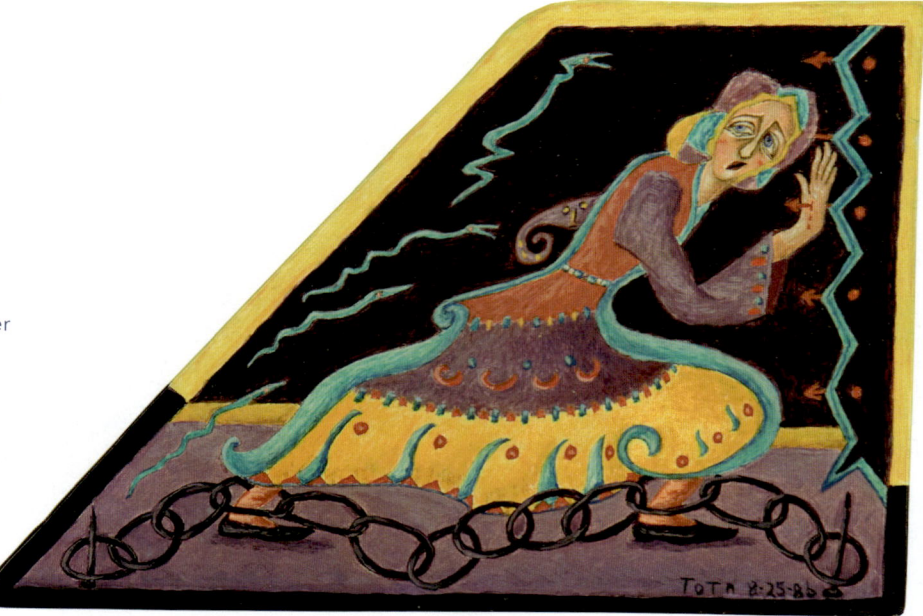

63. Untitled, completed July 8, 1986
Egg tempera on panel
12 x 16 ⅛ in.
Memorial Art Gallery of the University
of Rochester, Gift of Rosamond Tota,
2011.54

64. Untitled, completed August 25,
1986
Egg tempera on panel
6 ¹³⁄₁₆ x 9 ⅞ in.
Collection of Rosamond Tota, daughter

63

64

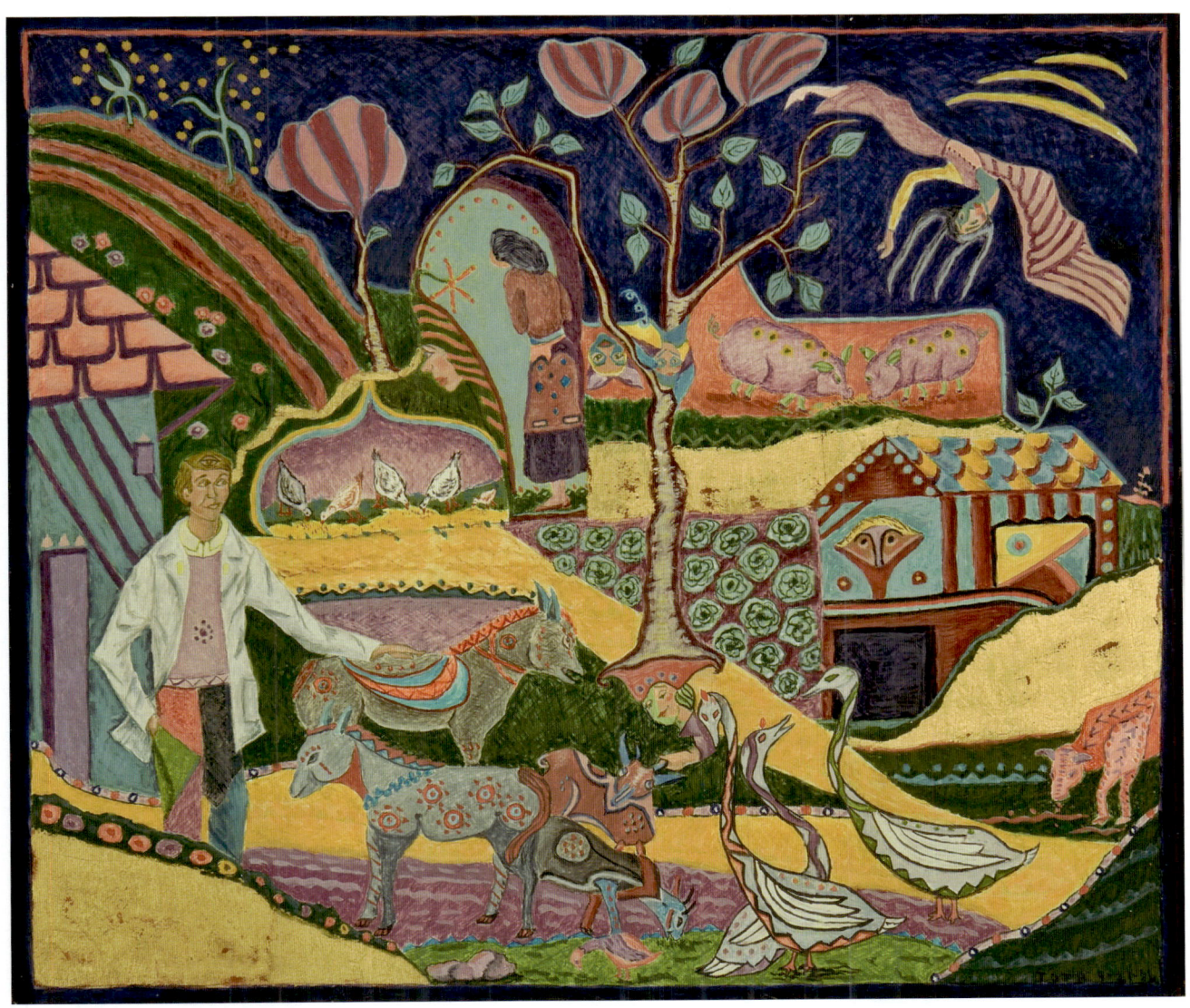

65

65. Untitled, completed September 21,
1986
Egg tempera and gold leaf on panel
13 ⅞ x 16 1/16 in.
On loan from Kathy and Ted Nixon, and
Erik and Mary Ellen Nixon

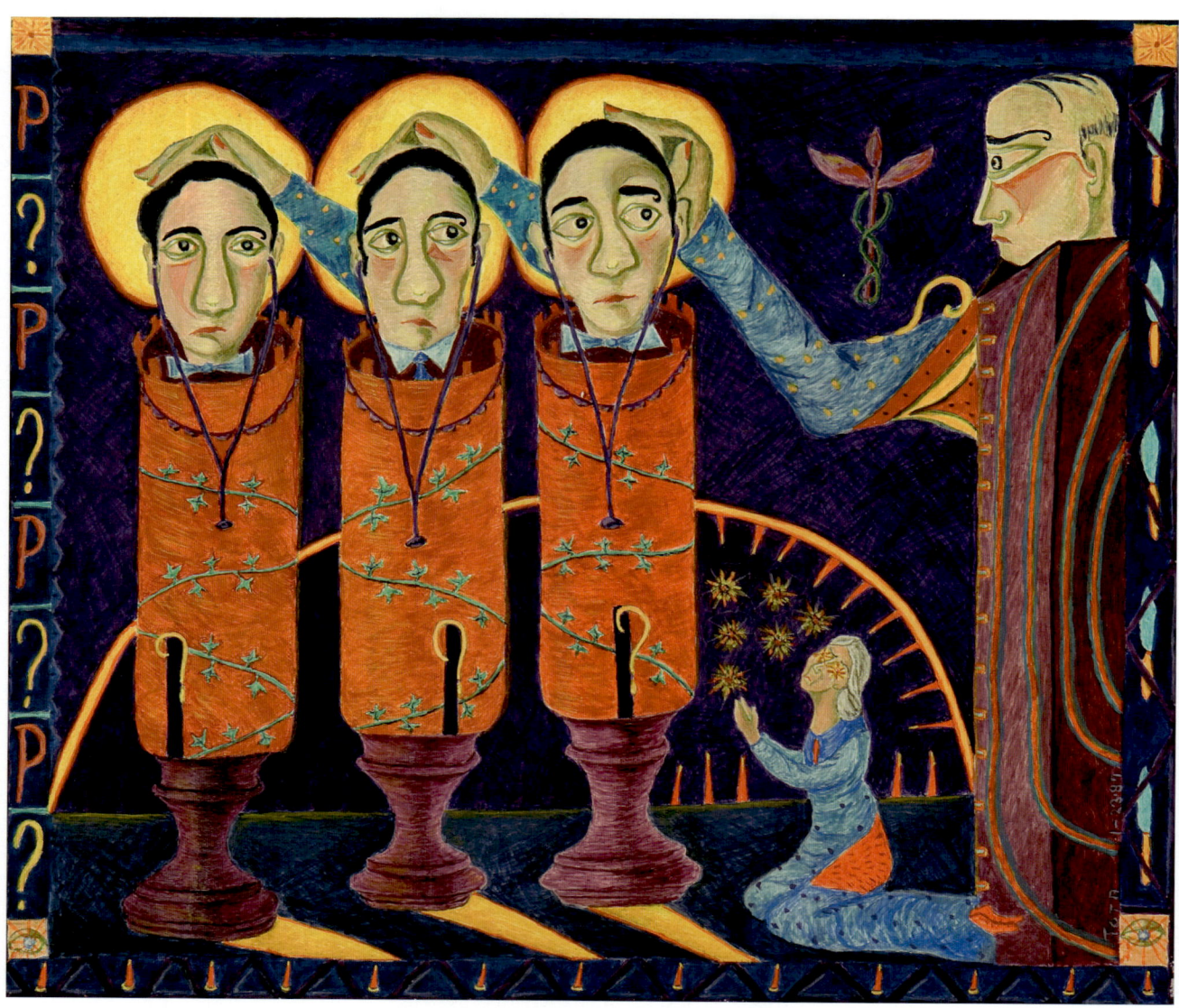

66

66. Untitled, completed January 23,
1987
Egg tempera on panel
14 ¹⁄₁₆ x 16 ⅛ in.
Memorial Art Gallery of the University
of Rochester, Gift of Rosamond Tota,
2011.56

67. Untitled, completed March 1987
Egg tempera and gold leaf on panel
16 ⅛ x 9 ¾ in.
Memorial Art Gallery of the University of
Rochester, Deaccession fund, 97.2

90

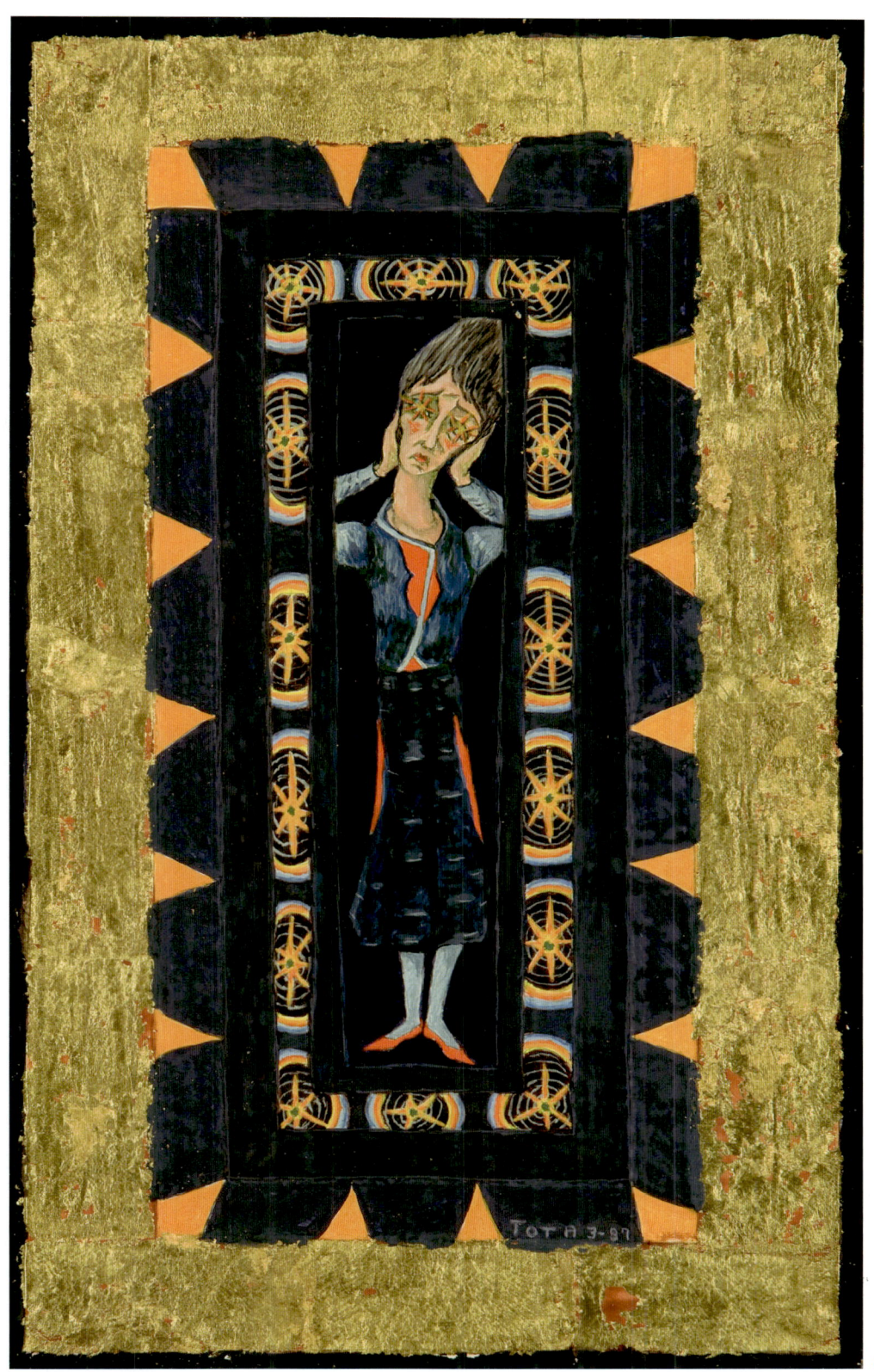

67

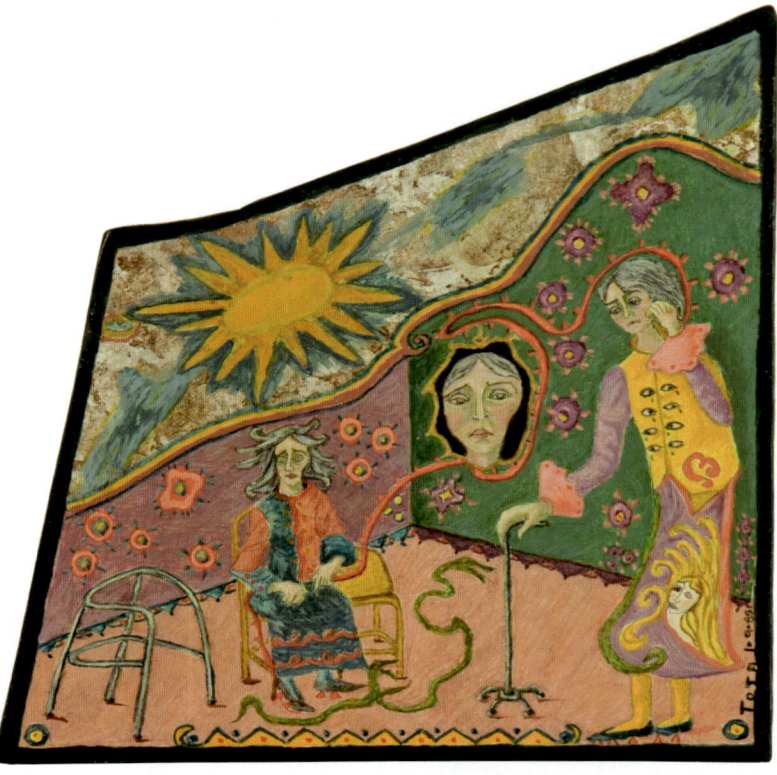

68

68. Untitled, completed January 9, 1988
Egg tempera and silver leaf on panel
8 ⅞ x 9 in.
Collection of Rosamond Tota, daughter

69. Untitled, completed January 26, 1988
Egg tempera on panel
7 ⅞ x 8 ¹⁄₁₆ in.
Private collection

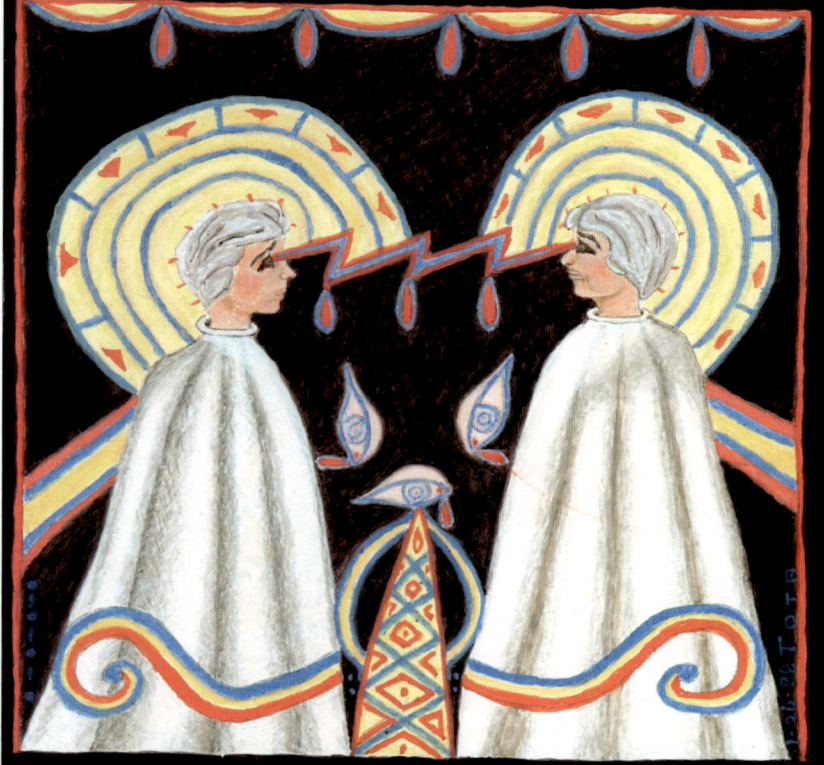

69

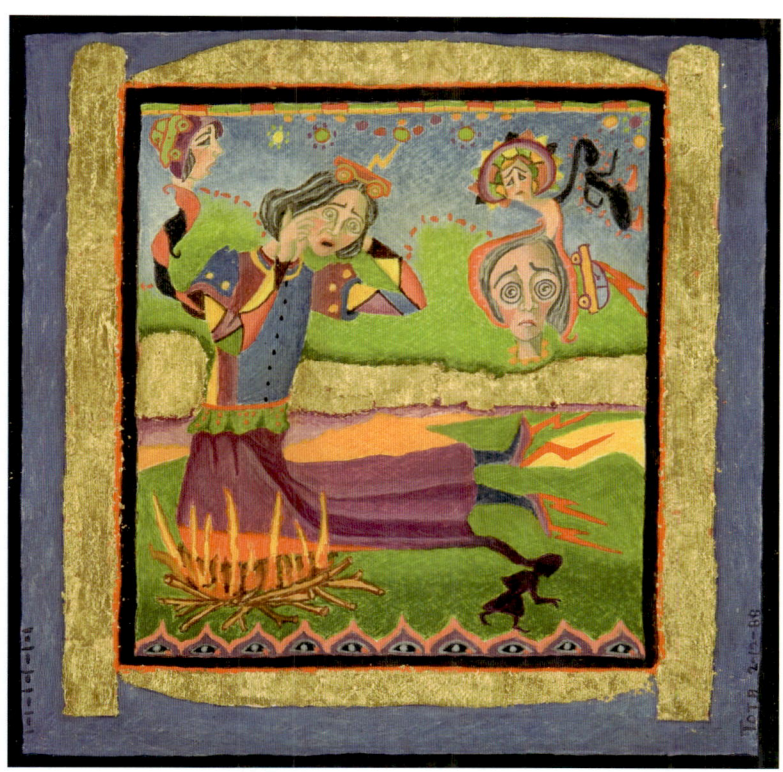

70. Untitled, completed February 12, 1988
Egg tempera and gold leaf on panel
12 x 11 ⅞ in.
Memorial Art Gallery of the University of
Rochester, Gift of Rosamond Tota, 2011.64

71. Untitled, completed June 18, 1988
Egg tempera and gold leaf on panel
10 ½ x 13 ¾ in.
Collection of Rosamond Tota, daughter

70

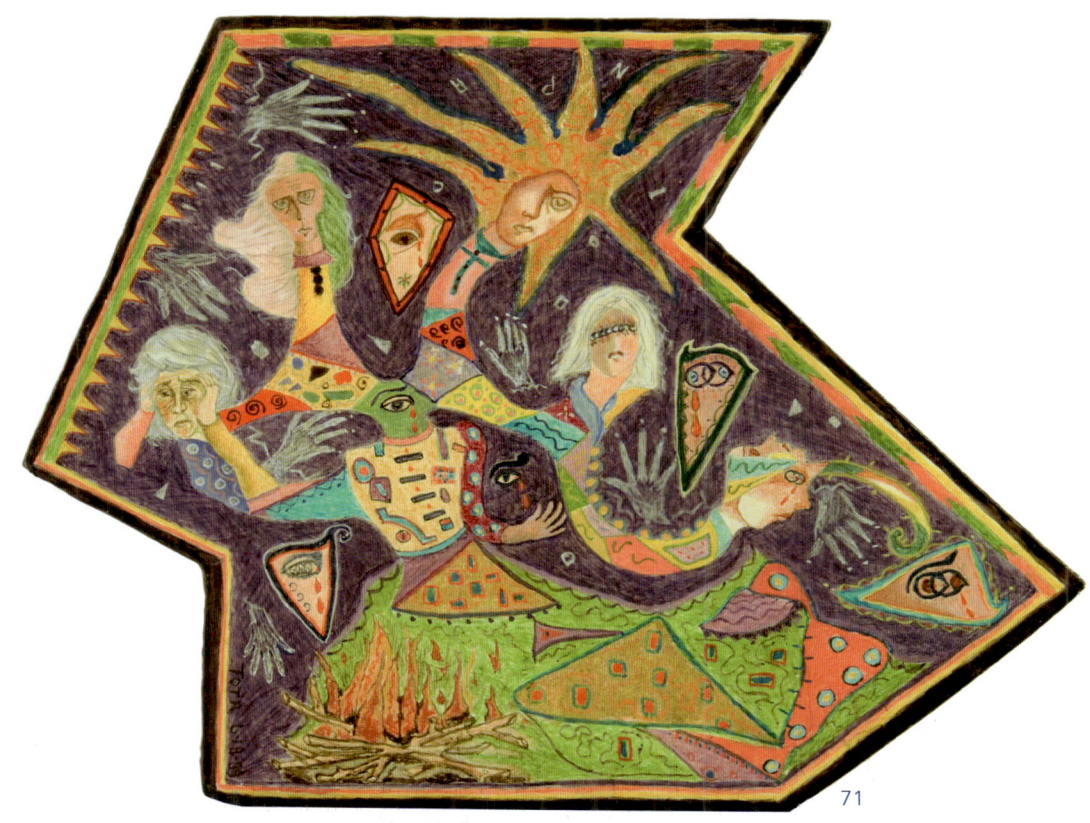

71

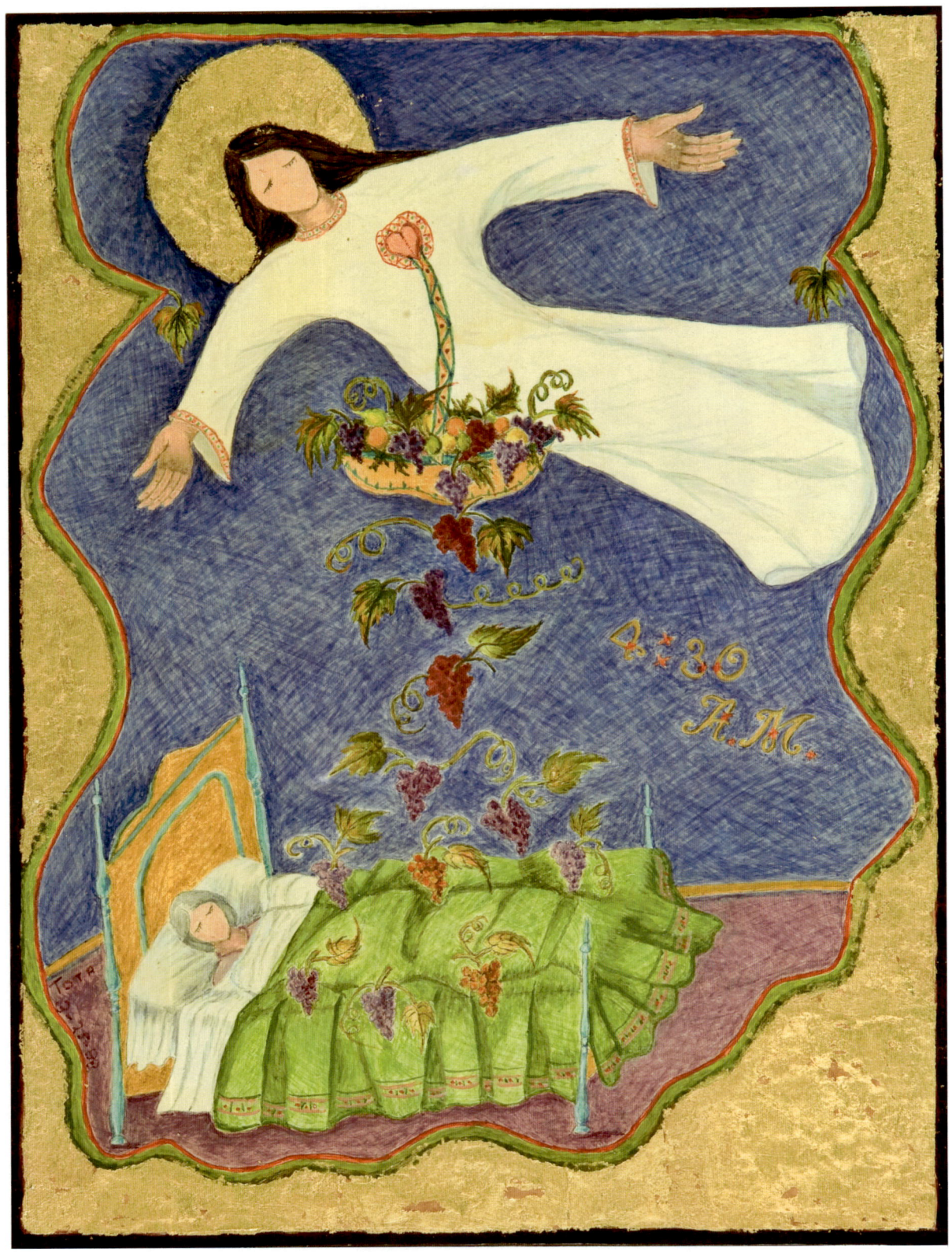

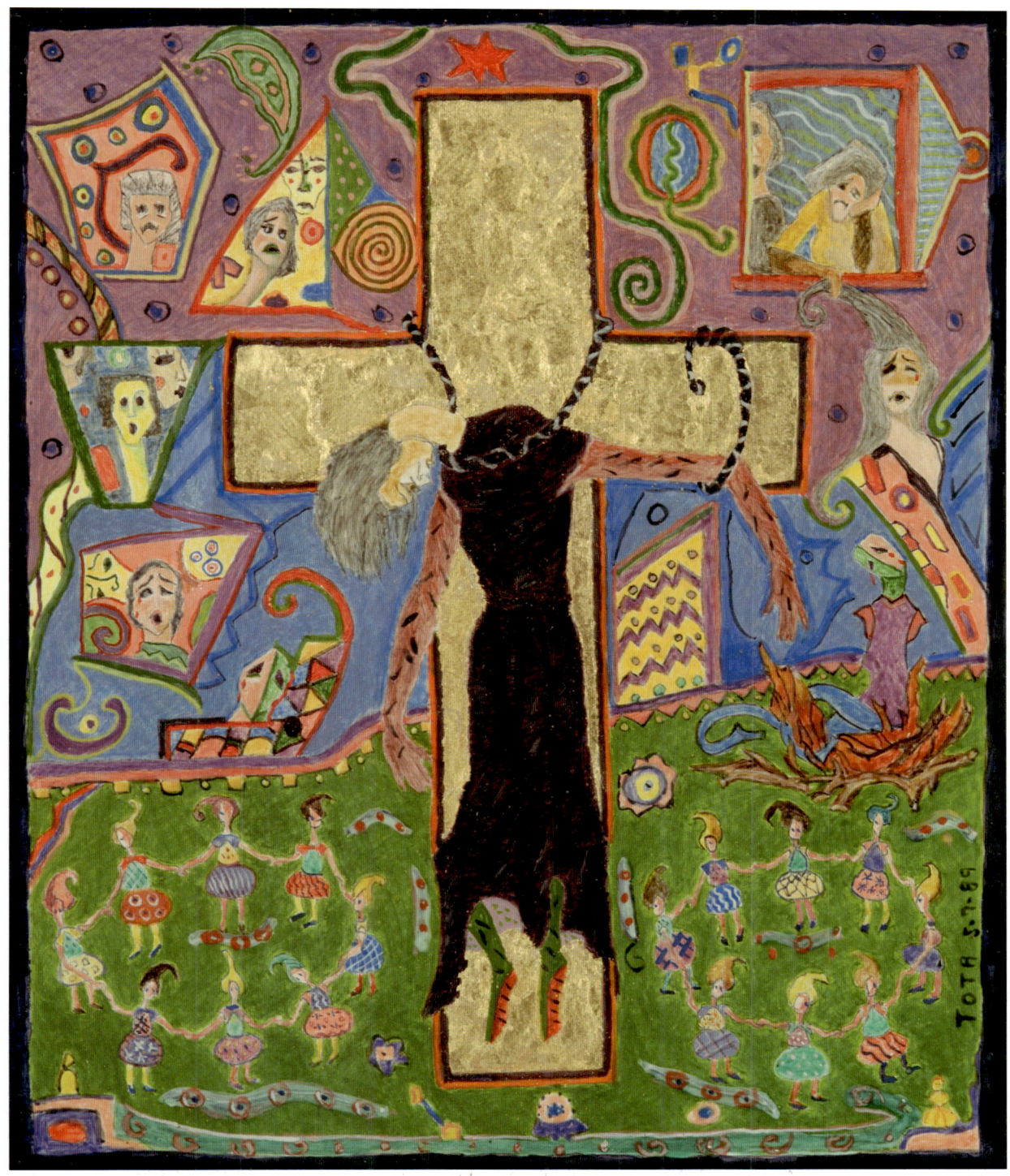

73

72. Untitled, completed March 25, 1988
Egg tempera and gold leaf on panel
16 ⅛ x 12 in.
Anonymous loan

73. Untitled, completed May 7, 1989
Egg tempera and gold leaf on panel
12 ⅟₁₆ x 10 ⅟₁₆ in.
Private collection

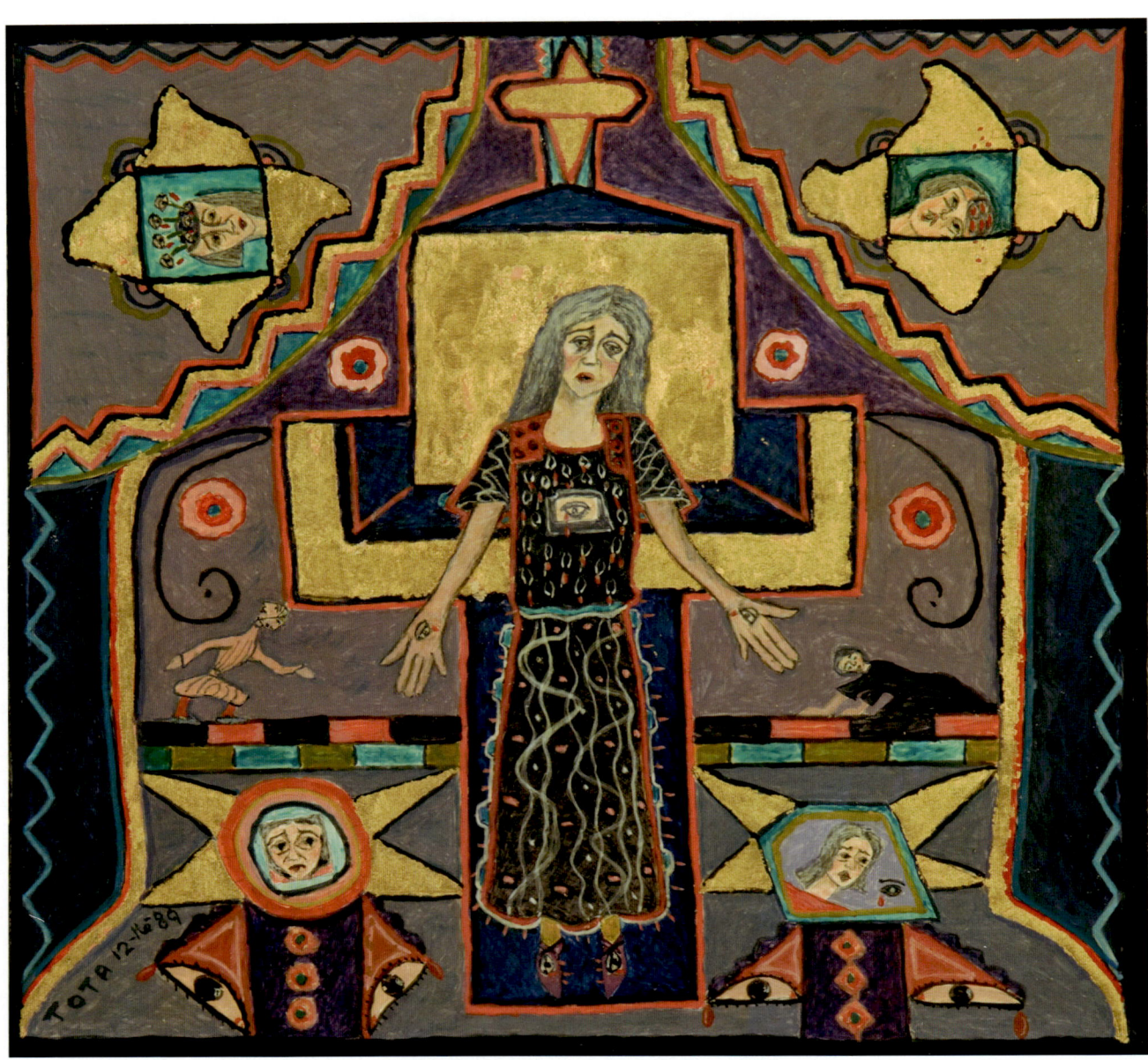

74

74. Untitled, completed December 16,
1989
Egg tempera and gold leaf on panel
11 ⅛ x 11 ¾ in.
Collection of Rosamond Tota, daughter

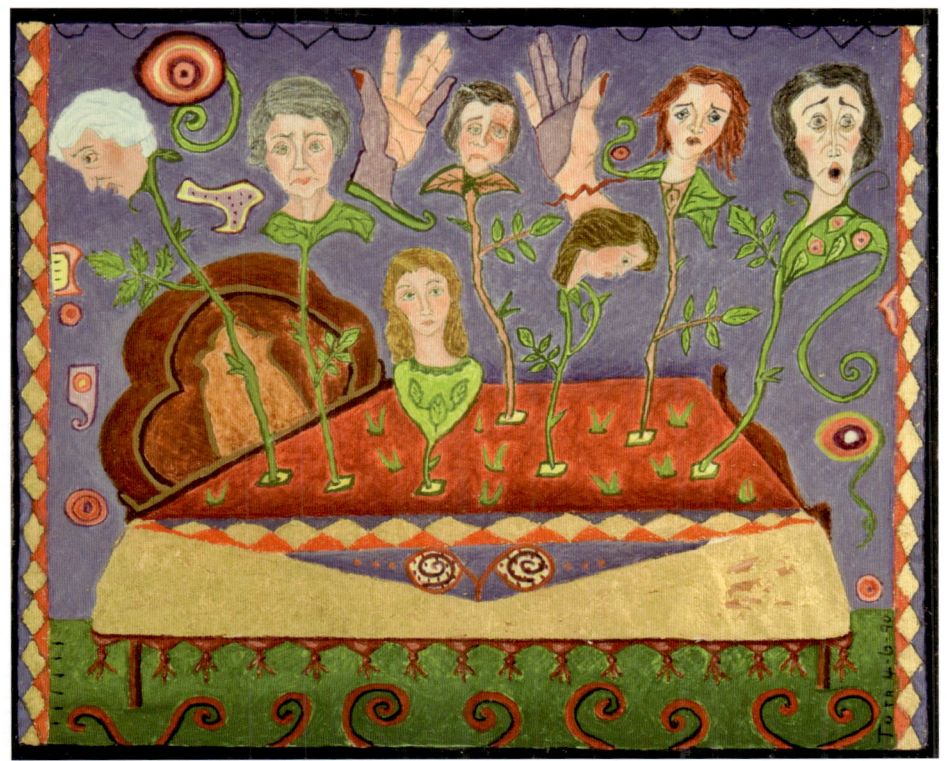

75

75. Untitled, completed April 6, 1990
Egg tempera and gold leaf on panel
10 ¹⁄₁₆ x 12 in.
Collection of Judith G. Levy

76. Untitled, completed June 1, 1990
Egg tempera and gold leaf on panel
8 ¾ x 7 ¾ in.
Collection of Rosamond Tota, daughter

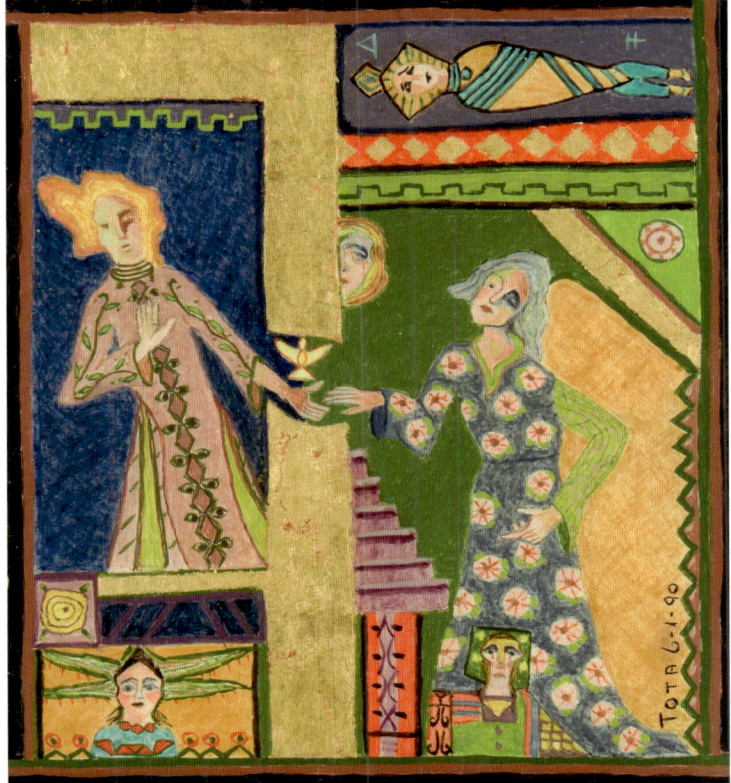

76

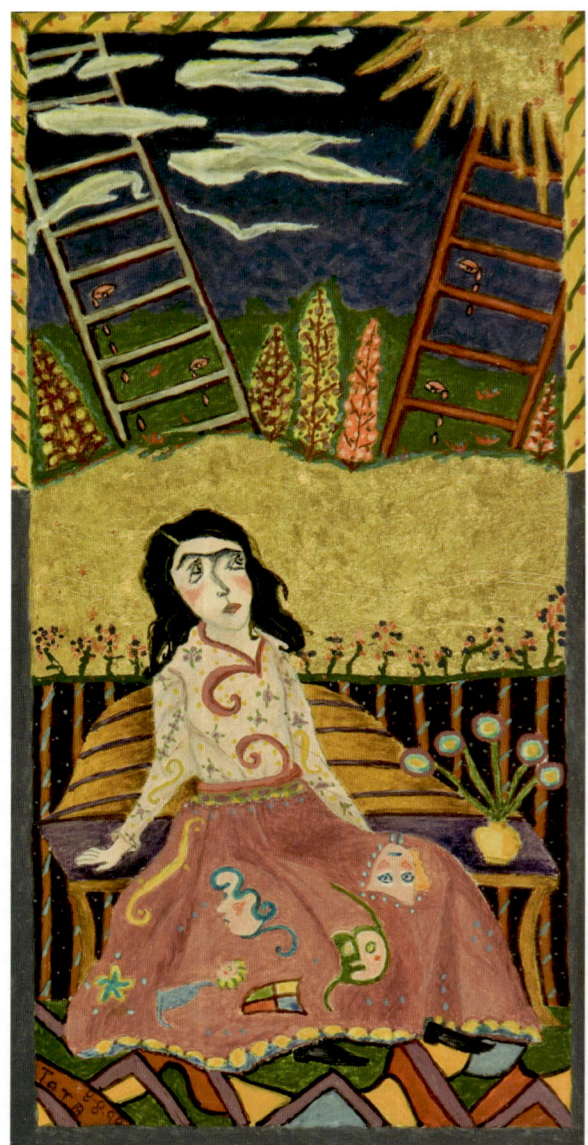
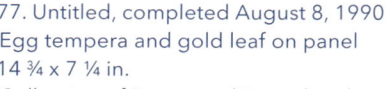

77

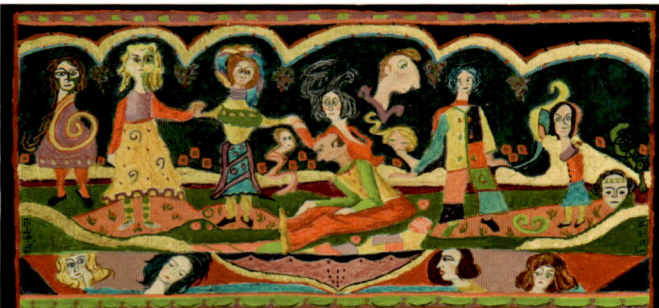

78

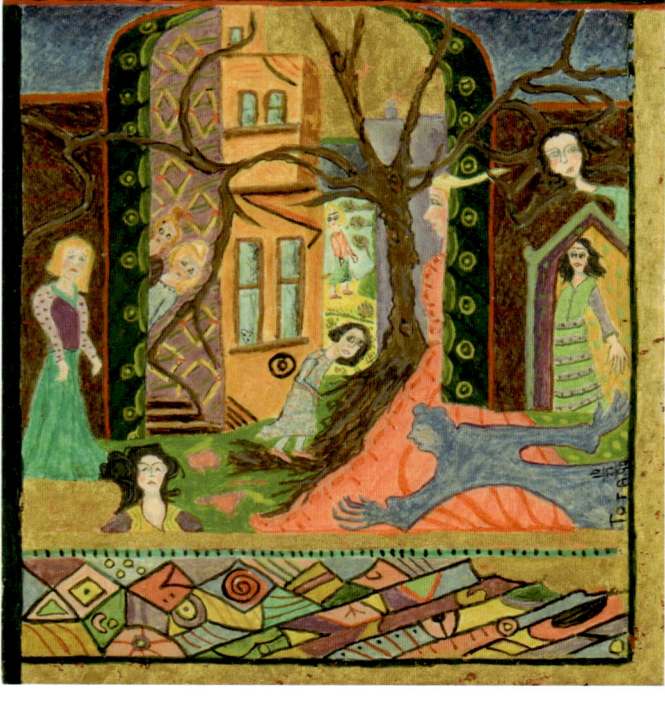

79

77. Untitled, completed August 8, 1990
Egg tempera and gold leaf on panel
14 ¾ x 7 ¼ in.
Collection of Rosamond Tota, daughter

78. Untitled, completed October 19, 1990
Egg tempera and gold leaf on panel
6 ⅛ x 12 ¼ in.
Collection of Rosamond Tota, daughter

79. Untitled, completed October 22, 1990
Egg tempera and gold leaf on panel
8 ¾ x 8 in.
Collection of Rosamond Tota, daughter

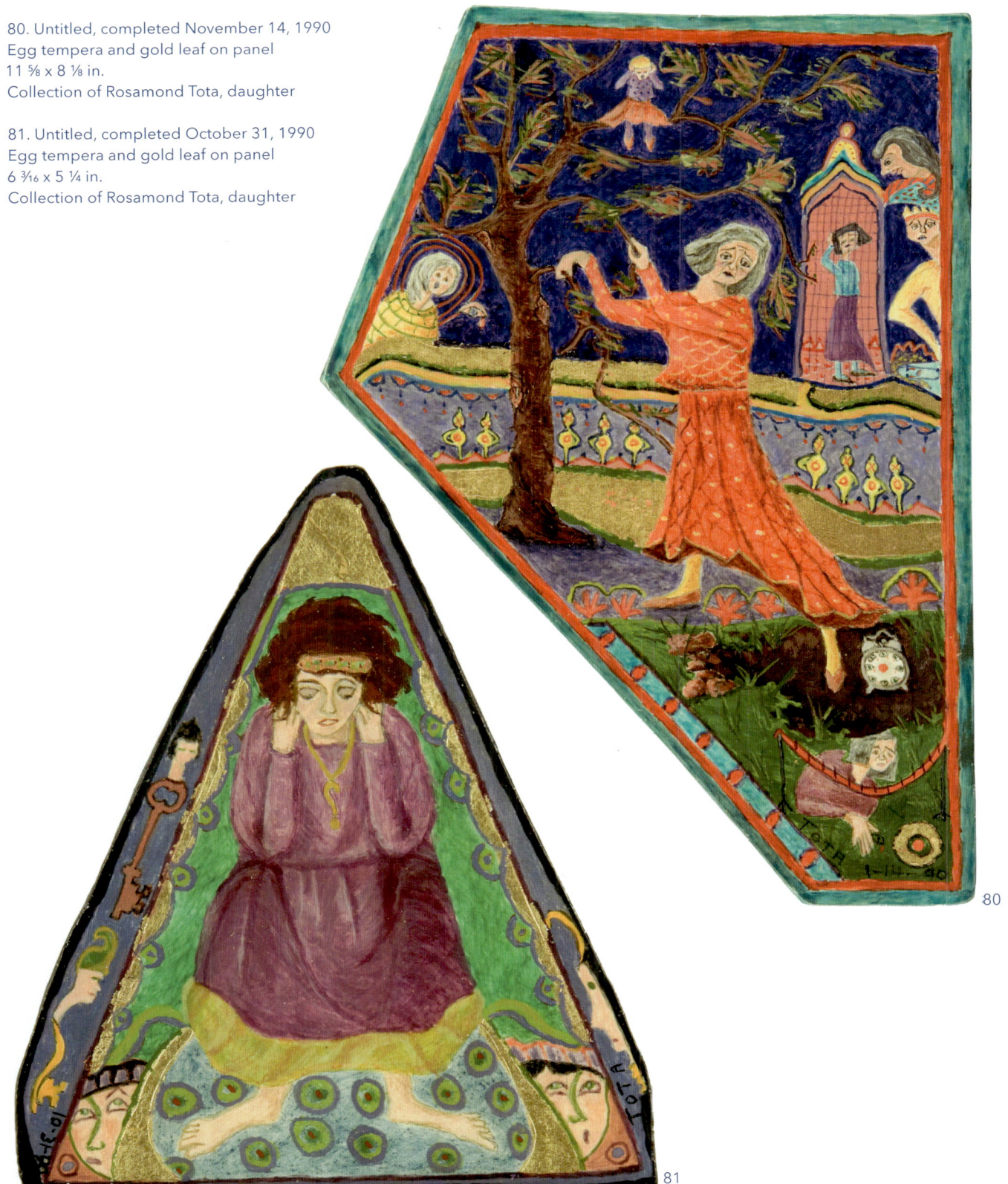

80. Untitled, completed November 14, 1990
Egg tempera and gold leaf on panel
11 ⅝ x 8 ⅛ in.
Collection of Rosamond Tota, daughter

81. Untitled, completed October 31, 1990
Egg tempera and gold leaf on panel
6 ³⁄₁₆ x 5 ¼ in.
Collection of Rosamond Tota, daughter

80

81

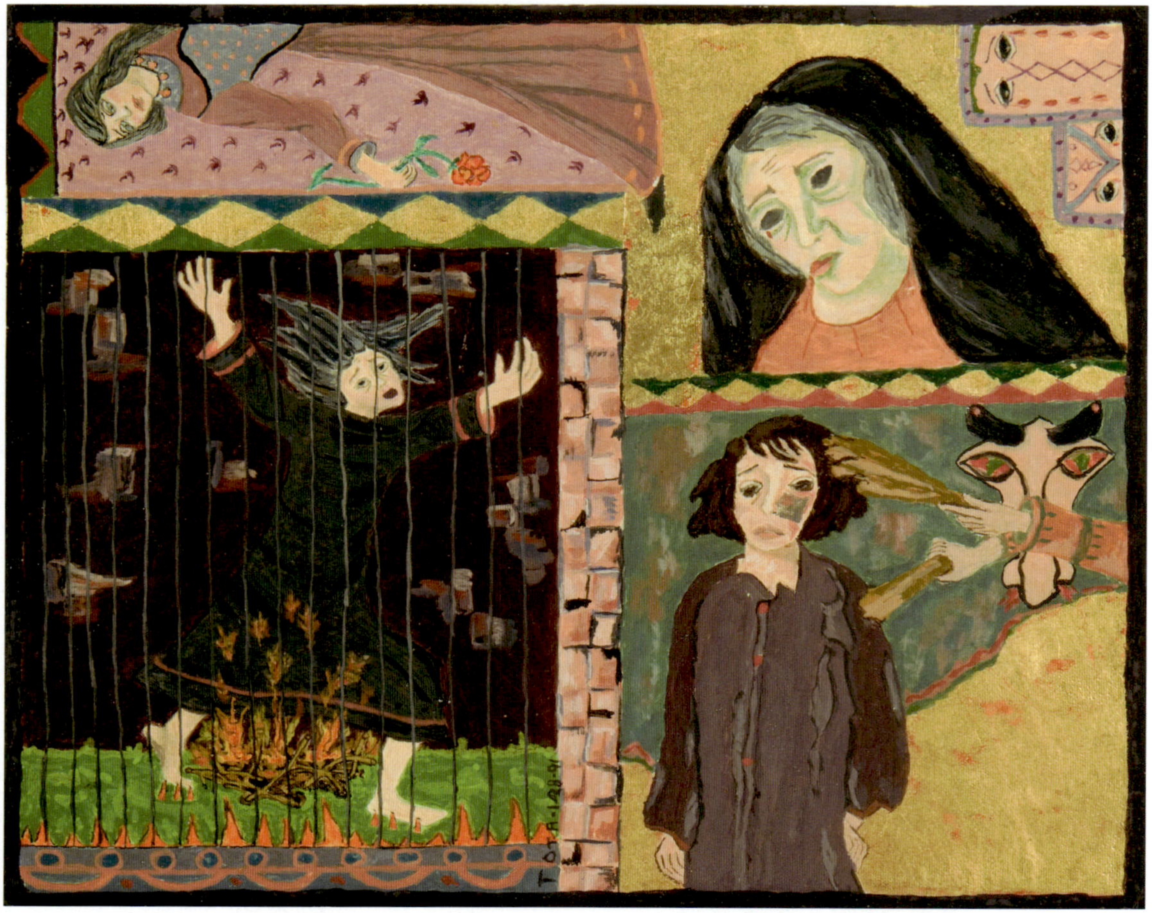

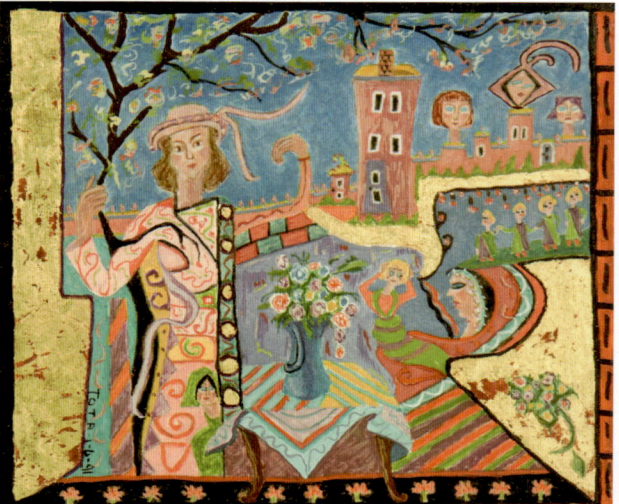

82

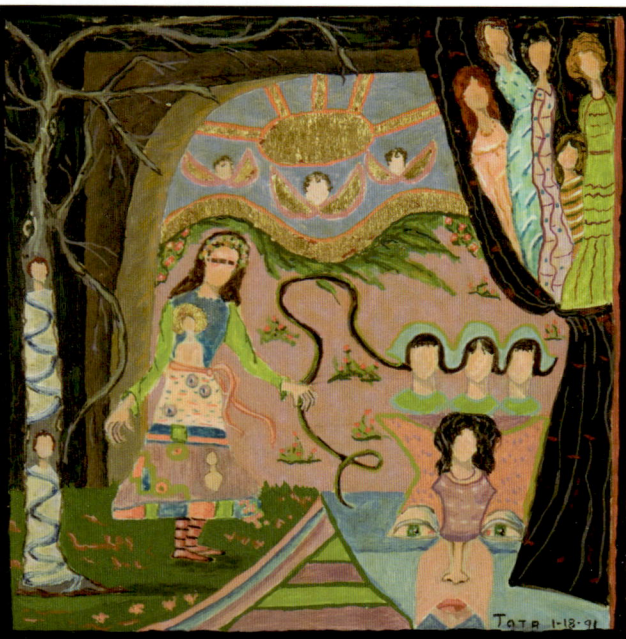

83

84

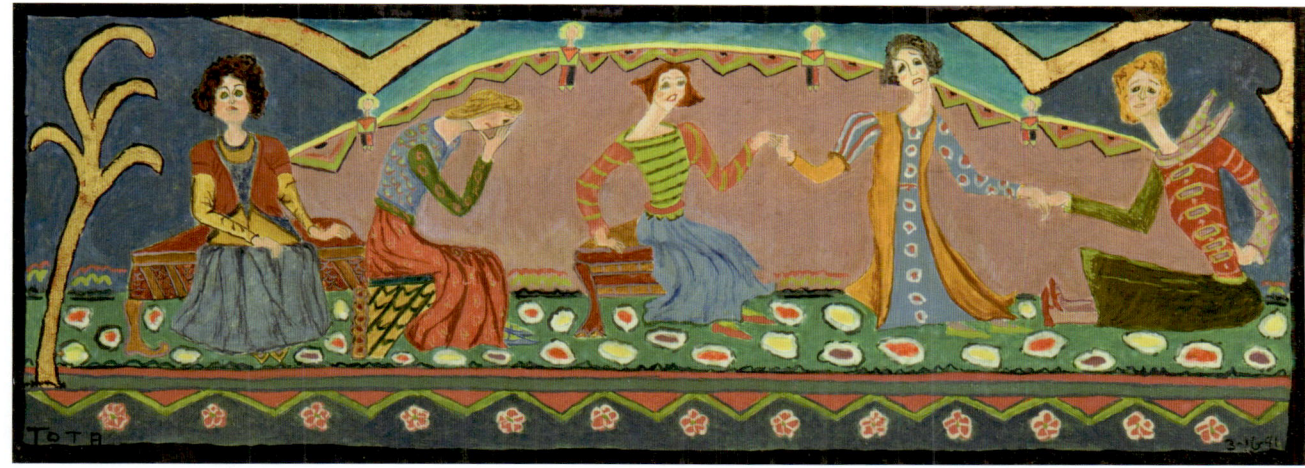

85

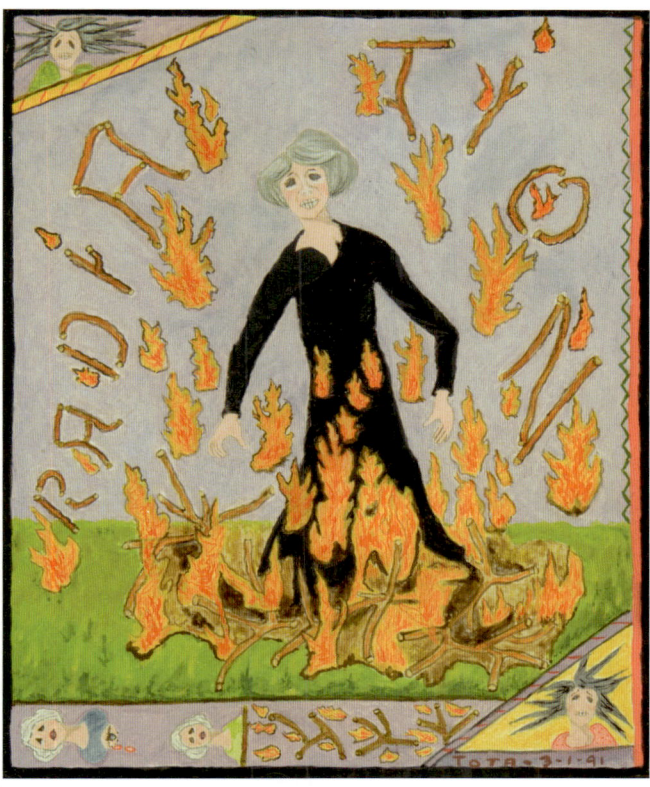

86

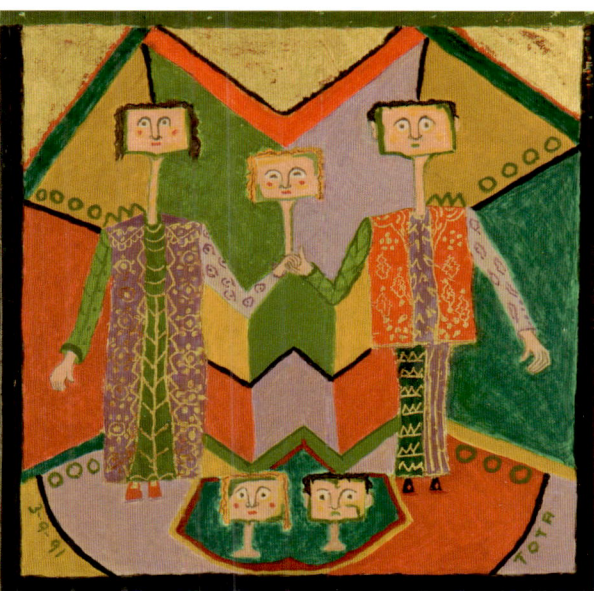

87

82. Untitled, completed January 28, 1991
Egg tempera and gold leaf on panel
9 x 11 ⅛ in.
Collection of Rosamond Tota, daughter

83. Untitled, completed January 6, 1991
Egg tempera and gold leaf on panel
7 x 8 ⅟₁₆ in.
Collection of Desiree P. Rodriguez

84. Untitled, completed January 18, 1991
Egg tempera and gold leaf on panel
8 ⅟₁₆ x 7 ¾ in.
Collection of Rosamond Tota, daughter

85. Untitled, completed March 16, 1991
Egg tempera and gold leaf on panel
6 x 16 ⅛ in.
Collection of Rosamond Tota, daughter

86. *Radiation*, completed March 1, 1991
Egg tempera on panel
11 x 9 ⅟₁₆ in.
Private collection

87. Untitled, completed March 9, 1991
Egg tempera and gold leaf on panel
8 ⅛ x 8 ⅛ in.
Collection of Rosamond Tota, daughter

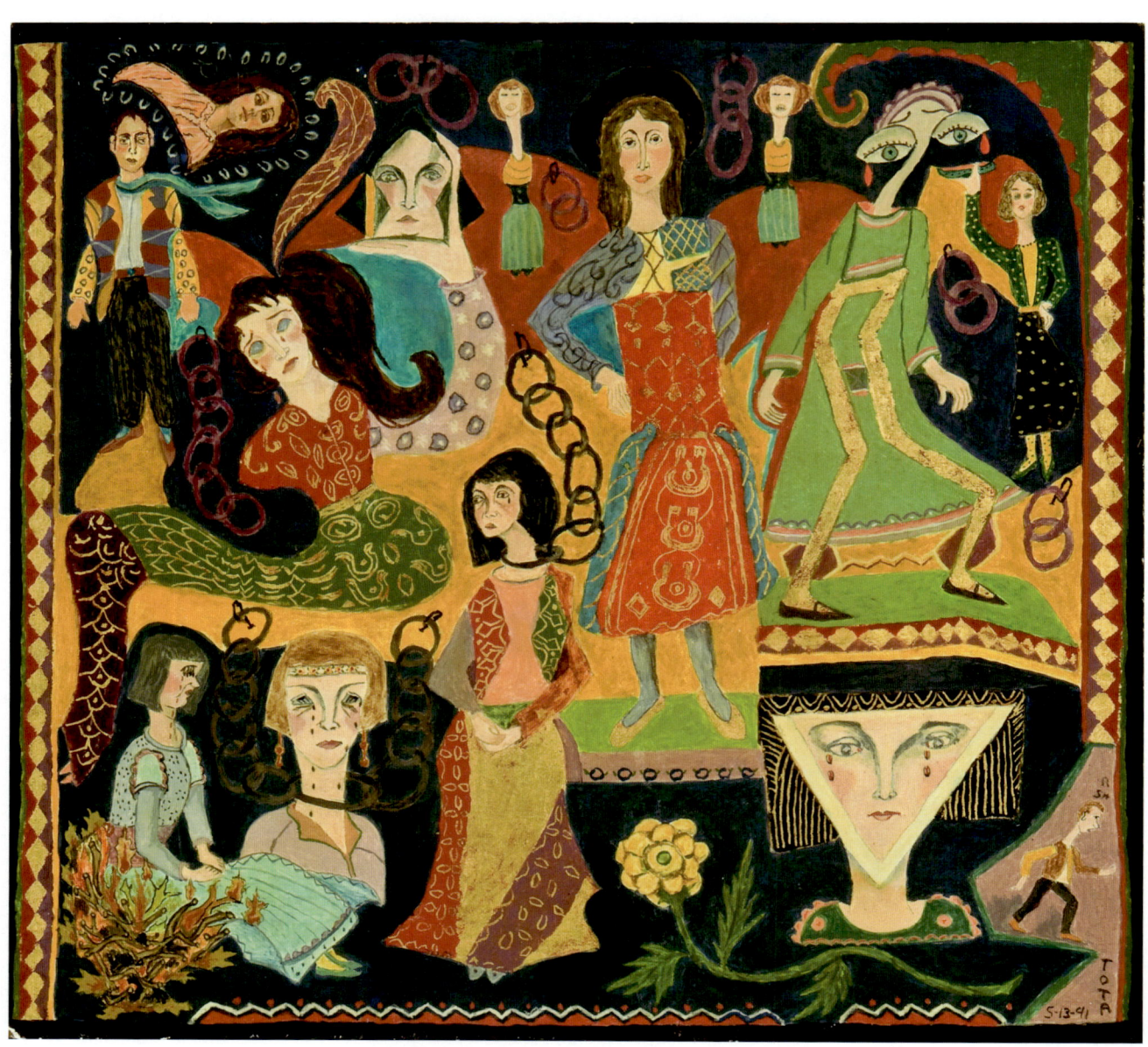

88. Untitled, completed May 13, 1991
Egg tempera and gold leaf on panel
16 x 18 in.
Collection of Rosamond Tota, daughter

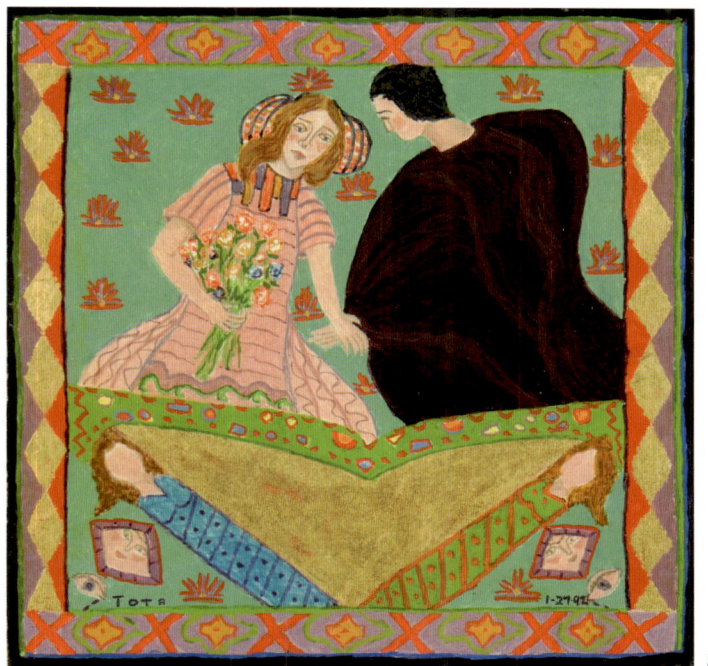

89

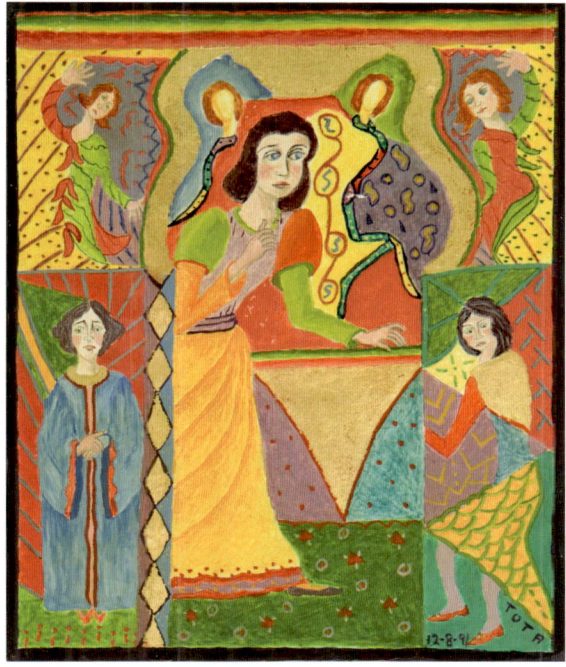

90

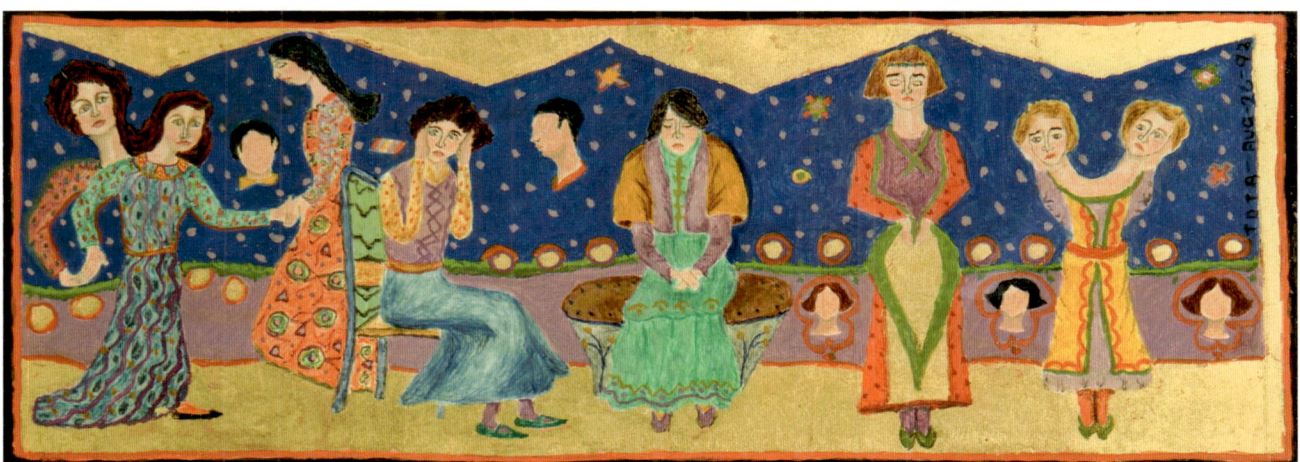

91

89. Untitled, completed January 27, 1992
Egg tempera and gold leaf on panel
8 x 8 1/16 in.
Collection of Rosamond Tota, daughter

90. Untitled, completed December 8, 1991
Egg tempera and gold leaf on panel
11 3/16 x 9 in.
Collection of Rosamond Tota, daughter

91. Untitled, completed August 26, 1992
Egg tempera and gold leaf on panel
6 x 16 1/8 in.
Collection of Rosamond Tota, daughter

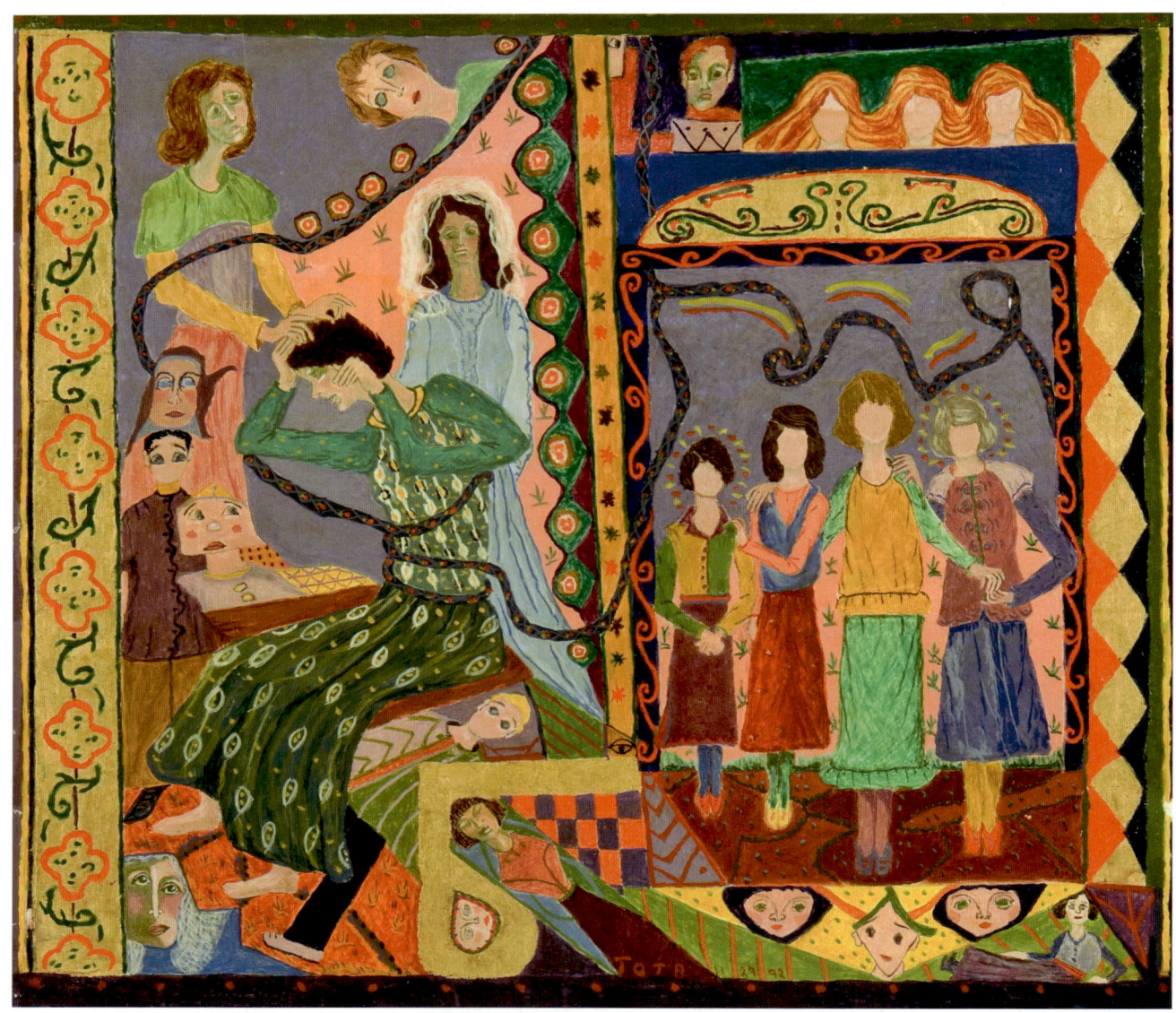

92. Untitled, completed November 29, 1992
Egg tempera and gold leaf on panel
16 x 18 in.
Collection of Rosamond Tota, daughter

93. Untitled, completed March 1, 1993
Egg tempera and gold leaf on panel
18 x 15 ⅞ in.
Collection of Rosamond Tota, daughter

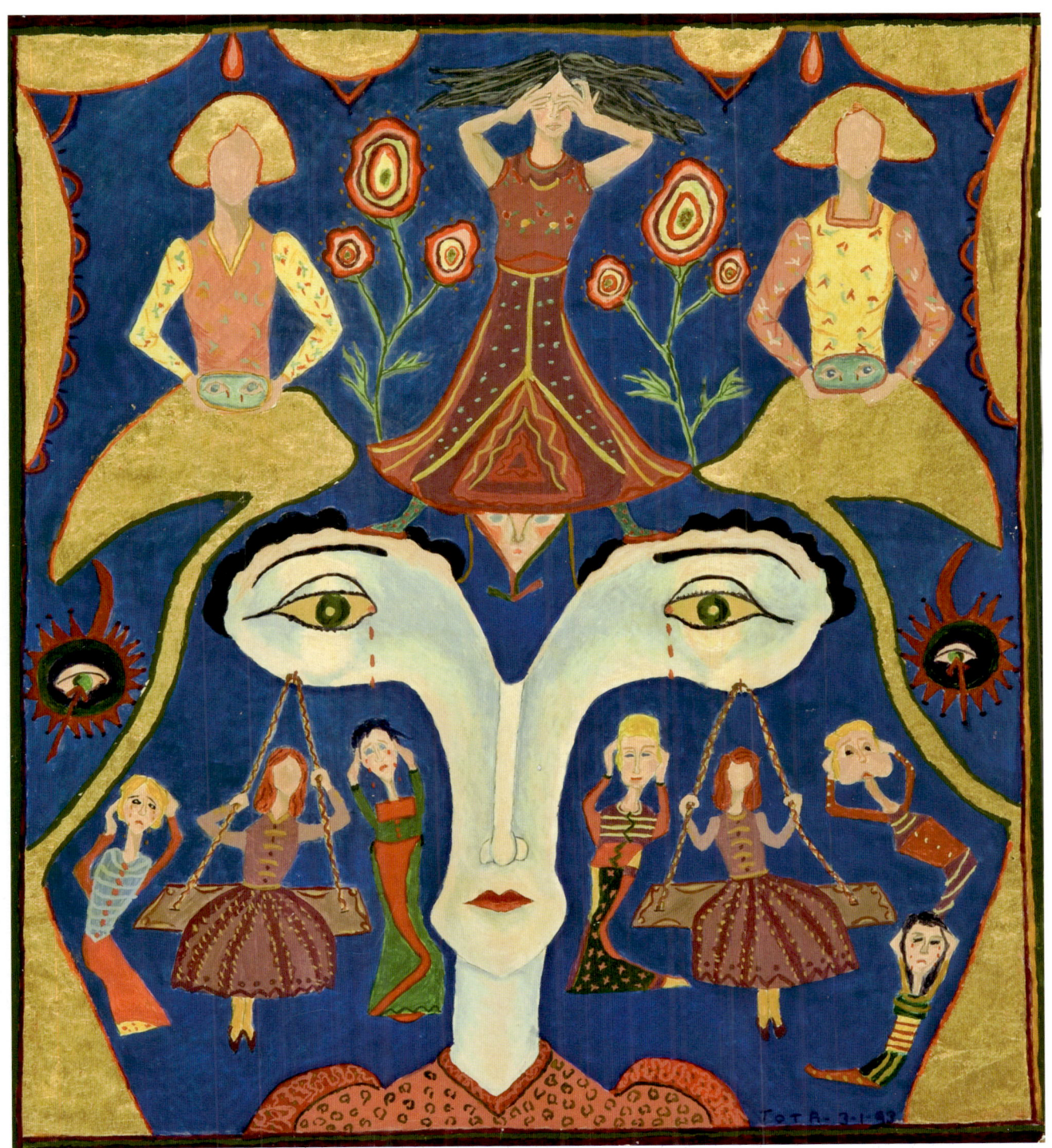

ACKNOWLEDGMENTS

Jessica Marten
Curator in Charge/Curator of American Art, Memorial Art Gallery of the University of Rochester

It is my pleasure to thank the people who have helped to bring *The Surreal Visions of Josephine Tota* to vibrant life. The exceptional stewardship of daughter Rosamond Tota and great-niece Lisa Rosica has been integral in maintaining Josephine Tota's artistic legacy with love, sympathy, and integrity. I am honored and grateful to them for trusting her legacy to me and for helping to bring her work to a larger audience.

This exhibition would not have been possible without the generosity of the lenders, many of them family or friends of the artist, who agreed to part with their beloved paintings long before the start of the exhibition. Some lenders prefer to remain anonymous; all other lenders are listed in the credit line for the individual works. I am very grateful for the long loan period that allowed the museum to study, conserve, photograph, and frame all of Tota's paintings.

Generous donors who have believed in and funded the project include Pamela Miller Ness and Paul Marc Ness, Rosamond Tota, the Gallery Council of the Memorial Art Gallery, and the Robert L. and Mary L. Sproull Fund. Additional support is provided by the James and Jacqueline Adams Fund, the June Alexander Memorial Fund, the Nancy E. Hyman Charitable Fund, and Marguerite and James Quinn, Jane Labrum, Lisa Rosica, and The Century Club of Rochester.

I am thankful to Jonathan Binstock, Mary W. and Donald R. Clark Director, who gave his full support to the exhibition. The acquisition of Tota's paintings was possible thanks to the support of Marjorie Searl, former Chief Curator; Grant Holcomb, Director Emeritus; and the museum's art committee members. I would like to thank Larry Merrill, former Director of the Creative Workshop, for bringing Tota's late paintings to MAG for her first exhibition and for his support of the current exhibition. The team of colleagues at the Memorial Art Gallery responsible for the success of this exhibition and catalog include Carol Acquilano, Preparator; Susie Daiss, Senior Associate, Division of Medical Humanities and Bioethics; Marlene Hamann-Whitmore, Director of Academic Programs; John King, Exhibition Designer; Dan Knerr, Exhibition Registrar; Ann Kuebel, Preparator; Courtney Lippa, Permanent Collection Registrar; Margot Muto, Exhibition Coordinator; Nancy Norwood, Curator of European Art; Kerry Schauber, Research Assistant; and Marie Via, former Director of Exhibitions. The entire MAG staff has contributed to the success of this exhibition and the museum in countless ways that cannot be expressed here.

For her significant contribution to this publication, I am thankful to Janet Catherine Berlo, Professor of Art History/Visual and Cultural Studies at the University of Rochester. Her important essay establishes a place for Tota within the history of twentieth-century visionary women artists. I would also like to thank Anne Timpano, Director of Traveling Exhibition Service, and the wonderful team at International Arts & Artists for their support of the exhibition tour.

Nearly every photograph of Tota's work was taken by Andy Olenick of Fotowerks, Inc. All paintings in need of stabilization and inpainting were treated by Susan Blakney and Chiara Kuhns at West Lake Conservators in Skaneateles, NY, and James Hamm, Fine Arts Conservation & Technical Services, Clarence Center, NY. I am also grateful for the people who have spent time thinking and talking about Josephine Tota with me and looking at her work: Lily Fiduccia, Jackie Germanow, Alec Hazlett, Jean Henty, Dr. Norman Pointer, and Hannah Solky.

I am thankful for the enthusiasm and expertise of the staff at RIT Press in the design and production of his book, especially Bruce Austin, Molly Cort, and Marnie Soom. I thank, too, Amy Mantell for her thoughtful and thorough editing.

For their unending supply of love and support, I would like to thank my husband, Christopher Price, and my children, Lucy and Henry PriceMarten.